DATE DUE

NO 2 9 00		
OC 9 00		

DEMCO 38-296

OTHER TITLES OF INTEREST FROM ST. LUCIE PRESS

The 90-Day ISO 9000 Manual and Implementation Guide

The Executive Guide to Implementing Quality Systems

Focused Quality: Managing for Results

Improving Service Quality: Achieving High Performance in the Public and
   Private Sectors

Introduction to Modern Statistical Quality Control and Management

ISO 9000: Implementation Guide for Small to Mid-Sized Businesses

Organization Teams: Continuous Quality Improvement

Organization Teams: Facilitator's Guide

Principles of Total Quality

Quality Improvement Handbook: Team Guide to Tools and Techniques

The Textbook of Total Quality in Healthcare

Total Quality in Higher Education

Total Quality in Managing Human Resources

Total Quality in Marketing

Total Quality in Purchasing and Supplier Management

Total Quality in Radiology: A Guide to Implementation

Total Quality in Research and Development

Total Quality Management for Custodial Operations

Total Quality Management: Text, Cases, and Readings, 2nd Edition

Total Quality Service

For more information about these titles call, fax or write:

St. Lucie Press
100 E. Linton Blvd., Suite 403B
Delray Beach, FL 33483
TEL (407) 274-9906 • FAX (407) 274-9927

S^t_L

Total Quality SERVICE

Principles, Practices, and Implementation

D. H. Stamatis

S^t_L

St. Lucie Press
Delray Beach, Florida

Library of Congress Cataloging-in-Publication Data

Stamatis, D. H., 1947–
    Principles of service quality / by D.H. Stamatis.
        p.   cm.
    Includes bibliographical references and index.
    ISBN 1-884015-83-2
    1. Customer service—Quality control.   I. Title.
    HF5415.5.S73   1996
    658.8'12—dc20   94-46634
                                                    CIP

Phone: (407) 274-9906
Fax: (407) 274-9927

S$\overset{t}{L}$

Published by
St. Lucie Press
100 E. Linton Blvd., Suite 403B
Delray Beach, FL 33483

DEDICATION

In memory of
my mother,
Venetia

TABLE OF CONTENTS

PREFACE

If total quality management was the ticket to success in the 1980s, then total quality service (TQS) is rapidly becoming the challenge of the 1990s. Companies that want to achieve a certain goal will be successful through a cultural transformation that produces a TQS organization. What is TQS? In its simplest form, it is a true commitment to operationalizing the concept of customer focus, establishing service performance standards, measuring performance against benchmarks, recognizing and rewarding exemplary behavior, and maintaining enthusiasm for the customer at all times. In its most complicated form, it increases sales and market share.

Smart companies will develop marketing information systems that will create a working union between sales and marketing and customer service and marketing research, the net result being superior service across the company (internal) and between suppliers and customers (external).

Too many businesses still think of quality in terms of manufactured goods instead of the products delivered by the vast and growing service sector. Management in the service industry views quality as a concept rather than a product subject to the same rigorous analysis and control taking place on the shop floor. It is estimated that only 10% of American service companies have any form of a quality improvement process in place. But quality is just as critical to the products and processes of the service industry, which accounts for approximately three-fourths of America's gross national product and nine of ten new jobs.

One of the first big challenges in improving quality is to get managers to view the business at the customer level, to develop a one-on-one mentality toward customers. They must strive to never disappoint a single customer. Businesspeople who are serious about quality service take quality as a personal responsibility and commitment. They regard their services and their companies as an extension of themselves and their own integrity and credibility, and they spread that message throughout the organization.

Real quality service, however, is not sales slogans, buzzwords, or lip service. It is a deep, organization-wide commitment to achieving the best. It starts with a personal and professional commitment by the CEO and is ingrained in the organization's culture to the point where every employee feels a strong sense of commitment. This is particularly important for companies such as large retailers, airlines, or banks with legions of front-line workers subjected to tremendous daily pressures from customers and managers. Many companies rely most on the people who are paid the least to leave the last impression with customers. The chances are slim that front-line workers will provide a satisfying experience for customers during a hassle-filled day if they do not feel there is a strong commitment to service at the top of the company. As dim as this sound, there are some practical steps a company can take to begin and maintain the process of delivering quality service:

- **Commitment:** Commit to improving quality and providing the resources to make improvement possible.

- **Delegate:** Designate a person or establish a unit reporting directly to the top. Look at everything as if you were dealing with customers or clients on a one-on-one basis.

- **Customer information:** Develop a comprehensive marketing information system through utilization of relational database management technologies.

- **Internal assessment:** Conduct internal assessments to determine how capable your company is of delivering quality service. Your own research will reveal employees' perceptions of how well they are doing, organizational commitment to quality, company performance standards, how employees view customers, and what they believe their customers believe.

- **Action:** Initiate a feedback system and use the information to adjust operations to respond to customer needs, wants, and expectations. Change procedures and even long-held policies, if necessary, and set more rigorous performance standards.

Companies that do not provide quality service not only will not compete, they will not exist. Just as true wisdom is knowing how much you do not know, true quality is knowing you can always do better. For quality service to exist and flourish, everyone in the organization must internalize the concept that quality is a journey, not a destination.

ACKNOWLEDGMENTS

As always, writing a book is the collective effort of many people with different contributions at different times. This book is no exception.

I want to take the opportunity and thank Ms. Sena Ford and the editors of *Quality Press* for giving me permission to use some of the material for Chapter 2 on product and service.

Also, I want to extend my thanks to Mr. W. Cowles and SkillPath Publications, Inc. for permitting me to use some material from *How to Deal with Difficult People* by Paul G. Friedman in the chapter on conflict.

I want to thank my wife, Carla, and my children, Christine, Cary, Stephen, and Timothy, for putting up with me during their vacation time and, furthermore, for giving me continual encouragement and support to finish as soon as possible.

I want to thank Ms. D. Fletcher for typing several early drafts without complaining.

I want to thank Mr. R. Munro and Ms. M. Peterson for their very valuable critique and suggestions during the entire writing project.

I want to thank the editors for their continual support and suggestions to make the manuscript better.

Finally, I want to thank all my seminar participants over the years who have helped with their questions, critiques, and ideas and without whose input much of the information here would not have been possible.

THE AUTHOR

Dean H. Stamatis, Ph.D., ASQC-Fellow, CQE, CMfgE, ISO 9000 Lead Assessor (graduate), is President of Contemporary Consultants Co. in Southgate, Michigan. He received his B.S./B.A. degree in Marketing from Wayne State University, his master's degree from Central Michigan University, and his Ph.D. in Instructional Technology and Business/Statistics from Wayne State University. He is a certified Quality Engineer through the American Society of Quality Control, certified Manufacturing Engineer through the Society of Manufacturing Engineers, and a graduate of BSI's ISO 9000 Lead Assessor training program.

A specialist in management and consulting, organizational development, and quality science, Dr. Stamatis has taught project management, operations management, logistics, mathematical modeling, and statistics at both the graduate and undergraduate levels at Central Michigan University, University of Michigan, and Florida Institute of Technology.

With over 28 years of experience in management and quality training and consulting, Dr. Stamatis has served numerous private sector industries, including but not limited to steel, automotive, general manufacturing, tooling, electronics, plastics, food, the navy, the Department of Defense, pharmaceutical, chemical, printing, hospitals, and medical device.

He has worked for such companies as Ford Motor Company, GM-Hydromatic Motorola, IBM, Texas Instruments, Sandoz, Dawn Foods, Dow Corning Wright, BP Petroleum, Bronx North Central Hospital, Mill Print, St. Claire Hospital, Tokheim, and ICM/Krebsoge, to name just a few.

Dr. Stamatis has created, presented, and implemented quality programs with a focus on total quality management, statistical process control (both normal and short run), design of experiments (both classical and Taguchi), quality function deployment, failure mode and effects analysis, value engineering, supplier certification, audits, cost of quality, quality planning, and the ISO 9000 and QS 9000 series. He has also created, presented, and implemented programs on project management, teams, self-directed teams, facilitation, leadership, benchmarking, and customer service.

Dr. Stamatis has written over 50 articles, presented over 20 speeches, and participated in both national and international conferences on quality. He is a contributing author on three books and the sole author of four books. His consulting extends across the United States, Southeast Asia, Japan, China, India, and Europe. In addition, he has performed over 100 automotive-related audits, 25 preassessment ISO 9000 audits, and has helped Rockwell International-Switching Division in the process of ISO 9001 certification and Transamerica Leasing in the process of ISO 9002 certification

He is an active member of the Detroit Engineering Society and the American Society for Training and Development, Executive member of the American Marketing Association, member of the American Research Association, and a Fellow of the American Society for Quality Control.

INTRODUCTION

In today's competitive market, no business can survive without satisfied customers. Findings from recent studies conducted by the Technical Assistance Research Program (TARP), a federal government-sponsored program, support this statement:

- Ninety-six percent of consumers who experience a problem with a small-ticket product (for example, small packaged goods) do not complain to the manufacturer. (Of these, 63% will not buy again.)

- Forty-five percent of consumers who experience a problem with a small-ticket service (for example, cable television or local telephone service) do not complain. (Of these, 45% will not buy again.)

- Not surprisingly, only 27% of unhappy consumers of large-ticket durable products (for example, automobiles, computers) do not complain. (Of these, 41% will not buy again.)

- Thirty-seven percent of unhappy consumers of large-ticket services (for example, insurance, loans, HMOs) do not complain. (Of these, 50% will not buy again.)

These numbers alone are significant and can make a major dent in future sales. But TARP has confirmed that negative word of mouth can create an even more formidable problem. Unhappy customers share their experience with others. A dissatisfied customer with a small problem typically tells ten other people; those with large problems tell sixteen others. Furthermore, 13% of dissatisfied customers tell their experiences to more than twenty people.

As bad as this sounds, the news is not all bad. Each customer whose small problem is satisfactorily resolved can be expected to tell five other people. Each customer whose large problem is satisfactorily resolved can be expected to tell eight other people. Of these people, some will then become new customers.

The significance of these numbers is that most customers whose complaints are satisfactorily resolved go on to buy again. These figures range from 92% of purchasers of small-ticket products to 70% of customers of large-ticket services.

Consider the following price tags on customer loyalty. The automobile industry believes that a loyal customer represents a lifetime average revenue of $140,000. So why fight over an $80 repair bill or a $40 replacement part? In banking, it is estimated that the average customer represents at least $80 a year in profit. In appliance manufacturing, brand loyalty is worth more than $2800 over a twenty-year period. The local supermarket counts on you for $4400 within a given year. So why quibble about some little nothing that the customer thinks is not right? People who believe in service superiority make things right—they want their customers to return and be satisfied. That is precisely the issue of total quality service.

Juran (1993, 1994) has observed that we are in the middle of a quality crisis and very few American companies have attained world-class class (less than 50 of the Fortune 500). The remaining companies are in various stages. Some have not yet started, some are starting over again, some are well along, and others have tried, failed, and given up. Juran notes that the seeds of failure are:

- Management ineptitude on quality issues

- Preoccupation with imports

- Quality lacks the necessary priority

- No appropriate measures

- Laissez-faire attitude

- Misguided leadership

- Unbalanced relations between headquarters and divisions

Juran's observations are quite appropriate and welcomed by everyone. However, do his observations hold true in the service industry? Yes, they do. In fact, they are more relevant than one would suspect. Consider the following:

- There is no other industry in which people skills are as important as immediate behaviors.

- There is no other industry where information has to be translated over and over again.

- There is no other industry where all employees have the responsibility and opportunity to deal effectively with the customer.

- There is no other industry where all employees must make the customer feel comfortable in the face of irate behavior.

- There is no other industry where the employee must answer the same questions over and over again with a smile, always showing concern and courtesy.

- There is no other industry where the employee must appease the irate customer so that the customer will feel satisfied.

Indeed, it is a proven fact: when treated well, shown respect, and kept informed, customers respond more favorably, complain less, are more cooperative, become loyal customers, and their perception of quality improves (TARP 1994; Petrina 1994; Bell 1994; Lyons 1994; Albrecht 1990; Albrecht 1985).

To be sure, one of the major problems we are still experiencing today is the notion that the quality of service is okay and does not need any improvement. According to a recent survey of several countries reported in *Newsweek* (1994), quality overall indeed is still not being taken seriously. However, of the countries reported in the survey, Japan is number one, with 38.5% of the people thinking that quality is important, and the United States is third, with 34.3%. Table I.1 shows the results in a percentage format.

Typical experiences are the published stories by Kitasei (1985) and Neuman (1994). How sad that, as Kitasei writes, "every employee I dealt with implied that it was my fault the store had both my money and the china." Neuman, on the other hand, is more descriptive. She writes, "'...How much longer do you think it will be?' I asked him. He looked at me as if I was a fly on his pastrami sandwich. 'There are a few cars in front of you,' he said. No smile. No apology for the delay. To make a long, loooooong [her emphasis] story short, I waited for three hours before my car was ready. Nobody told me it was ready even then..."

Bad quality service may be several things or it may be as simple as putting one poor sucker on the job to handle far too many customers. It may be that the person in charge of the service does not have the appropriate skills, attitude, or aptitude for the job. In any case, bad quality service is the result.

TABLE I.1   Quality Counts

Country	Percent Approval
Japan	38.5
Germany	36.0
United States	34.3
England	21.9
France	20.6
Canada	18.3
Italy	16.0
Spain	10.3
China	9.3
Taiwan	9.0
Mexico	6.2
Russia	5.8

Quality service is the key to attaining uncommon, unprecedented customer satisfaction—the kind of satisfaction marked by bragging customers and clients, repeat business, and increased market share and profitability.

In this book, we will address the principles that concern service quality, with special focus on the following:

- Quality from a service perspective

- Implementation of service quality

- The ingredients of service quality—teams and empowerment

- Communication

- Benchmarking

- How to deal with difficult people

- Customer satisfaction and its measurement

- Surveys

- Appropriate tools

REFERENCES

_____ (March 14, 1994). "The International News Magazine." *Newsweek.* p. 3.

Albrecht, K. and Bradford, L. J. (1990). *The Service Advantage: How to Identify and Fulfill Customer Needs.* Dow-Jones-Irwin, New York.

Albrecht, K. and Zemke, R. (1985). *Service America: Doing Business in the New Economy.* Dow Jones-Irwin, New York.

Bell, C. R. (January 1994). "Creating and Maintaining Elegant Service Delivery." *Quality Digest.*

Juran, J. M. (July/August 1993). "Why Quality Initiatives Fail." *Journal of Business Strategy.*

Juran, J. M. (May 24, 1994). "The Upcoming Century of Quality." Address at the 1994 ASQC Annual Quality Congress, Las Vegas.

Kitasei, H. H. (October 1985). "Japan's Got Us Beat in the Service Department, Too." *Quality.*

Lyons, D. (June 1994). "Grace Under Pressure." *World Travel.* Northwest Airlines.

Neuman, P. E. (July 24, 1994). "Good Service Does Not Require Laying Down Your Life." *Heritage News-Herald.* Southgate, Mich.

Petrina, B. (Spring 1994). "The Golden Opportunity of the 90s." *Training Suppliers... Voice.* ASTD.

TARP (1994). White House Office of Consumer Affairs, Technical Assistance Research Programs, Washington, D.C.

1

QUALITY

It has been said that quality is in the eyes of the beholder. Therefore, quality has many definitions and means different things to different people. This chapter focuses on the term *quality*. Specifically, our focus is to identify the ingredients and the strategy that service organizations must understand, internalize, and implement in order to define the term as it applies to them.

GENERAL OVERVIEW

Quality has been defined in many ways over the years. However, the most common definitions are basically the following:

1. Conformance to requirements (Crosby 1979)

2. Fitness for use (Juran 1979)

3. Continual improvement (Deming 1982)

4. As defined by the customers (Ford 1984, 1990)

5 Loss to society (Taguchi 1987)

6. Six sigma (Harry and Stewart [Motorola] 1988)

7. Zero defects (Crosby 1979)

Certainly these definitions are acceptable. However, the question still remains: What are the ingredients of a quality system that define, plan, develop, and improve quality in order to ultimately satisfy, or even delight, the customer?

To answer this very fundamental question, we must explore and understand some basic strategies dealing with the human element in any organization. We must do so because quality begins with the single individual, regardless of position, and not the quality department, as some still think today. Let's examine these strategies, which become the prerequisites of defining quality.

Define and Provide a Clear Objective

Companies must have a clear objective in order to be successful in defining quality. Planned, if not controlled, expansion (in every domain within the organization), timely change, and effective continual innovation will permit steady growth and respectable profits, as long as the vision and objectives of the organization are defined. In order to remain competitive, growth and profitability have to depend on internal creativity and financial powers, to be sure. This is illustrated in Figure 1.1, which shows in a graphic format the phases of

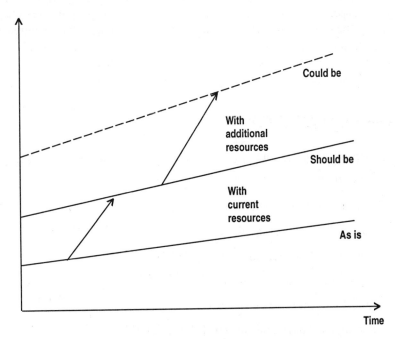

FIGURE 1.1 Phases of performance

performance. However, the objectives based on some form of customer requirements or quality are the foundations of that growth and profitability. (From the author's experience and literature research, the *only* exception to this rule is Stevens's (1991, pp. 74–76) thesis that "quality does not sell quick printing." Rather, Mr. Stevens's contention is that a good marketing plan is of importance. Mr. Stevens concludes his article by admitting that "quality is expected but it does not help to advertise it."

It is important that the definition of quality for the service organization account for all the main ingredients for which the organization is known (Figure 1.1, *as is*) and identify (Figure 1.1, *as could be*) and totally support them. It must be noted that in order to do this, sometimes paradigms must shift and the culture must be renewed.

Initiate or Redefine the Culture

Initiating or redefining the corporate culture is aimed not at problem solving, but at improving basic conditions within the organization, so that all employees can work more successfully. A typical redefinition of culture and expectations is shown in Table 1.1. The goal of this new culture is to foster a spirit of commitment within the entire organization that will further the corporate aims contained in the company's basic principles and management guidelines. This is demonstrated through Table 1.2. This goal should be encapsulated in the definition of quality.

When we are about to initiate and/or redefine the culture of the organization, much thought must be given to the values and ethics within the organization. The two are not the same. For example:

Values	*Ethics*
Define the individual	Translate values into actions
Are constant	Are changing
Are internally derived	Are situationally determined
Are concerned with virtue	Are concerned with justice
Are general	Are highly specific
Are stated morally	Are stated behaviorally
Are judged as good or bad	Are judged as present or absent
Set priorities	Set limits for appropriate behavior

TABLE 1.1 Typical Redefinition of Culture and Expectations

Category	Previous	Future
1. Jobs and people	Functional, narrow scope, management controlled	Service/service task forces, shorter cycle time, ownership, reduced inventory, employment stability, job flexibility
2. Technology and workplace layout	Product trends: management driven	Continuous flow, work-space-need oriented, perfection of processes
3. Role of manager	Plan, organize, motivate, control	Lead continual improvement, develop people, visionary—committed to total organization
4. Information and communication	Downward, limited, need-to-know	Greater sharing of needed information, integrated databases, continued emphasis on personal communication
5. Reward system	Pay by job and longevity, few team incentives	Reward for performance, improve performance appraisal system—link to pay, gainsharing for group involvement/rewards
6. Organization and structure	Authoritarian: top to bottom	Organization-project matrix oriented, fewer layers of management, suppliers as extensions of internal flows
7. Personnel policies and symbols	Hierarchy: status symbols	Reinforce core values, fewer procedures, enhancement of presenteeism program
8. Recruitment, selection, orientation, and training	Skills and knowledge	Behavior, ability, skills, long-term needs

TABLE 1.2 Assumptions of a Control versus a Commitment Company

Characteristic	Control	Commitment
1. Trust	People are untrustworthy, irresponsible	People are inherently responsible, committed to quality
2. Motivation	People work for pay; carrots and sticks apply	People are motivated by work itself, achievement, recognition, growth; responsibly respond to "ownership"
3. Results	Achieved via controlling behavior through policies and procedures; use of checks and balances	Achieved via (1) very high performance goals, (2) supportive relationships, (3) teamwork, (4) positive climate
4. Organization of work	Broken down into narrow elements; jobs specialized, individualized; coordinated and controlled with hierarchies	Integrated functions through teams; teams linked vertically and horizontally
5. Management–worker relationships	Arms-length; different goals; status reinforced with perks; adversarial, win–lose group-to-group; fear useful; people expendable	All employees share common destinies; people are most precious resources; open, problem-solving atmosphere; core values reinforced
6. Priority and focus	Financial performance achieved by cost and schedule via compliance with procedure; "good enough" quality achieved by specifications and inspection	Quality to the customer is foremost; this results in cost and schedule performance, which produces superior financial results

The attitude and behavior of each individual are integral to establishing cooperation within the company. High morale, enthusiasm for a job well done, punctuality, loyalty, and diligence on behalf of both the company and the employee build mutual cooperation. A corporate culture is more likely to change if there is harmony between the company and the employees. To facilitate this change, it is imperative that the culture of the organization do everything in its power to communicate throughout that quality is nothing less than the ticket to both current and future prosperity. One can actually see this in the word *quality* as an acronym:

QUALITY =
QUality is the Act for Liberty and Income Through the Years

Indeed, quality is an initiative that allows freedom—without fear—for both the organization and the people in the organization to take charge of continual improvement, so that they both can prosper. Maybe that is what P. Crosby meant when he said that "quality is free." To be sure, this is easier said than done. How, then, can the organization make sure that the appropriate culture is developed, so that quality can become a way of doing business? The following are some suggestions:

1. **Be friendly.** A friendly atmosphere between managers, employees, and customers will do wonders toward quality service. For example, a smile may be the difference between success and failure. Friendliness facilitates communication, and communication allows for an exchange of ideas, concerns, issues, and so on.

2. **Keep everyone informed.** Information generates knowledge, and knowledge generates sound decisions. Therefore, the communication channels in the entire organization should be open at all times for both vertical and horizontal hierarchies. Furthermore, the communication must be both top-bottom and bottom-up. The voice of the customer must be heard at all times by everyone.

3. **Keep together through mutual cooperation, consideration, and openness.** Focus on win–win situations as opposed to win–lose situations. With a win–win attitude, both parties learn to compromise at an optimum, whereas with a win–lose attitude, one of the parties is looking to take advantage of the other. The first is built on trust and honesty; the second is based on mistrust.

4. **Make decisions based on facts, not opinions.** Decisions should be made based on quantifiable data instead of opinion or hearsay. Be a data-driven organization.

5. **Keep procedures simple and nonbureaucratic.** Use the KISS (keep it simple and short) principle as often as possible. Long and bureaucratic procedures are complicated and difficult to implement. They present major communication problems in both sending and receiving messages.

6. **Manage by example.** Quality is not the responsibility of one individual or even one department; it is the business of every employee. All employees need to have exacting and fastidious attitudes about their job functions. All employees must want to produce quality service not because they are told to, but for their own self-worth. These attitudes need to be present in management discussions, in the work that takes place, and all across the company's boundaries, including the customer service department.

These requirements are incumbent upon management. Management must set an example of courtesy and consideration. Managerial leadership derives from competence. All managers in quality service organizations should have a good understanding of how to operate all of the organization's services and know how their basic features and benefits work, so that they can set up clear objectives for individual tasks and provide the necessary motivation. In service industries, it is of paramount importance that all managers make the effort to encourage staff members to find creative solutions to problems. Delegate, empower, and do the right things. Biemesderfer (1994) presents a very good example of this.

Consistent Communication

Listening is very important throughout the company. Listen to both employees and customers to attain a clear understanding of goals, objectives, priorities, and satisfaction. Consistent communication helps everyone understand that their individual contribution can make a difference. The organization must develop an open forum for routine company-wide communication through either regular meetings or newsletters. Cultivate openness and eliminate fear of asking appropriate questions.

Listening to the customer provides an accurate perception of the product or service to be provided. With a clear understanding of service capabilities and/or individual performance, neither party will be disappointed in the end result. The better the communication between the customer and the company, the higher the degree of success and customer satisfaction.

Institute Education and Training

Training is important for everyone. The better an employee is trained, the better his or her performance will be. The better trained the customer is, the more

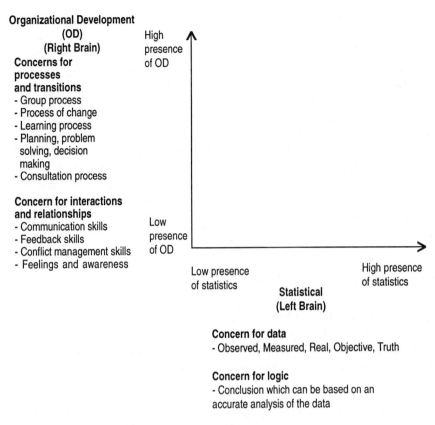

**Organizational Development
(OD)
(Right Brain)**
**Concerns for
processes
and transitions**
- Group process
- Process of change
- Learning process
- Planning, problem
  solving, decision
  making
- Consultation process

**Concern for interactions
and relationships**
- Communication skills
- Feedback skills
- Conflict management skills
- Feelings and awareness

High
presence
of OD

Low
presence
of OD

Low presence
of statistics

High presence
of statistics

**Statistical
(Left Brain)**

Concern for data
- Observed, Measured, Real, Objective, Truth

Concern for logic
- Conclusion which can be based on an
  accurate analysis of the data

FIGURE 1.2   Overall training perspective

reliable the service will be. In service, it is imperative that skill and education work together. When that happens, the organization stays on the leading edge and maintains a congruency of quality all across the organization.

As important as education and training are, they must always be kept with two perspectives in mind. The first is the organizational development side and the second is the statistical side. No organization is at 50–50. It is management's responsibility to define the optimum for the organization. An example of this perspective is shown in Figure 1.2.

Promote Continual Improvement

Continual improvement quality programs place the customer first. These programs are called *customer-based* because the elements that constitute quality are ever-changing. Changes in both definitions and policies may be necessary, especially in light of the ISO 9000 standards. The term *continual* as opposed to continuous is used here to denote that improvement is always the focus. It does not matter if a plateau is reached or the improvement is very small. Continuous, on the other hand, is not a realistic goal because the implication is always improvement—something that is not possible.

Further distinguishing continual improvement from other programs is the fact that there are no quotas. Management and employees work together. Everyone pitches in wherever and whenever needed, eliminating the "not my job" mentality. Quality must be a way of life rather than a project. It must be instituted throughout the entire organization as a philosophy rather than a dead-end opportunity. It must be always looked upon as a dynamic evolution rather than a static project waiting to expire.

THE GURUS' DEFINITION

While the preceding are very generic strategies to define the term quality in a given service organization, the literature provides a variety of options. Some examples of defining both quality and the implementation of total quality service in different sectors of the service industry are provided in Chapter 4. The most common ones are based on the theories of:

1. **Juran:** Juran's quality improvement strategy stresses project-by-project implementation and the breakthrough sequence. He warns against taking shortcuts from symptom to solution without finding and removing the cause. Juran also provides several problem-solving tools in addition to statistical process control (SPC). With his definition of quality as fitness for use, he is strongly oriented toward meeting customer expectations. His philosophy is summarized in Table 1.3.

2. **Crosby:** Crosby's approach gives attention to transforming the quality culture. He is able to involve everyone in the organization in the process by stressing individual conformance to requirements. His fourteen steps provide management a blueprint and an easy-to-understand approach for management to launch the journey toward world-class quality. His approach is a top-down process. Crosby's fourteen points are summarized in Table 1.3.

3. **Deming:** Deming's strategy is based on statistical tools. It tends to be a bottom-up process. The emphasis of the strategy seems to be on con-

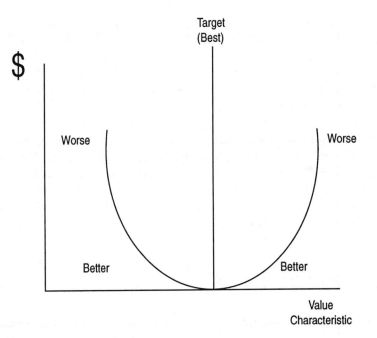

FIGURE 1.3   The loss function

tinual improvement and measurement. (Deming does not recognize the cost of customer dissatisfaction because, as he says, it is impossible to measure). Deming's strategy is to look at the process to remove the variation, because most of the variation (92%) is management controllable. He is a strong believer in empowering the workers to solve problems, provided management gives them the appropriate tools. Deming's fourteen points are summarized in Table 1.3.

4. **Taguchi:** Taguchi's strategy is focused in the loss function, which defines any deviation from the target as a loss that someone will pay. Taguchi's strategy is somewhat difficult for the novice; however, it provides specific guidelines for improvement and cost considerations, especially in the service industry. His philosophy is summarized in Table 1.3, and the loss function curve is illustrated in Figure 1.3.

None of the specific definitions of the gurus is all-inclusive. None is perfect. Rather, each definition is an attempt by one of the gurus to demonstrate that everyone needs an operational definition of quality. An operational definition is a description in quantifiable terms of what to measure and the steps to follow in

TABLE 1.3 Comparison of the Four Major Quality Philosophies

Juran's Philosophy	Crosby's Philosophy	Deming's Philosophy	Taguchi's Philosophy
1. Assign priority to projects	1. Management commitment	1. Create constancy of purpose for improvement of product and service	1. An important dimension of the quality of a product/service is the total loss generated by that producer to society
2. Pareto analysis of symptoms	2. Quality improvement team	2. Adopt the new philosophy of refusing to allow defects	2. In a competitive environment, continual quality improvement and cost reduction are necessary for staying in business
3. Theorize on causes of symptom	3. Quality measurement	3. Cease dependence on mass inspection and rely only on statistical control	3. Continual quality improvement includes continuous reduction in the variation of product performance characteristics about their target values
4. Test theories, collect and analyze data	4. Cost of quality evaluation	4. Require suppliers to provide statistical evidence of quality	4. The customer's loss due to a service's performance variation is approximately proportional to the square of the deviation of the performance characteristic from its target value
5. Narrow list of theories	5. Awareness	5. Constantly and forever improve production and service	5. The final quality and cost of a product/service are determined to a large extent by the engineering designs of the product/service and its process
6. Design experiment(s)	6. Corrective action	6. Train all employees	
7. Approve design, provide authority	7. Zero defects planning	7. Give all employees the proper tools to do the job right	
8. Conduct experiment, establish proof of cause	8. Quality education	8. Encourage communication and productivity	
9. Propose remedies	9. Zero defect day	9. Encourage different departments to work together on problem solving	
10. Test remedy	10. Goal setting	10. Eliminate posters and slogans that do not teach specific improvement methods	
11. Action to institute remedy	11. Error cause removal	11. Use statistical methods to continuously improve quality and productivity	
	12. Recognition		
	13. Quality councils		
	14. Do it all over again		

12. Control at new level

Note: Items 1–8 define the journey from symptom to cause and items 9–12 define the journey from cause to remedy. Juran distills his philosophy in the famous trilogy which identifies: (1) plan, (2) control, (3) improve

Note: Crosby distills these fourteen points to four absolutes:
1. Definition of quality
   Conformance to requirements
2. System
   Prevention
3. Performance standard
   Zero defects
4. Measurement
   Cost of quality

12. Eliminate all barriers to pride in workmanship
13. Provide ongoing retraining to keep pace with changing products, methods, etc.
14. Clearly define top management's permanent commitment to quality

Note: Deming distills these fourteen points into the following model: Plan-Do-Check (Study)-Act. This model (1) symbolizes the problem analysis process and quality improvement cycle and (2) provides focus on defect correction as well as defect prevention.

6. Performance variation can be reduced by exploiting the non-linear effects of the product or process parameters on the performance characteristics

Note: Taguchi distills his philosophy down to the loss function, which recognizes that any deviation from the nominal (target) is costly and somebody pays for it

order to consistently measure it. The purpose of this measurement is to determine the actual performance of the process.

FUNCTIONAL CHARACTERISTICS OF THE TERM "QUALITY"

Each of the gurus in the field of quality presents positive and negative points. No definition is perfect. Therefore, each service organization must define quality based on its own objectives, expectations, culture, and customers. In fact, it is not unusual for an organization to combine the best points and create its own definition of quality. This combination is based primarily on three points:

- **Quality characteristics**, which are the characteristics of the output of a process that are important to the customer. Quality characteristics require knowledge about the customer in every respect.

- **Key quality characteristics**, which are the most important quality characteristics. Key quality characteristics must be operationally defined by combining knowledge of the customer with knowledge of the process.

- **Key process variables**, which are the components of the process that have a cause-and-effect relationship of sufficient magnitude with the key quality characteristics such that manipulation and control of the key process variables will reduce variation of the key quality characteristics and/or change their level to either a quality or a key quality characteristic.

In defining quality service, there are additional characteristics to be accounted for. Garvin (1988), for example, identified eight dimensions of quality, with each dimension contributing to a set of requirements. In quality service, it is paramount that those dimensions be accounted for and planned in the service process. However, regardless of how the organization defines and/or derives its definition of quality in service, it must be understood by everyone that quality service must incorporate as many of the dimensions as possible. The dimensions in a modified version are:

- **Function:**   The primary required performance of the service

- **Features:**   The expected performance (bells and whistles of the service)

- **Conformance:**   The satisfaction based on requirements that have been set

- **Reliability:**   The confidence of the service in relationship to time

- **Serviceability:** The ability to service if something goes wrong

- **Aesthetics:** The experience itself as it relates to the senses

- **Perception:** The reputation of the quality

To be sure, Garvin's dimensions have become the *de facto* requirements in service. However, in addition to these dimensions and characteristics, it is important to recognize that in order for service to be effective and efficient, the following additional characteristics *must* be present:

- Be accessible

- Provide prompt personal attention

- Offer expertise

- Provide leading technology

- Depend on subjective satisfaction

- Provide for cost effectiveness

The acronym **COMFORT** helps to ensure that these assumptions are accounted for. It stands for:

Caring

Observant

Mindful

Friendly

Obliging

Responsible

Tactful

This is addressed in greater detail in Chapter 7 on customer satisfaction.

REFERENCES

Biemesderfer, D. (June 1994). "Modus Operandi." *World Traveler*. Northwest Airlines.

Crosby, P. (1979). *Quality Is Free*. McGraw-Hill, New York.

Deming, W. Edwards (1982). *Out of the Crisis*. Massachusetts Institute of Technology, Cambridge, Mass.

Ford (1984). *Continuing Process Control and Process Capability Improvement*. Ford Motor Company, Statistical Methods Office, Operations Support Staffs, Dearborn, Mich.

Ford (1990). *Planning for Quality*. Ford Motor Company, Corporate Quality Office, Dearborn, Mich.

Garvin, D. A. (1988). *Managing Quality: The Strategic and Competitive Edge*. Free Press, New York.

Harry, M. J. and Stewart, R. (1988). *Six Sigma Mechanical Design Tolerancing*. Motorola University Press, Schaumburg, Ill.

Juran, J. M., Gryna, F. M., and Bingham, R. S. (1979). *Quality Control Handbook* (3rd Ed.). McGraw-Hill, New York.

Stevens, M. (July 1991). "Quality Does Not Sell Quick Printing!" *Quick Printing*.

Taguchi, G. (1987). *System of Experimental Design* (Vol. 1–2). UNIPUB/Kraus International Publications, White Plains, N.Y.

2

PRODUCT VERSUS SERVICE

An overview of product and service quality is provided in this chapter. Specifically, the similarities and differences between the two are addressed and the service process is defined. In addition, the concepts of variation and the cost of quality as they relate to service are discussed.

OVERVIEW

Schwartz (1992) presents a very thought-provoking argument as to why the difference between product and service is important and why it is not a mere semantic issue. He claims, and rightfully so, that failure to distinguish between products and services contributes to lack of quality in both.

In a summary format and somewhat paraphrased, the following is what Schwartz (1992) has to say. A product is a transformation of matter and energy into a presumably desirable form, at presumably desirable locations, at presumably desirable times. Economists use the word "product" to represent the output, or result, of economic activity. Economists break down the overall category of product into two classes:

- The tangible product, which they call goods

- The intangible product, which they call services

The word "product" is sometimes used in the quality literature to refer to both goods and services, consistent with the economists' definition. For example, Juran and Gryna (1980, pp. 1–3) state that "we will frequently use the word 'products' as a short generic term to designate both goods (milk, clothes, houses, vehicles) and services (electrical energy, bus rides, health care, education)." When the word "service" is used to designate a product, the same word, used in the expression "product and service," sometimes refers to either of two different additional meanings.

The first meaning is field, customer, or product support. Service then means support such as warranty repairs or helpful advice. The second meaning is the behavior of the service provider, technically known as "service manner." Examples include friendliness and patience. The word "service" in the expression "product and service" all too frequently, however, refers to a vaguely formulated shifting composite of both support service and service manner.

The word "product" is also used in the quality literature to refer to a goods product and the word "service" to refer to a service product. In such cases, the expression "product and service" usually refers to the combination of the economists' two kinds of products: *goods* and *services*. Feigenbaum (1951) uses this terminology and then helpfully and consistently refers to what he calls "product service" as the separate support functions. Typical differentiation between the two concepts can be illustrated as follows:

The Majority of GOODS Are	The Majority of SERVICES Are
Tangible (100%)	Intangible (100%)
Storable (close to 100%)	Perishable (100%)
Transportable	Service providers are transportable
Immediate purchase is for capability of later performance	Immediate purchase is for immediate performance

DISTINCTION BETWEEN GOODS AND SERVICES PRODUCTS

Pure products are very rare. A bank's acceptance of a deposit might seem to be a typical pure service product, but, in fact, the deposit receipt, a component of the deposit services product, is no less tangible to a customer than a sheet of steel.

Whereas the skills for product (manufacturing) quality have been addressed in the literature quite extensively (Burr 1976; Small 1977; Duncan 1986; Ishikawa 1985; Crosby 1985; Gitlow et al. 1989; Gulezian 1991; and many others), the issues of service quality are—as of this writing—still developing. However, what has emerged are some skills that seem to be the foundation of service. These skills are:

- Determining and specifying quality of design

- Setting standards

- Measuring for conformance

- Rejecting defects

- Regulating the production process using feedback from inspection to improve the quality of service/product shipped

- Redesigning the service/product and the process using feedback from quality engineering to improve the quality of product made

Chase (1978) and Rathmell (1974) have made it clear that the degree of customer involvement is a fundamental distinguishing characteristic among services and their management. Using the degree of customer involvement as a criterion of distinction among services reveals that goods production and low customer contact, production-centered service operations, such as insurance companies and bank back offices, have more in common than do low customer contact, production-centered service operations and high customer contact, customer-centered service operations. This concept can be illustrated as follows:

Goods and Production-Centered Service Operations	*Customer-Centered Service Operations*
Customer involved in very few production processes	Customer involved in many production processes
Production and delivery processes are separate	Production and delivery processes overlap to: • varying degrees and • might even be identical
Production is independent of consumption	Production is frequently simultaneous with consumption

Goods and Production-Centered Service Operations	Customer-Centered Service Operations
Product design is centered on the customer, and process design is centered on the employee	Both product design and process design are centered on the customer
Production results show less variability	Production results show more variability
More amenable to standards, measurements, inspection, and control	Less amenable to standards, measurements, inspection, and control
Technically more complex	Technically less complex
Employee–customer relationships are generally not complex	Employee–customer relationships are generally very complex
Technical skills dominate operations	Interpersonal skills dominate operations
Training is heavily physical	Training is heavily psychological
Most producers do not deal directly with the customer	Most producers deal directly with customer
Economies of scale are generally readily attainable	Economies of scale are less readily attainable

It becomes clear that the degree of customer involvement ranges between being virtually continuous and being virtually zero. Examples of this concept are:

Close to Continuous	Close to Zero
Retail store shopping	Retail store stocking
Depositing a check	Processing a check
Restaurant dining	Restaurant cooking

The consequences of these characteristics are that involved customers can rush, slow down, disrupt, and alter production processes. Involved customers can influence the treatment of subsequent customers by the effect they have on service providers. Because of these major differences, in quality service we must become cognizant of what a process is and how variation affects the quality of service. Let's look at the process first.

PROCESS

Traditionally, a process has been defined as a series of actions which repeatedly come together to transform inputs provided by a supplier into outputs received by a customer. The output is simply what is produced by the actions. The actions which repeatedly come together are a combination of all or part of the following:

- Manpower
- Machine
- Material
- Method
- Measurement
- Environment

The focus of a process is to generate an output given an input. The greater the ratio of that output to input, the more efficient the operation is. This is illustrated in Figure 2.1, which provides a visual representation of a process in relationship to its components.

In service quality, the definition of a process is the same except that the actions which come together may be viewed as a combination of:

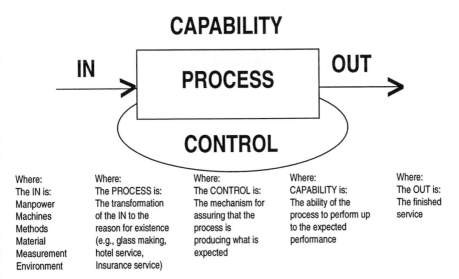

Where:	Where:	Where:	Where:	Where:
The IN is:	The PROCESS is:	The CONTROL is:	CAPABILITY is:	The OUT is:
Manpower	The transformation	The mechanism for	The ability of the	The finished
Machines	of the IN to the	assuring that the	process to perform up	service
Methods	reason for existence	process is	to the expected	
Material	(e.g., glass making,	producing what is	performance	
Measurement	hotel service,	expected		
Environment	Insurance service)			

FIGURE 2.1 A generic process model

- **Structure:**   The resources put together to deliver the service

- **Process:**   The service itself

- **Outcomes:**   The value results of the service

The focus of this process is to generate an outcome (benefit) that meets and/or exceeds the needs, wants, and expectations of the customer. Figures 2.2, 2.3, and 2.4 illustrate the relationship of the service process and its components, as well as the appropriate fit with the customer. What is interesting about the definition of the service process is that within the structure, process, and outcomes, the traditional components of the manufacturing process may indeed have to be accounted for.

For example, consider the case of a restaurant. The structure may be defined as the cooks, waiters, bus personnel, hostesses, facilities, tables, standard procedures, health regulations, and so on. The process may be defined as the food, the servicing of the food, procedures, attention to the tables, the ratio of waiters to tables, and so on. The outcome may be defined as the ambiance of the facility, the overall service, the level of satisfaction, and so on. Note that in each of these three categories, a number of traditional ingredients are included as part of the ultimate delivery of the service.

Another important issue in the quality of service is the concern of the owner. Who is the real owner of the process? The owner turns out to be the same as in the traditional manufacturing environment. That is, the owner of the process is

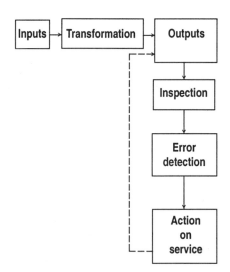

FIGURE 2.2 Traditional method of quality

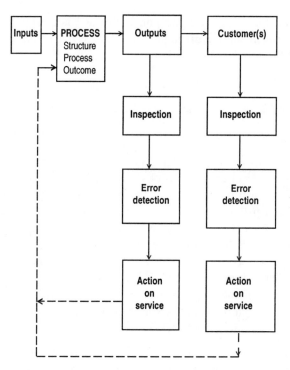

FIGURE 2.3   Traditional method of ensuring service quality

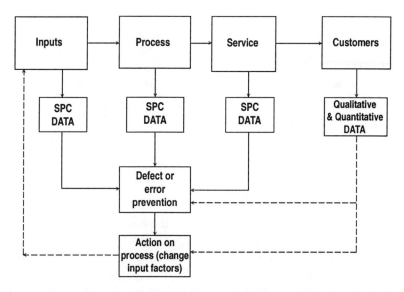

FIGURE 2.4   Deming's method of service quality: extended process

the person who has or is given responsibility and authority for leading the continuing improvement of a given process. Process ownership is driven by the boundaries of the process. For example:

Individual process	←———————→	Individual ownership
Functional process	←———————→	Unit-based ownership
Cross-functional process	←———————→	Unclear ownership

In the service environment, it is also not unusual to operate both sequentially and in parallel at the same time. This obviously is more difficult, and it becomes more complicated to precisely define the boundaries of the process. For example, consider a patient entering the hospital through the emergency department. While the patient is in the emergency ward, other departments are also required to be present for the services they provide (e.g., X-ray, respiratory, laboratory, medical records, and so on). Who is the customer here and what is the process? It depends on how the boundaries are drawn. Any department could be the customer of another department. The services provided to the patient not only are sequential, but in some cases are performed in parallel stages (e.g., X-ray services and laboratory work). Other examples of processes from the health care industry include:

Information flow	**Service delivery flow**
Admission/transfer/discharge	Operating room turnover
Revenue cycle	Emergency room waits
Budget development	Test result turnaround
Material/supply flow	**Patient diagnosis flow**
Meal tray delivery	Ambulatory surgery
Linen exchange	Labor and delivery
Supply restocking	Coronary artery bypass graft

VARIATION

Deming's (1982) message on variation is: "If I had to reduce my message to management to just a few words, I'd say it all had to do with variation." But what is variation? Simply defined, variation is the difference in the reproducibility of a particular action. Another way of defining variation is to say that it is the difference between a particular action and the target outcome. For a detailed explanation of variation, see Wheeler (1993).

Variation is an important concept in the scheme of quality, and as such it must be understood by all employees. Everyone—managers, workers, suppliers, customers, and investors—must play a role in the continual reduction of variation and the improvement of quality. Variation is what produces defectives (errors of any kind) and less uniform services. Reduction and control of variation will lead to the improvement of service. To do so, the work force must become involved in using statistical methods to provide management with information that will lead to improvements.

There are two kinds of variation: (1) common cause, sometimes known as inherent cause, and (2) special cause, sometimes known as assignable cause. Common cause variation occurs in all processes and in all organizations. It is produced by interactions of aspects of the process that affect every occurrence and/or aspects that are controlled by management and are part of the system. Examples of common cause variation are:

• Poor lighting

• Lack of training

• Poor office design

• Obsolete equipment

These kinds of problems can only be corrected by management intervention. In controlling this type of variation, it is management's responsibility to:

• Understand that responsibility for the process belongs to management. The process has an inherent capability which will not change unless the process is changed by management.

• Improve the process. It is management's responsibility to recognize that the process has to be improved and/or changed. (However, with empowerment in place, this may be a moot point.)

• Stop blaming others. Management must identify the aspects of the process that contribute to the common cause. Furthermore, management must determine which aspect of the process to change or improve in order to reduce variation or must adjust the middle (target) value of the process.

• Change the organizational view.

• Plan for the culture change as well as the process change.

• Never blame the workers for common cause variation.

• Not try to interpret individual variations of the process or explain the differences between highs and lows.

Special cause variation occurs in the process but does not affect every outcome. It is due to special circumstances, and any individual worker may address this kind of variation. Examples of special cause variation are:

- New form
- New employee
- New machine
- New schedule

These kind of problems may be addressed by the people who are closest to the process—the employees. The worker's responsibilities in controlling this type of variation are to:

- Communicate to management the specific problem(s)
- Learn the process so that the worker can identify any difference
- Be open to teamwork

This is not meant to imply that workers and management should have their own agendas, should pursue different courses of action, or are independent of each other. Rather, the two should always work together. Both have responsibilities. In general, the responsibilities of workers and management in controlling variation are to:

- Immediately try to understand when a special cause has occurred
- Determine what was different when the special cause occurred
- Identify ways to prevent the special cause from recurring, once it is understood
- Not make fundamental changes in the process
- Not tweak the process

INITIATIVE FOR THE APPROPRIATE ACTION DUE TO VARIATION

Depending on the kind of variation that has been identified in the process, either the worker or the manager may take the initiative for the appropriate action. Keep in mind, however, that in all cases of variation, both management and workers must work together to eliminate the variation. A pictorial representation of this cooperation is as follows:

	Who Typically Initiates Action	Need Help From
Special cause	**Worker**	**Management**
Common cause	**Management**	**Worker**

It is important recognize that this pictorial representation may change with empowerment. In fact, in Chapter 5 the distinction is made between empowerment with a lower-case "e" and an upper-case "E" to differentiate the contribution of the worker versus management.

The significance of initiating some action regarding the variation is that only if variation is eliminated from a process can that process become stable and capable of being improved. Everyone (management and nonmanagement) should always focus on the goal of reducing variation, because losses (however defined) begin to accrue as soon as products deviate from the nominal target. This, of course, is the philosophy of Taguchi, as expressed by the loss function (see Figure 1.3). The never-ending reduction of process variation around the nominal is maximally cost efficient and provides the degree of customer satisfaction demanded in today's marketplace.

COST OF QUALITY

Morse, Roth, and Poston (1987) define quality as a set of attributes that enable a service to conform to customer expectations. The assumption, of course, is that some design specifications have been developed and must be followed for the service in question. As long as all the specifications are being met, the customer is satisfied. When the specifications are not met, not only is the customer not satisfied, but that dissatisfaction can be measured.

The cost of quality is the cost that is incurred because poor quality, however defined, may or may not exist. Two broad categories of quality costs, prevention and appraisal, are incurred because poor quality may exist.

Prevention costs are those costs incurred to prevent poor quality products from being produced. Examples are analysis and planning for quality, quality training, development of process controls, and so on.

Appraisal costs are the result of activities undertaken to prevent poor quality services from being processed beyond the point at which they become nonconforming or from being delivered to customers. Examples include the inspection and testing of raw materials and products as well as services.

Those products that do not conform to quality standards often cause the organization to incur failure costs. Depending on the point at which quality problems are identified, failure costs are often classified as internal or external.

Internal failure costs are the costs associated with materials or services that fail to meet quality standards and are identified before the product or service is delivered to the customer. Examples include scrap, rework, and so on.

External failure costs are the costs incurred because poor-quality products are delivered to customers. Examples include the costs of handling complaints, product liability, warranty, returns and allowances, customer ill-will, and so on.

A general list of cost-of-quality items in service is provided in Appendix G. The list is not intended to be exhaustive; rather it is provided as a guideline to identify some critical characteristics in the service industry on a departmental basis.

REFERENCES

Burr, I. W. (1976). *Statistical Quality Control Methods*. Marcel Dekker, New York.

Chase, R. (November–December 1978). "Where Does the Customer Fit in a Service Operation?" *Harvard Business Review*.

Crosby, P. (1985). *Quality Improvement through Defect Prevention*. Philip Crosby Associates, Winter Park, Fla.

Deming, W. E. (1982). *Out of the Crisis*. Massachusetts Institute of Technology, Cambridge, Mass.

Duncan, A. J. (1986). *Quality Control and Industrial Statistics* (5th Ed.). Irwin, Homewood, Ill.

Feigenbaum, A. V. (1951). *Total Quality Control*. McGraw-Hill, New York.

Gitlow, H., Gitlow, S., Oppenheim, A., and Oppenheim, R. (1989). *Tools and Methods for the Improvement of Quality*. Irwin, Homewood, Ill.

Gulezian, R. (1991). *Process Control: Statistical Principles and Tools*. Quality Alert, New York.

Ishikawa, K. (1985). *What Is Total Quality Control? The Japanese Way*. Prentice-Hall, Englewood Cliffs, N.J.

Juran, J. M. and Gryna, F. M. (1980). *Quality Planning and Analysis* (2nd Ed.). McGraw-Hill, New York.

Morse, W., Roth, H., and Poston, K. (1987). *Measuring, Planning and Controlling Quality Costs*. Institute of Management Accountants, Montvale, N.J.

Rathmell, J. (1974). *Marketing in the Service Sector*. Winthrop Publishers, Cambridge, Mass.

Schwartz, M. H. (June 1992). "What Do the Words 'Product' and 'Service' Really Mean for Management?" *Quality Progress*.

Small, B. B. (1977). *Statistical Quality Control Handbook*. Western Electric, Easton, Pa.

Wheeler, D. J. (1993). *Understanding Variation: The Key to Managing Chaos*. SPC Press, Knoxville, Tenn.

3

COMMUNICATION
AND MANAGEMENT

As we already have seen, communication surfaces quite often in a variety of ways and in many circumstances throughout the quality service organization. Communication is perhaps one of the most important ingredients in the total quality service scheme. It is essential that managers in service industries be able to communicate by talking, listening, writing, and reading in the business environment. This is precisely the reason why the focus of this chapter is communication and management. Communication is defined, and a theoretical background for the need to integrate communication and management is provided.

The communication process contains elements involving sending and receiving a message as well as feedback. A pictorial representation of the communication process is shown in Figure 3.1. When people communicate, they engage in the act of sending and receiving a message. The sender encodes (forms) the message that the receiver decodes (develops meaning). Himstreet and Baty (1981) note that in order for communication to take place, there must be a sender and a receiver of the message. One cannot receive a message if no message has been sent.

Fitzgerald (1985) presents an analogy that brings together an understanding of communication. The analogy is the image of a ball being thrown and being caught. The ball is the message that goes back and forth. The pitcher, who

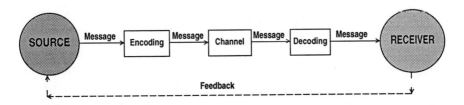

FIGURE 3.1   A simple model of the communication process

throws the ball, must concentrate on the mound, much like the communicator. The catcher, on the other hand, is the receiver and receives what is thrown, or what is being communicated. A major mistake in either a game of catch or in communication is taking a person or a situation for granted.

Just as every sender is different and cannot throw every type of ball well, every receiver (catcher) is also different and cannot catch every ball. Receivers may indeed have different skill levels, which must be taken into account. As a consequence, it is of paramount importance for each of us to know our weaknesses and strengths.

Communication in service industries can be either verbal or nonverbal. Verbal communication occurs on a one-to-one basis, in small groups, and in meetings and presentations. Telephone usage is another form of verbal communication.

Nonverbal communication can take the form of writing business letters, memos, newsletters, graphs, or reports. Other aspects of nonverbal communication are body language, eye contact, and dress.

In any organization, management communicates by formal and informal communication channels. Formal forms of communication includes reports and newsletters. Informal communication is evident in grapevines and social groups that exist within organizations.

Communication processes can occur horizontally, vertically, upward, and downward in an organization. Managers need to understand these processes and how they can use them in order to communicate more effectively. Today's managers must be effective communicators if they want to reach their goals of upper-level management positions, as well as deliver a quality service with customer satisfaction (Beck 1986; Parkinson and Rowe 1977). Communication is indeed the cornerstone of service.

Sheppard (1986) describes Dr. Albert Mehrabian's study on verbal and nonverbal communication as having three dimensions in face-to-face communication: verbal (the words actually spoken), vocal (the pitch, tone, and timbre of a person's voice), and facial expressions. He goes on to say that the relative weight for verbal impact is 7%, vocal 38%, and facial 55%. Thus, nonverbal communication is extremely important for managers, especially in the service industry.

"Nonverbal communication (body language) conveys our frame of mind with much greater accuracy than our most carefully selected words" (Lewis 1980, p. 150). When verbal and nonverbal communications contradict each other, people generally tend to believe the nonverbal. As an example, Sheppard (1986) cites a picture of President Gerald Ford bumping his head and tripping on steps. This said more about his capabilities than his verbal skills and inevitably led some people to question his actual abilities.

Another example was experienced by the author in the fall of 1992 during a project management training seminar in Singapore. The seminar started at 9:00 a.m. with no problem—until it was noticed that everyone in the seminar sat with their hands folded in front of their chest and there were no questions and/or comments. That went on until lunchtime. In the meantime, the author had tried to engage the participants in discussion to no avail. He was crushed. He thought he was not communicating and not well received. During lunch, he approached the seminar organizer to tell him of this predicament and ask if there was anything he could suggest to salvage the rest of the seminar. The seminar organizer began to laugh hysterically. When he finally stopped laughing, he said, with tears in his eyes, "I have personally asked the participants how they like it so far. Nothing to worry about, everybody loves your presentation and loves the topic. Your enthusiasm has made the difference." The author could not believe what he was hearing because he had already judged the situation based on his experience with body language in the United States. As it turned out, that was the wrong way to benchmark his success or failure because he was trying to compare two different cultures. Since then, he has visited Singapore several times and is both more sensitive to and knowledgeable about interpreting body language.

Two types of nonverbal communication are kinesic and metacommunication. "Kinesic messages are conveyed through actions, wink, frown, smile, sigh, grooming, attire, posture and temper" (Himstreet and Baty 1981, p. 8). Managers need to be more conscious of their own and others' facial and body expressions. Nonverbal communication is the articulation of one's feelings and behavior expressed in a very subtle manner. It is so common and prevalent that even an old saying continues to emphasize its importance: *the eyes are the windows to our souls.* Eyes show a person's real feelings. Clothing is another aspect of nonverbal communication. Many books, such as Malloy's *On Dressing for Success*, discuss the image a person projects by his or her clothing.

Metacommunication was described by Himstreet and Baty as reading messages between the lines. "Almost everyone has read business letters and can recall messages that were picked up 'between the lines'" (Himstreet and Baty

1981, p. 8). These messages are not literally expressed in words, but they accompany messages that are expressed in words (Himstreet and Baty 1981, p. 8). Receivers of these messages must listen to the message(s). This is quite appropriate in handling customer complaints.

The concept of listening can be thought of as receiving a message. Lewis (1980, p. 91) indicates that normal listening patterns result in 50% retention immediately after a 10-minute presentation, with a decline to 25% retention after a 48-hour period. These figures show that the average person experiences a 75% loss of information because of poor listening skills and illustrate the importance of ensuring that you not only listen (hear with comprehension) to others but that others are also listening to you when you speak. Hunt (1980) lists four functions of listening as:

1. Enables us to gain work-related information

2. Enables us to be more effective in interpersonal relationships

3. Enables us to gather data to make sound decisions

4. Enables us to respond appropriately to the communication messages we hear

Hunt (1980, pp. 82–85) lists the following ten ways to improve listening skills:

1. Listen for the sender's central idea

2. Concentrate on what the sender is saying

3. Do not let emotions influence listening

4. Do not reject what you hear as too familiar, unfamiliar, or trivial

5. Do not just listen for the facts

6. Avoid formulating arguments against the sender's ideas before you fully understand them

7. Try to ignore uncomfortable surroundings

8. Try to personalize the sender's topic

9. Be perceptive to the sender's nonverbal communication

10. Do not be afraid of difficult expository messages

People have to work hard to communicate well. They have to depend on both formal and informal systems as well as downward and upward modes of disseminating information through the organization. As a case in point, how can a customer service representative (CSR) without appropriate communication techniques resolve a customer complaint? If the CSR is not actively listening, the organization will have a bad reputation in the customer's opinion and the CSR will be frustrated since there can be no mutual resolution. The result is that everyone loses.

Upward communication is initiated by lower level employees and is directed toward top management. This enables top management personnel to know what is happening in the organization. Upward communication can take the form of interoffice memos and formal reports. Downward communication comes from the top down. Forms of this type of communication are bulletins, newsletters, and company newspapers. All the above are types of formal communication.

Informal communication includes the social (club) activities whereby managers can gain information. The company grapevine is another important type of informal communication. Although the grapevine is based mainly on rumors, Swindle and Swindle (1985, p. 13) indicate that about 90% of all rumors in business settings turn out to be accurate. Managers can make effective use of this type of informal communication by testing (leaking) information to see how it will be accepted or rejected. This approach is used by the government to test public reaction to sensitive policy decisions.

Writing letters is a type of formal communication. Good writing is a powerful tool; it can make a message stand out from the mass of writing competing for attention in the everyday production of messages in a corporation (Dumaine 1983, p. xi). Executives must impart ideas in a manner that will elicit the responses they are seeking. The first step in writing is for the writer to determine the purpose of the letter. A letters is written to persuade the reader to take the action the writer wants. An important rule is to write the information down while it is fresh in your mind. Everyone is busy, including the reader. Wells (1978) used the acronym "KISS" (Keep It Short and Simple) as a rule to be adhered to in writing. If a letter is too long, it will not be read. If a letter is poorly written, it will not be effective in communicating to others, no matter how good the idea may be. The reverse can and does happen; the reader is given the impression that the writer does not know what he or she is talking about.

Two common types of business letters are letters to say "no" and letters to handle complaints. Both require a prompt answer. When saying no, it must be said gracefully and in a friendly way. The writer should explain why he or she is saying no and emphasize the positive. Turn the letter into a sales letter (Rosenthal and Rudman 1968, p. 88). Handling complaints is another type of communication where the positive must be emphasized. Never minimize the complaint or blame the person who is complaining (Rosenthal and Rudman 1968, p. 125). Conflicts or complaints can be communicated in person as well as in writing.

Graphic aids are another form of presentation that enhance written communication (Lesikar 1979). Proper selection of the most appropriate format and appropriate placement of graphs can supplement writing. Graphic aids may be used in presentations well as meetings.

Meetings in an organization consist of the gathering of a number of people for a specific purpose. Preston (1979) identifies meetings as an opportunity for face-to face-communication. Properly run meetings serve a purpose, but a number of factors (long meetings, no set agenda) must be monitored to ensure that communication channels remain open.

Managers need to properly plan meetings, including proper arrangement of chairs and tables, deciding who will sit where, and the audiovisual aids that will be used. Managers must run effective meetings so that information can be shared by all members. Kerzner (1995, pp. 275–285) lists the following guidelines for effective meetings:

- Start on time. Waiting for people rewards tardy behavior.

- Develop agenda "objectives." Generate a list and proceed; avoid getting hung up on the order of topics.

- Conduct one piece of business at a time.

- Allow each member to contribute in his or her own way. Support, challenge, and counter. View differences as helpful; dig for reasons or views.

- Silence does not always mean agreement. Seek opinions.

- Be ready to confront the verbal member.

- Test for readiness to make a decision.

- Make the decision.

- Test for commitment to the decision.

- Assign roles and responsibilities.

- Agree on follow-up or accountability dates.

- Indicate the next step for the group.

- Set the time and place for the next meeting.

- End on time.

- Evaluate whether the meeting was necessary.

Dumaine (1983) identifies speeches as yet another channel through which information is imparted. The image a speaker projects is important in his or her effectiveness. Giving a speech can be very nerve-racking. In getting people to listen, good posture, eye contact, and a strong pleasant voice will aid the speaker. A speech must communicate what was planned rather than any feelings the speaker may be trying to overcome. The speaker should talk neither too slowly (boring) nor so fast that the audience is still trying to figure out what was said after the speech has ended. Always communicate at a level that will be understood by the least educated/experienced participants. Avoid jargon as much as possible.

Barriers such as noise affect communication. Managers need to be able to identify these barriers and take appropriate action to eliminate them. Kerzner (1984, p. 267) identifies some of these barriers as follows:

1. Receiver hearing what he or she wants to hear. This results from people doing the same job for so long that they no longer listen.

2. Sender and receiver having different perceptions. This is vitally important in interpreting contractual requirements, statement of work, and proposal information requests.

3. Receiver evaluating the source before accepting the communication.

4. Receiver ignoring conflicting information and doing as he or she pleases.

5. Communicator ignoring nonverbal cues.

6. Receiver being emotionally upset.

In addition to the above barriers, managers must also understand that communication in an organization can be filtered. Both managers and employees filter information for various reasons. They may not want unfavorable information to come to their supervisor's attention, may mistrust the message, or may be insecure about the outcome.

Another situation that both managers and employees deal with, especially in the service industry, is conflict. Communication during any conflict is emotional and must be dealt with sensitively. Baker and Morgan (1986, p. 21) suggest following four steps when facing a highly charged emotional conflict:

1. Recognize the feelings.

2. Encourage others to express their feelings.

3. Check the correctness of your perceptions.

4. Verbalize your own feelings.

Because conflict is so important, it is addressed separately in greater detail in Chapter 6.

Why is communication important in the service industry? It is especially important in the service industry because communication is indeed the lifeblood of service. Without it, nothing happens. It does not matter whether the communication is formal or informal. What does matter and what will facilitate the exchange of the service is understanding the message, however that message is transmitted.

Why must communication be addressed in the discussion of total service quality? The answer is provided by Swindle and Swindle (1985, p. viii). They report that "business managers spend as much as 80% of their time each day communicating." This in itself indicates that in order for a manager to be successful, he or she must communicate effectively. Ineffective communication will be interpreted as a manager who is ineffective. Communication skills can be learned, but they must also be practiced. Communication in the future will change somewhat with technological improvements such as the computer, which will be another tool that managers have at their disposal. Regardless of any changes that may occur, people will remain the real communicators in an organization.

REFERENCES

Baker, H. K. and Morgan, P. (1986). "Building a Professional Image: Using 'Feeling-Level' Communication." *Supervisory Management.* 31:20–25.

Beck, C. E. and Beck, E. A. (1986). "The Manager's Open Door and the Communication Climate." *Business Horizons.* 29:15–19.

Dumaine, D. (1983). *Write to the Top: Writing for Corporate Success.* Random House, New York.

Fitzgerald, P. E. (1985). "How to Play Catch." *Supervisory Management.* 30:26–31.

Himstreet, W. C. and Baty, W. M. (1981). *A Guide to Business Communication.* Learning Systems, Chicago.

Hunt, G. T. (1980). *Communication Skills in the Organization.* Prentice-Hall, Englewood Cliffs, N.J.

Kerzner, H. (1995). *Project Management: A Systems Approach to Planning, Scheduling, and Controlling* (5th Ed.). Van Nostrand Reinhold, New York.

Lesikar, R. V. (1979). *Basic Business Communications.* Richard D. Irwin, Homewood, Ill..

Lewis, P. V. (1980). *Organizational Communications: The Essence of Effective Management.* Grid Publishing, Cleveland, Ohio.

Parkinson, C. N. and Rowe, N. (1977). *Communicate: Parkinson's Formula for Business Survival.* Prentice-Hall, Englewood Cliffs, N.J.

Preston, P. (1979). *Communication for Managers.* Prentice-Hall, Englewood Cliffs, N.J.

Rosenthal, Irving and Rudman, H. W. (1968). *Business Letter Writing Made Simple.* Doubleday, New York.

Sheppard, I. T. (1986). "Silent Signals." *Supervisory Management.* 31:31–33.

Swindle, R. E. and Swindle, E. M. (1985). *The Business Communicator.* Prentice-Hall, Englewood Cliffs, N.J.

Wells, G. (1978). *How to Communicate.* McGraw-Hill, New York.

4

TOTAL QUALITY SERVICE IMPLEMENTATION STRATEGY

Earlier, total quality service (TQS) was defined as a true commitment to operationalizing the concept of customer focus, establishing service performance standards, measuring performance against benchmarks, recognizing and rewarding exemplary behavior, and maintaining enthusiasm for the customer at all times, so as to increase sales and market share.

In this chapter, that definition is formalized and a strategy for implementation based on the project management approach, the ISO 9000 standards, and the Deming philosophy is recommended. The project management approach has been chosen because it is one of the best tools for implementing a project in a given organization. Furthermore, it allows for proper planning, scheduling, and keeping track of the budget, resources, and schedule. The ISO 9000 standards have been chosen because they provide a very strong foundation for a quality system that systematically covers the entire organization. The Deming approach has been chosen primarily because it offers a more holistic approach to quality with specific goals.

OVERVIEW

A formal definition of the TQS concept is that TQS is a strategic, integrated management system which involves all managers and employees and uses both

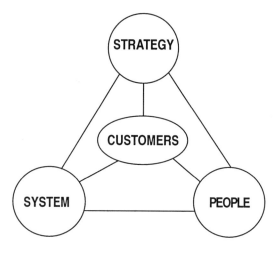

STRATEGY: A clear and well-communicated statement of the organization's position and goals on customer service.

SYSTEMS: Organizational programs, procedures, and resources designed to encourage, deliver, and assess convenient and quality services to the customer.

PEOPLE: Employees—in ALL positions—who possess the capacity and desire to be responsive to customer needs.

OVERALL OBJECTIVE:
Achieving customer satisfaction
Giving everyone responsibility
Making continual improvement

FIGURE 4.1   The total quality service system

qualitative and quantitative methods to continuously improve an organization's processes in order to meet and exceed customer needs, wants, and expectations. This relationship is summarized in Figure 4.1. The focus of TQS is on five areas, as follows.

1. Customer focus.   Identification of the customer is the number one priority. The organization must in no uncertain terms define who the customer is. The customer may be internal, external, and/or the service itself. Once the customer has been identified, then the customer's needs, wants, and expectations must be defined and planned for and a system designed to deliver the particular service. At this point, a measurement system should be developed, or at least planned for, in order to establish compliance with the requirements as the organization has defined them.

In addition to this customer definition, it is imperative that the organization develop a partnering relationship with key customers and suppliers on a win–win basis. The reason for this is to operationalize the customer requirements and ultimately to be able to measure effectiveness in meeting them.

The customer refers to the person or unit receiving the output of a process or system. The supplier is the person or unit that provides the service, information, material, etc. A customer may be the supplier for another service, just as a supplier may be the customer of a previous service.

2. Total involvement. Total involvement means commitment. Management must provide quality improvement opportunities for all employees and demonstrate leadership qualities all across the organization. Management must also delegate both responsibility and authority for improving work processes to those who actually do the work. Encourage job enrichment rather than busywork. An example of a job enrichment approach is shown in Table 4.1. Management must

TABLE 4.1 Job Enrichment Model

1. Recognize that there is a problem (symptoms: scrap, turnover, errors, grievances, etc.)

2. Vertical awareness in the organization and initial commitment to sanction the project (time, money, manpower, involvement, etc.)

3. Measurements of workers' feelings about job content

4. Top management confrontation with data

5. Selection of a task team (not workers whose jobs will be enriched)

6. Initial meeting with task team (role definition of team and resource person)

7. Team receives cognition base training (behavioral science understanding)

8. Presentation by supervisor of job characteristics and expectations (the job *as is* now)

9. Brainstorm the *as is* job

10. Separation of tasks into favorable and unfavorable items

11. Identify the hygiene items

12. Identify the motivators for the hygiene items

13. Develop the motivators into statements and definitions

14. Prioritize motivators

15. Potential problem analysis

16. Prioritize and review the hygiene items for possible implementation and combining with motivators

17. Combine both hygiene and motivators in the process

18. Presentation to management (the implementation plan and request for pending commitment)

19. Meeting with employees (communicate the plans)

20. Meeting with all others (internal and external) who will be influenced by the change

21. Implementation throughout the identified tasks; it must be gradual and it must involve all the effected and affected employees

22. Post-measurement

23. Review data with all interested parties

24. Improve and modify as needed

25. Enrich the task as needed

26. Do it all over again

empower the workers. As part of this empowerment, management must also create a climate in which multidisciplinary and cross-functional work teams are responsible for designing and improving products, services, processes, and systems.

The direct management commitment to quality improvement can be summarized as follows:

- Create a vision and establish a mission for your department
- Set quality improvement goals
- Identify your customers and their needs, wants, and expectations
- Start the improvement process
- Lead a team
- Serve on the steering committee
- Lead the improvement
  - o Provide the opportunity to form teams
  - o Recognize the need for training
  - o Train the employees
  - o Empower the employees to resolve issues affecting and effecting their work
  - o Encourage the employees to participate without fear
  - o Listen
  - o Provide feedback
  - o Support/direct/coach the employees
- Communicate with top management and steering committee
- Reward and recognize your employees for teamwork, improvement, performance, and contribution to quality
- Deming's improvement cycle (shown in Figure 4.2 as Plan-Do-Check (Study)-Act)
- Move from a "control" to a "commitment" organization (see Table 1.2)
- Move the organization to a new paradigm
- Utilize the human resources effectively (see Tables 4.1 and 4.2)

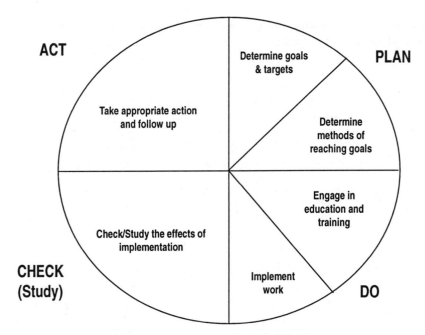

FIGURE 4.2 Deming's improvement cycle (PDC(S)A)

The indirect management commitment to quality improvement can be summarized by the following illustration:

3. Measurement. The need here is to establish some form of baseline measures internal/external to the organization and with customers. A generic and very simple measurement system is shown in Figure 4.3. The ingredients of this measurement system can take the form of:

TABLE 4.2 Effectiveness of Organizational Development (OD) and Quality Professionals

	Least Effective	Average	Most Effective
1. Mission	Teach and consult on methods and tools	Coach application of methods and tools and problem solving to quality and productivity improvement	Become involved in and coach improvement to competitiveness via diagnosis and system changes in all aspects of the organization
2. "Hooks" into organization	Training or quality assurance programs	Managing continuous improvements	Most vital organization-wide issues of the business
3. Language	OD and quality jargon	Quality statistics, costs	The many dialects of the business (laboratory, design, factory, field, customer, operations, financial, etc.)
4. Behavior	Work in classroom or within functional "silos"	Work in classroom, "silos," and with problem-solving teams	Work with management and groups of employees in their workplace, supplemented by appropriate training
5. Tools and techniques	Encourage standard tools and problem-solving sequences	Simple methods and tools for factory, more sophisticated methods and tools for professionals	Help apply whatever tools/methods are necessary for change—only as sophisticated as needed
6. Focus	Example problems	Real problems and processes in engineering, manufacturing, and other functions	Problems, process improvement, and system change

OD and quality professionals are most effective when:

- They are an integral part of addressing the most pressing issues of the business
- They speak many dialects and bring a broad range of tools or methods
- They are hands-on involved in the workplace instead of just consulted
- They help management change systems and help people add value to products and services

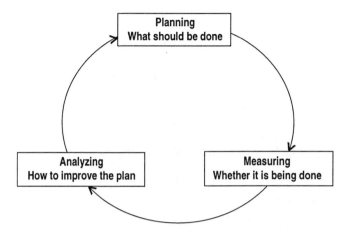

FIGURE 4.3   A generic measurement cycle in quality service

- Developing process and results measures

- Identifying outputs of critical work processes and measuring compliance with customer requirements

- Correcting and improving your own work

4. Systematic support.   Management's responsibility here is to manage the quality process by:

- Building a quality infrastructure tied to the internal management structure

- Linking quality to existing management systems such as:

  o Strategic planning

  o Performance management

  o Recognition, reward, and promotion

  o Communication

5. Continual improvement.   Everyone's responsibility is to:

- View all work as a process

- Anticipate changing customer needs, wants, and expectations

- Make incremental improvements

- Reduce cycle time

- Encourage and gladly receive feedback—without fear

At this point, it is logical to wonder why you should bother with TQS since service is an intangible item and, more often than not, is an instantaneous experience. The answer is simple. The following benefits can result from implementing TQS:

1. Increased quality satisfaction index by any measure

2. Increased productivity and efficiency

3. Increased profit

4. Increased market share

5. Increased employee morale

6. Increased customer satisfaction

How then is a quality system implemented in the service industry? The process begins by recognizing that some kind of change (paradigm shift) must occur within the organization in its current organizational structure, responsibilities, procedures, processes, and resources. A typical first change is the visionary and implementation roles shown in Figure 4.4. The process continues by beginning to add the systematic actions necessary to provide adequate confidence that the service will satisfy the customer, given the requirements defined on his or her behalf. A generic model of a quality system is illustrated in Figure 4.5.

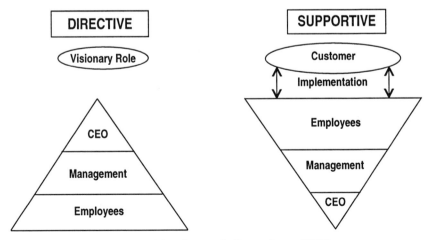

FIGURE 4.4   Visionary and implementation roles of TQS

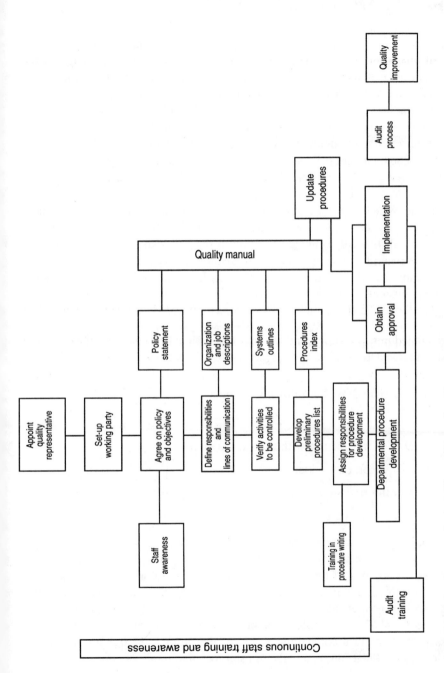

FIGURE 4.5   A generic quality system development

CHANGE AND PARADIGM SHIFT

It has been said that *the only thing in life that is for certain is change.* In the world of quality, change in any organization creates misunderstanding, confusion, and indecision. Change is difficult indeed. The reason for this difficulty is that each individual operates with his or her own set of paradigms.

A paradigm is a set of assumptions that enable us to create our own reality. In fact, these assumptions create their own rules or regulations that describe and sometimes control boundaries and tell us what to do in order to be successful within those boundaries. Paradigms are very powerful and help create constancy of the *status quo.* On the other hand, they also stifle and contribute to obsolescence of ideas as well as organizations. Some examples from the past may prove the point. Who would have thought that the following statements could have been made by such noted personalities: "Radio has no future" (Lord Kelvin, President, British Royal Society), "Who in the hell wants to hear actors talk" (Harry Warner, founder, Warner Brothers Studio), "The significant problems we have cannot be solved at the same level of thinking with which we created them" (Albert Einstein).

The basic question then is, how do we know when it is time to change and to what extent? The answer to this simple and straightforward question is that if you want to bring about change, you must be dissatisfied with the way things are right now (if you are not dissatisfied, why change?) and have a positive vision of what the future would look like if it were different. This simple concept can be represented by the following formula:

$$D \times V \times F > R$$

where D = dissatisfaction with the current situation

   V = vision of a better future

   F = the first steps of a plan to convert D to V

   R = resistance to change

It is clear see that unless resistance is less than the product of *DVF*, change will not occur. On the other hand, it is equally important to recognize that an increase in any one of the variables (D, V, or F) will not cause a change. The reason for this is that if any variable is missing (stays the same), the product will be zero (not greater than R).

The moral of this formula is that once everyone in a group shares a common dissatisfaction and a compelling vision of the future and commits to specific actions toward that future, a paradigm shift occurs. In other words, their way of making sense out of the current world changes. Organizational change, then, just as personal change, begins as resistance falls away.

In quality service, one of the many problems we are faced with is that management leaders have been brought up to micromanage and with a "don't rock the boat" mentality. Even if a manager moves to a new organization, there is a tendency to manage the same way because his or her paradigm has not shifted. A social analogy may prove the point. It is said that second marriages often fail for similar reasons as the first marriage did. In other words, people often remarry the same person in a different package—unless they change their whole way of looking at the world.

That is why a quality system and continual improvement are so difficult to implement. Until we can see a new way, we cannot bring it about. In that context, continual improvement looks like a band-aid—a little better here, a little better there—rather than articulating the dissatisfaction (whatever the level) and doing something about it in a systematic way.

At least three components define a positive quality transformation in a service organization: the values of the organization, the structure of the organization, and the style of the organization. Each one of these components must be addressed and evaluated from two points of view. The first is the now or current situation, and the second is the should be or needed situation. The following matrix identifies some of the components of each of the categories:

	Now	*Needed*
Values	Risk adverse	Innovation
	Caring	Service quality
	Competitive	Collaboration
	Quality is high	Continual improvement
	Quality costs	Quality prevention
Structure	Bureaucratic	Flat, decentralized
	Department independence	Collaboration
	Turf protection	Customer concerned
Style	Budget	Customer satisfaction
	Bottom line	Customer satisfaction
	Control	Empower/support
	Intuition	Quantify/measure
	Independence	Synergy

A GENERAL MODEL FOR CONTINUOUS IMPROVEMENT

Before considering a specific implementation program for quality service, let's examine a generic model. The purpose of this generic model is to present some of the basic concepts of implementation. To this end, an overview of some of the most common tools that are used in the implementation process is presented in Appendix F. The generic model follows a six-step approach, as follows.

Step 1: Identify the value-added service you provide to the customer. The focus of this step is on value added and service. Value added is the service that adds value to the customer. It must contribute to customer satisfaction. Service, on the other hand, is the result of what you do which is intended for some recipient outside of your function or process.

Step 2: Identify the customer and determine his or her expectations as closely as possible. The focus of this step is to identify the customer to whom you provide your service. Remember, the customer may be either internal and/or external. Regardless who the customer is, however, it is your obligation to strive toward delighting that customer.

Satisfying the customer may require a variety of actions, as each customer may have different needs and priorities. Some typical examples of customer expectations in the service industry are to:

- Be responsive and return phone calls promptly

- Be easy to contact

- Be reliable in meeting commitments

- Be responsive to complaints as well as empowered to solve problems

Step 3: Identify your critical needs that will enable you to satisfy the customer. In this step, the organization examines the critical requirements associated with each of the essential inputs that have been defined as important and in need of further study.

To use Motorola's terminology, the organization must in no uncertain terms identify and define **all** disconnects as they relate to the service. As defined by Motorola, a disconnect is a step, procedure, interface (input or output), or measurement in the process that is missing, unnecessary, performing poorly, or does not add value to the customer.

Step 4: Define the process for doing work. In this step, the organization defines the process of interest *as is*. This definition may be facilitated by using either a process flow or a process map or a combination of the two. The purpose of identifying the *as is* process is to help quantify the improvements. The definition of the *as is* and the expected improvement was illustrated in Figure 1.1.

Step 5: Mistake-proof the process and eliminate wasted effort. In this step, the benefits of measuring process performance are realized as the critical requirements are evaluated with the sole objective of improving the service, creating a new service, or discontinuing the current service. Examples of such measuring characteristics include cycle time (from writing up an order to receipt of the order), or cost of nonconformance, billing problems, and number of customer problems not solved by the first call.

Step 6: Ensure continuous improvement by supporting continual feedback. In this final step, the focus is to recognize the need to continually monitor for changes—of any kind—in customer requirements. Part of this recognition must deal with the appropriate definition of data selection and analysis as well as the desire to measure and monitor the improved process.

The specificity of this continual improvement can be summarized in the FOCUS model, as follows:

- **Find a process to improve.** This is where it all begins. Unless you find a process to improve, you cannot proceed in the improvement process. The question then becomes, how does an organization go about identifying the process to improve? The following questions provide some guidance and structure:

  1. What is a simple statement that describes the process and its boundaries?

  2. Who provides inputs to the process?

  3. What is provided by the supplier(s)?

  4. What is done with the inputs?

  5. What is produced by the process?

  6. Who receives the outputs? (Who benefits from the improvement of this process?)

  7. Why is it important to improve the process at this time?

  8. What is the opportunity statement that will serve as the mission of the improvement effort? (It should include items 1, 6, and 7 above.)

- **Organize a team that knows the process.** In this step, the process participants are identified as specifically as possible for appropriate action. The closer they are to ownership of the process, the better. The assumption that drives this step in the FOCUS model is the notion that the person who performs a task is the most knowledgeable about that process. How do you go about focusing on this ownership? The following considerations provide some guidance and structure in answering this question:

  1. Who should own the improvement of this process?

  2. Who will lead the team? If that person is not the owner of the process, is the process owner a member of the team?

  3. Is there representation from all the customer/supplier relationships within the process boundaries?

  4. Are the employees who work closest to the process part of the team?

  5. Who is the facilitator/advisor who will provide technical guidance and educational assistance to the team?

  6. What is the plan or road map for the team?

- **Clarify current knowledge of the process.** In this step, try to find out as much as possible about the current process. You must know where you are if you want to go someplace else. Good or bad news at this stage is not important. What is important is to define the process *as is* and then use that information as a benchmark for improvement. How do you go about focusing in this investigative process? The following considerations provide some guidance and structure in answering this question:

  1. What is the actual flow of the process as depicted by a flowchart?

  2. After studying the flowchart, have obvious improvements been identified?

  3. Does the team agree that making the obvious improvements will not adversely affect any other process?

  4. How should PDCA be used to make the obvious improvements? (See Figure 4.6.)

  5. Does everyone carry out the process in the same way? If not, why not?

  6. What steps should the team take to reach agreement on the "best" way for the process to work based upon current knowledge? How should

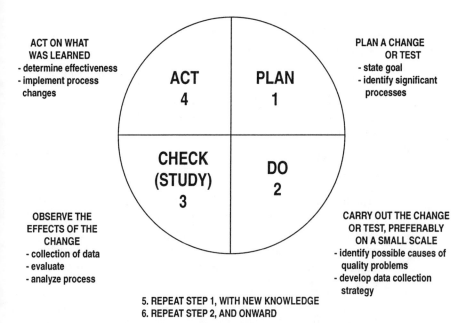

ACT ON WHAT
WAS LEARNED
- determine effectiveness
- implement process
changes

ACT
4

PLAN
1

PLAN A CHANGE
OR TEST
- state goal
- identify significant
processes

CHECK
(STUDY)
3

DO
2

OBSERVE THE
EFFECTS OF THE
CHANGE
- collection of data
- evaluate
- analyze process

CARRY OUT THE CHANGE
OR TEST, PREFERABLY
ON A SMALL SCALE
- identify possible causes of
quality problems
- develop data collection
strategy

5. REPEAT STEP 1, WITH NEW KNOWLEDGE
6. REPEAT STEP 2, AND ONWARD

FIGURE 4.6 The Plan, Do, Check (Study), Act cycle during continual improvement

PDCA be used, with emphasis on training everyone in the best process? (See Figure 4.6.)

7. Should the boundaries of the process be changed?

8. Based on what is now known, should refinements to the original opportunity statement and team membership be made?

- **Understand causes of process variation.** As discussed in Chapter 2, the concept of variation is very important. It is important because the type of variation that exists (common or special) affects the type of action plan(s) that will be required. How do you go about identifying this variation? The following questions may help in this process:

1. Has a dialogue been established with the customers of this process to build your knowledge about what is important to them?

2. What characteristic of the process output is most important to the customer (key quality characteristic, KQC)?

3. How was the customer involved in determining the KQC?

4. What is the operational definition of the KQC?

5. How should PDCA be used to establish a chart of the KQC?

6. Do the initial 20 to 25 data points indicate a special cause? If so, how should PDCA be used to find out what was different and take appropriate action?

7. Who will maintain and monitor the chart for signs of special causes on an ongoing basis?

8. Does the chart of the KQC indicate only common cause variation? If so, how should the flowchart and other knowledge of the process be used to identify the process variables? How can a cause-and-effect diagram be useful to systematically explain variables in methods, materials, measurements, environment, equipment, and people?

9. Based on this investigation and the interest in reducing variation in the KQC, what is the most important process variable (key process variable, KPV) to change and statistically control?

10. How should PDCA be used to establish a chart or time line for the KPV?

11. How should the cause-and-effect relationship between the variables and the KQC be investigated? Would a scatter diagram be helpful?

- **Select the process improvement.** In this final stage, you make the commitment to improve a specific process. Fundamentally, there are three questions that you must answer before you proceed:

  1. What are the alternative process variable changes?

  2. What criteria will be used to choose among them?

  3. What is the clear, simple description of the proposed process improvement?

To help you and your organization focus on the right process with the right plan of expectations, you may also want to employ the rationale of the Shewhart/Deming cycle, otherwise known as PDCA. In its simplest form, the PDCA model as applied in the service industry is as follows:

The PDCA cycle in the service industry

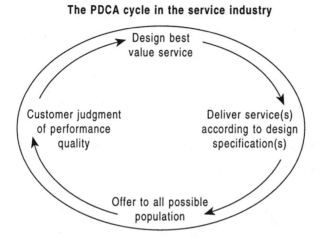

For a more traditional view of the PDCA cycle, see Figures 4.2 and 4.6. PDCA can be used to help address the following issues and concerns:

- **Plan the improvement and continued data collection.**   In this initial phase, planning is challenged for appropriateness, effectiveness, soundness, and so on. The following questions are designed to help in this challenging phase:

  1. Does the plan include what the improvement will be and who will make it?

  2. Does the plan include when, where, and how it will be made?

  3. How should the change be piloted?

  4. Does the plan include the who, what, when, where, and how of the continued data collection?

  5. How will the charts of the KQC and KPV be used to test the theory?

- **Do the improvement, data collection, and analysis.**   In this phase, the focus is on data and all its ramifications (e.g., appropriate sampling, collection mechanisms, usage of analysis, and so on). The following questions are designed to help in this questioning process:

  1. Is the improvement being implemented according to the plan?

  2. Who is monitoring the plan?

  3. Has maximum use been made of graphical means of data display?

- **Check and study the results.** In this phase, focus is on evaluation of the results. Some direct questions to be asked include the following:

  1. Did the process improve as expected?

  2. Did it improve from the customer's point of view?

  3. Did the process improve from the point of view of those who work in the process?

  4. What aspects of the team effort went well?

  5. How could the collaboration be improved?

  6. Were any easily measured savings identified?

- **Act to hold the gain and to continue to improve the process.** The focus here is on monitoring and feedback. You are interested in holding any gains you may have achieved as a result of the specific action you took, but also are interested in continuing improving from where you currently are. The following questions are designed to help focus on these two issues:

  1. What parts of the improved process need to be standardized?

  2. How will the flowchart be changed?

  3. What policies and procedures need to be revised?

  4. Who needs to be trained?

  5. Who needs to be made aware of the change?

  6. Who will continue to maintain the charts of the KQC and KPV?

  7. Based on the new knowledge, should the owner of this process be changed?

  8. Repeat appropriate steps of FOCUS-PDCA for as long as its remains economically feasible.

THE PROJECT MANAGEMENT MODEL FOR IMPLEMENTATION

Quality systems have been failing in the implementation process all across the spectrum of industries, to the point where some sectors believe that quality systems may not apply to them at all (Griffiths 1990; Hall 1990; Latzko 1986; English and Josh 1987; Nader 1987). The reason(s) why TQS has not been a success may be due to several causes; however, the most critical appear to be the lack of commitment to TQS, as well as lack of an overall strategy for implementation (Clemens 1987; Hausmann 1987; Lipscomb 1991; Schein 1985; Stamatis 1994). All this unfocused energy can be characterized by the story of several blind men trying to describe an elephant. Each man's description was dependent upon which part of the elephant he was touching, which resulted in an inaccurate description of the animal. In fact, as the story goes, the blind men identified each part of the elephant as an independent part having nothing to do with the elephant's anatomy. Lack of communication between the men and an inability to see the "whole" produced a result that had nothing to do with the elephant.

Some companies have made the same mistake as the blind men (i.e., failure to see the "whole" picture). As a consequence, companies emphasize Deming, Juran, Crosby, Q101, Targets for Excellence, Pentastar, Six Sigma, and many more individual routes to improvement. They fail to recognize the concept of quality in its totality. Rather, they focus on the individual program to get them through the improvement process, as well as satisfy the customer in the most expedient way.

QUALITY MANAGEMENT

The inability to define quality as it relates to all functions within a company has resulted in the unsuccessful implementation of quality improvement programs. In what some would call a typical American approach, quick fixes have been applied to the symptoms of problems instead of applying corrective action to root causes.

The failure has been the result of defining quality problems by looking at only portions of the implementation process, as opposed to viewing the process as an integrated whole. Examples of such approaches include quality circles, worker involvement, employee empowerment, statistical process control, participative management, design of experiments, quality function deployment, failure mode and effect analysis, just-in-time, preventive maintenance, and many more.

Companies that have tried these individual programs have had limited, if any, success. Success here is viewed as **total** improvement in any given organization. To be sure, many companies have very successful individual programs, but they do not tie them together. Pockets of success are therefore the end result, rather than a complete understanding of the overall goal of the organization. The holistic approach (i.e., incorporating all of these programs throughout all disciplines and functions within the organization) is missing.

Where successes have been published, such as the Four Seasons Hotel, Henry Ford Hospital, all the companies in the National Demonstration Project (Berwick et al. 1990), Ford Motor Company, Motorola, Holiday Inn, Federal Express, Hewlett-Packard, and others, it appears that multidimensional programs may have a greater chance of success if for no other reason than they involve more people. However, if these multidimensional programs are implemented only in the quality department, companies will still be frustrated by the lack of results. The lesson may be that a complete formula without a method for company-wide implementation will not guarantee the desired final product.

Like a recipe for a cake without baking instructions, a quality improvement program without an implementation strategy is unlikely to produce the desired results. The methods by which companies implement their strategies for improved quality are, therefore, more important than the complete list of ingredients. In order for a quality program to be implemented with the desired success, a project management approach must be instituted throughout the organization. Project management is recommended because it involves cross-functional and multidisciplined people in implementing the project. Quality here is viewed as just another project. (It is important to recognize that we are referring to implementation of quality rather than the concept of quality, which is not a project but rather a philosophy of doing things). The distinction between a project and philosophy is that one of the key ingredients of a project is that it has definite start and end dates (Kerzner 1992). In contrast, a philosophy has a definite start but no end date.

IMPLEMENTATION OF TOTAL QUALITY SERVICE

Stamatis (1992a, 1992c, 1991) has defined the steps for implementing TQS as:

1. Energize the organization with quality awareness.

2. Change the culture of the organization.

3. Define the scope of your commitment to the organization as a whole.

4. Identify key process and product variables.

5. Implement statistical process control.

6. Incorporate process improvement activities in the organization.

7. Assess the quality improvement in the organization.

Detailed discussion of these seven steps can be found in Stamatis (1991). However, in order for these steps to be effective, the organization must be willing to invest resources in high-performing project teams. A high-performing team is a team that performs at a level of excellence far beyond that of comparable systems (the concept of synergism). Some of the ingredients of a high-performing team are:

1. It produces high-quality and high-value products and services.

2. It consistently performs well against known internal and external standards.

3. It uses significantly fewer resources than would be expected.

4. It generates a sense of enthusiasm and excitement among its members and those who come in contact with the team.

5. It serves as a source of ideas and inspiration for others.

To get to these ingredients, a company must be willing to change. One change must be in the area of employee empowerment. It is imperative that the organization communicate to the employees the concept of "what's in it for me" rather than "do it because it's good for the organization." This change can be facilitated through a project management approach, since this integration of change will involve everyone in an organization. This integration will help in project planning.

Quality implementation is not a linear transformation, but rather a burst function (matrix structure) that crosses the entire organization. A pictorial view of this is provided in Figure 4.7 (Stamatis 1992a). The idea of the "burst" is that it allows the whole organization to actively participate toward achieving a

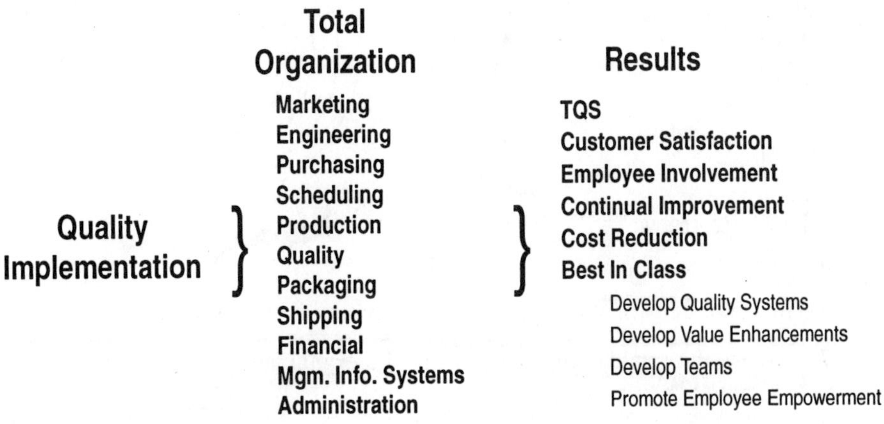

Total Organization **Results**

| Quality Implementation } | Marketing
Engineering
Purchasing
Scheduling
Production
Quality
Packaging
Shipping
Financial
Mgm. Info. Systems
Administration | } | TQS
Customer Satisfaction
Employee Involvement
Continual Improvement
Cost Reduction
Best In Class
Develop Quality Systems
Develop Value Enhancements
Develop Teams
Promote Employee Empowerment |

FIGURE 4.7   Burst function

common goal. However, the pace of individual departments may be at different levels, as required.

TOTAL QUALITY SERVICE AND PROJECT MANAGEMENT

The burst function is dynamic and constantly changes to connect people in different ways as the need arises for innovation and problem solving. This kind of flexibility will ensure that the organization remains adaptive to change. Furthermore, this matrix organization will speed up the cumbersome communication paths of the typical hierarchical structure present in most organizations. The relationship between project management and TQS is illustrated in Figures 4.8 and 4.9 (Stamatis 1992a).

The overall relationship between project management and TQS is illustrated in Figure 4.8, which visually presents the essential components of both project management and TQS. In Figure 4.9, the relationship between project management, TQS, and the organization as a whole is depicted. In Figures 4.10 and 4.11, the overall relationship between project management and TQS as it applies to the organization is illustrated. Specifically, Figure 4.10 visually demonstrates

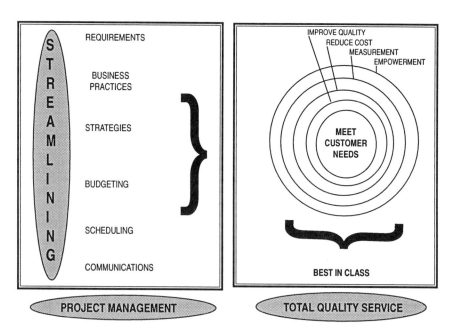

FIGURE 4.8 The relationship between project management and TQS

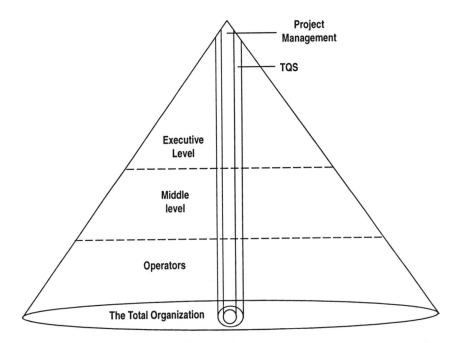

FIGURE 4.9 The relationship between project management, TQS, and the organization

that TQS is indeed the core of the organization, and Figure 4.11 visually demonstrates that the pegs called TQS are in fact the connecting points for the levels in the organization. Precisely what are the characteristics that TQS provides and that project management facilitates? The following list is only a sample:

1. **Shared vision, mission, goal, and common purpose:** The executive, middle, and operating management share the vision, mission, goal, and common purpose to the point of understanding their existence and, as a consequence, building a strong bond for their successful implementation.

2. **Visionary leadership:** The management of the organization acts as a champion for the objectives set in item 1. This championship is of paramount importance as management seeks consensus and commitment among the entire organization as well as help in the widespread communication of the message.

3. **Efficient use of resources:** Management and all personnel must utilize all resources with high efficiency.

FIGURE 4.10   The relationship between the organization and TQS

4. **Well-defined and managed boundaries:** Management must recognize its limitations and stay within its own environment.

5. **Optimum flexibility:** Management must be stable enough to operate efficiently, yet flexible enough to respond quickly and effectively to changing conditions, demands, and opportunities not only in the horizontal mode of the organization but also in the vertical structure as well.

6. **Effective teamwork:** Management must encourage cooperation and teamwork and lead by example.

7. **Customer focus:** Management in each of its levels must be cognizant of customer needs, wants, and expectations. As a consequence, it gives high priority to items that will be of value to the customer.

8. **Effective renewal process:** Management must develop formal processes that enables it to readily adapt to changes in internal or external needs, demands, and conditions.

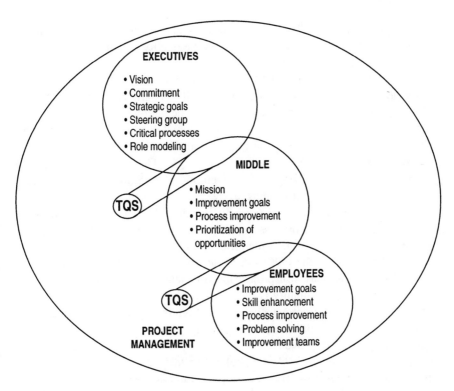

FIGURE 4.11   Project management and the relationships of TQS in the organization

9. **Emphasis on learning, development, achievement, and support-oriented work cultures:** Management must recognize that learning is a continual process and is essential for any organization. A balance between achievement and support orientation in the work environment is also essential.

10. **Effective performance and evaluation:** Management must focus on tasks and objectives rather than personalities.

THE INFLUENCE OF PROJECT MANAGEMENT IN THE IMPLEMENTATION PROCESS

At this point, one may wonder why the quality department cannot do all the above. The answer is very simple. Quality departments do not produce quality products. Rather, they serve as the executers and integrators of TQS in the organization. In fact, in some organizations the quality department serves only as a "scorekeeper" of quality.

The execution and integration of TQS may indeed be facilitated by the quality department. However, unless the quality department utilizes the principles of project management, successful implementation may indeed be doubtful. Project management may be used, since project planning and project monitoring are the ingredients of a true quality commitment in the organization.

How does project management fit into TQS? The answer is given in a pictorial form in the following figures (Deming 1986; Stamatis 1992a). Figure 4.2 identifies the Shewhart/Deming cycle and applies the basic principles of project management. Figure 4.6 identifies the Plan-Do-Check(Study)-Act (PDC(S)A) cycle and the process improvement, with even more detail for the expected functions. Figure 4.12 identifies the model for total quality management in relationship to the PDC(S)A cycle. In fact, it ties the implementation steps of TQS to the phases of project management.

Modern thinking on quality is that work must be done through teams. The purpose of a team is to improve a process through the use of the knowledge and skills of that team of individuals who have the greatest day-to-day knowledge of the process. That improvement of course is the decision of the team, based on consensus. The team is *always* seeking to make those changes within its authority and responsibility that will improve the process.

Why is it, then, that teams fail even though they work on opportunities, concerns, and/or problems within their process? Bradford (1976) identifies some of the reasons as:

1. **Assignment too broad:**   The project is too big for individual (specific) resolution.

2. **Responsibilities unclear:**   No clear-cut authority and responsibility for the project.

3. **No measurability:**   No mechanism for effective feedback.

4. **Lack of management support:**   Everybody talks about the project, but nobody really does anything about it (the proverbial "lip service").

5. **Project irrelevant to the team members (no ownership):**   Dictation of a problem from outside sources rather than development of the problem within the scope of the team.

6. **Team members do not have the appropriate skills:**   Lack of fundamental knowledge in team dynamics and group behavior, as well as problem-solving techniques (basic to advanced).

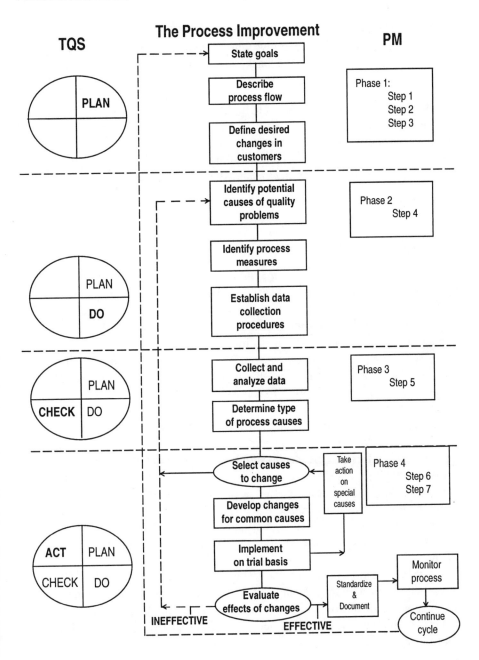

FIGURE 4.12   The relationship of process improvement to TQS and project management

7. **No clear-cut reporting relationships:** With no authority and responsibility, nobody really knows what is going on. Poor reporting facilitates poor to unacceptable feedback, and the result is a poor decision on the part of management.

How does project management help the implementation process? In order to answer that question, we must first address the issue of what project management is. By definition, project management focuses on the project (Kerzner 1992). A project, on the other hand, is an undertaking that has a beginning and an end and is carried out to meet established goals within specific:

- Costs

- Schedules

- Quality objectives

Project management brings together and optimizes (puts the focus on the allocation of resources) rather than maximizes (going all out at the expense of something else; maximization leads to suboptimization) resources, which include skills, talents, cooperative efforts of teams, facilities, tools, information, money, techniques, systems, and equipment.

Since the implementation process of TQS was defined as a project, it follows that the allocation of resources in any organization must be of importance, and, therefore, the appropriate tool for such a task is indeed the project management approach.

A second question is of value in dealing with the appropriateness of project management: How does project management differ from other management principles? It differs in at least two significant ways. First, it focuses on a project with a finite life span, whereas other organizational units expect perpetuity. Second, projects need resources on a part-time and full-time basis, whereas permanent organizations require resource utilization on a full-time basis. The sharing of resources may lead to conflict and requires skillful negotiation to see that projects get the necessary resources to meet objectives throughout their life spans.

A third question regarding the implementation of TQS may be: How and what will project management do to facilitate this implementation? Project management will follow and assure success of the implementation process by following the four phases of a project's life (Kerzner 1992). The four phases are as follow.

1. Defining the project. When the decision to implement TQS has been made by management, the first order of business is to clarify the project and arrive at an agreement among all concerned about the specific definition and scope as well as the basic strategy for carrying it out. Some of the activities that project management will address in this stage include:

- Study, discuss, and analyze the focus of the project and its relation to the organization.

- Write the project definition. Writing the definition will demonstrate confidence and understanding of the project. Of course, at this stage the definition may prove to be preliminary and may be revised as more information flows into the organization.

- Set an end result objective. Using the preliminary definition, plan the end result objective(s), preferably on a milestone and/or critical path chart.

- List absolute and desirable needs. Plan or list the outcomes that will define the success of the project.

- Generate alternatives. Because project management focuses on allocation of resources, it follows that the more alternatives that are provided early on, the more likely it is that the led objective will be met.

- Evaluate alternatives. The focus here is on realistic expectations that reflect the end result rather than sheer optimism or what we wish we could achieve.

- Choose a course of action. Evaluation in the previous step will help in the selection of an action plan that meets the project definition and objective.

2. Planning the project. Planning means listing in detail what is required to successfully complete the project along the critical dimensions of quality, cost, and time. Specifically, in this phase the following may be addressed:

- Establish the project objective. Review, and if need be revise, the objective to reflect the new information.

- Choose the strategy for achieving the objective.

- Break down the project into small steps. The smaller the steps, the better the control and understanding. Recall the earlier discussion about failure(s) being attributed to projects that are too large.

- Determine the performance standards. Unless the standards of success are defined in this phase, problems may arise later on in the evaluation phase.

- Determine the time requirements. Be realistic. Time is very important, not only from a resource allocation perspective but also in terms of the morale of the participants. Time limits that are too conservative ask the impossible. On the other hand, time limits that are too loose portray the project as less important. This element of defining the time is perhaps the most crucial in the entire implementation process.

- Determine the sequence of implementation: who, where, what, why, and how. This sequence is relevant for a successful implementation.

- Design a cost budget. It is important to know how much the implementation is going to cost, not only to satisfy the financial department but for planning purposes as well.

- Design the staff organization. Know who is going to do what and determine whether or not the organization has the available personnel to carry out the implementation.

- Determine the appropriate training. What is necessary in terms of training? Who is going to do the training? Will it be done internally or externally? Will outside consultants play a major, minor, or no role in the implementation?

- Develop policies and procedures. What are the goals and the general vision of the implementation and how will they be carried out? The policies and procedures are the guideposts for the entire implementation process. However, they may change because implementation itself is a dynamic process.

3. Implementing the plan.   The entire project is coordinated on an ongoing basis. Some of the responsibilities of this coordination include controlling and/or monitoring the work in progress according to plan; negotiating changes to the plan, services, and supplies; providing appropriate feedback (formal or informal) to all concerned; resolving differences; and making sure that a corrective action plan exists and is being followed.

4. Completing the project.   The goal of project management is to obtain management acceptance of the project result. This means that management agrees that the quality specifications of the project parameters have been met. For this agreement to take place as smoothly as possible, an objective evaluation must occur based on measurable criteria defined in the early stages of the implementation. As part of the completion phase, it is imperative that follow-up steps be defined to make sure that the TQS now in place will not fade away. The definition of this follow-up should be very specific, so that the continuation of the TQS will be self-sustained.

This recommendation is based on the fact that TQS is people dependent and, furthermore, that people are of cross-functional and multidisciplined backgrounds. Project management is strongly recommended to manage such diversity.

THE ISO MODEL FOR IMPLEMENTATION

The ISO standards are a very basic form of defining a quality system. They provide the structure and elements of a complete quality system as well as a means for standardization throughout the world. The intent of this section is not to give an elaborate rationale for the existence and application of ISO; rather, the intent is to provide a simple overview of the standards and the implementation process for a service organization. For a more detailed discussion, see Peach (1992), Lamprecht (1992), and Stamatis (1992b), among others.

Global competition requires that our attitudes and values toward work be dynamic, engaging, and collaborative. The ISO 9000 standard series is one way to revitalize people, their attitudes, and their approaches to work. It is indeed the core minimum of all quality systems taking into consideration the entire organization. An overview of this relationship is illustrated in Figures 4.13 and 4.14. Note that in Figure 4.13 ISO is not only the center of all the functional departments in a given organization (the base of the cone) but also cuts through all levels of personnel (both management and nonmanagement). Figure 4.14 shows the relationship between project management, ISO, and TQS.

There are surprisingly few basic principles associated with ISO, but actually integrating them into the fundamental work of the business may be the toughest thing a management team does. If these basic principles are allowed to develop, they may change the very nature of work itself. To focus on this work with a specific goal of *improvement,* at least three issues must be considered:

1. **Establish important goals and objectives:** Management must identify why it is interested in ISO and, perhaps more importantly, must define reality from the organization's point of view. Is management pursuing ISO because of outside influences or because of a general philosophy to be the *best?*

2. **Formulate actions via policies, programs, and procedures to achieve the desired goals:** Management must be committed to rather than merely involved in whatever it says and does. The mode of operation should be to *lead by example* rather than to lead by memo and/or direc-

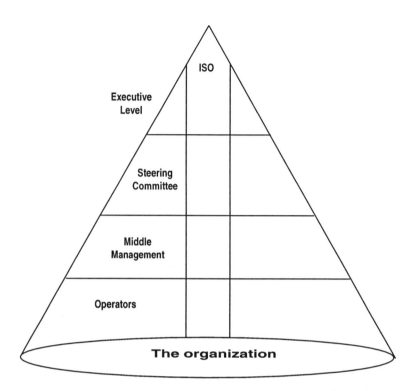

FIGURE 4.13 The relationship between the organization and ISO

tive. It is imperative that policies, programs, procedures, and goals be based on being purpose led (vision), planning oriented, people centered, process focused, and performance based. All effort should be directed toward eliminating bias and partial information.

3. **Understand the source(s) of resistance and neutralize them:** All work creates stress. All work contributes to resistance once the work is understood. It becomes the *status quo*. It is the job of senior management to make sure that everyone in the organization understands that conflict occurs, and more often than not it is normal. However, with effective vertical and horizontal communication, tactical and operational plans can be developed by empowered associates who know where the organization is going and are acutely familiar with the strengths and weakness of both the company and its competitors.

To facilitate these basic principles, it is recommended that a project management approach be at the center of the implementation process, as illustrated in

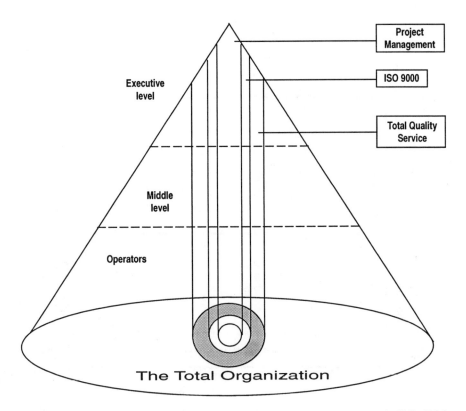

FIGURE 4.14 The relationship between project management, ISO, TQS, and the organization

Figure 4.14. Project management by definition defines the project—its beginning and end, budget, scheduling, and allocation of resources. (The ISO implementation process is defined as a project.)

A typical approach to project management is to define the project initiation, understand the process, meet the ISO training strategy and requirements, and monitor the process. An example of some of the specific items included in project management is provided in Figure 4.15.

Once project management is established and understood by the organization, it is time for the full ISO 9000 implementation process. Note that this implementation task is indeed a process. It is not necessarily a linear process, but it follows four phases, each of which defines a certain level of content and understanding of the process. An overview of this implementation is provided in Figure 4.16. This figure, in conjunction with the general model that follows, defines the individual tasks and responsibilities of each phase. The model of ISO implementation is based on the following phases:

Phase 1	Phase 2	Phase 3	Phase 4
Management Commitment	*Set up the structure*	*Implementation of procedures*	*Registrar*
Project initiation	**Understand process**	**ISO training**	**Monitoring progress**
Management planning and goal setting	Team flowcharting for process understanding and analysis	Executive training	Employee control in process
Department business and technical commitment	Cause-and-effect analysis	Department training	Define quality manual, procedures, instructions and forms as they relate to the specific department area
Quality team selected and active	Critical in process parameters identified	Identification of shortcomings in the system of quality i.e., specific areas	Internal audit
Training philosophy and tools of quality	Standard operating procedures review, equipment repair, preventive maintenance and calibration	Define boundaries of responsibility	Visit by the Registrar
Process definition and selection	Process input and measurement evaluation	Define limitations of resources	Official audit
Critical characteristics identified	Static process data collection	Review system for completeness	Follow up and maintenance of certification

This grid takes into consideration that the activities in previous phases may or may not be completed. The advantage of implementing ISO 9000 in any organization is that the implementation process can be parallel, horizontal, and/or vertical. The pace and rate of implementation may indeed be different for each individual department. **The long-term goal is to receive and keep the certification.**

FIGURE 4.15   The ISO 9000 status grid

Phase 1	Phase 2	Phase 3	Phase 4
Management Commitment	*Set up structure*	*Implementation*	*Registrar*

Establish an ISO implementation team of one person from each functional area. Define a steering committe
 	
Train those selected in ISO knowledge
	Define company objectives in ISO format:
	  Mission
	  Goals
	  Focus on continual
	    improvement
	  Policies and
	    procedures
	  Quality management
	    commitment
		Define the goal of ISO implementation and/or certification
		
		Examine internal structure and compare it to ISO:
		  Determine department
		    objectives
		  Review structure of the
		    organization
		  Review job descriptions
		  Review current processes
		  Review control mechanisms
		  Review training requirements
		  Review communication
		    methods
		      Reports
		      Meetings
		      Record keeping
		  Review all approval processes
		  Review risk considerations and
		    how are they addressed
		  Review all outputs
		  Review all action plans
			Registrar requirements
			  Audit
			  Surveillance
			  Corrective action
			  Certification
			  Re-certification

FIGURE 4.16 Requirements under each of the phases of project management

Phase 1: Management commitment

- Gain commitment

- Develop a strategy

Phase 2: Set up the structure

- Develop the organization

- Train the employees

Phase 3: Implementation of procedures and documenting the quality system

- Identify all pertinent procedures, policies, and practices to meet ISO 9000.

- Prepare the documentation. The full relationship of documentation is displayed in Figure 4.17.

    1. Quality manual: A road map to the system, outlining the policies and objectives that relate to specific aspects of the system.

    2. Procedures: Provide process descriptions and flowcharts of activities and give detail as to what, who, where, and why an activity is carried out.

    3. Work instructions: Step-by-step description of how to carry out a task. They are often called standard operating procedures (SOP), standard job practices (SJP), or operating guides. Work instructions must be revised and integrated into the overall documentation system.

    4. Forms and records: Forms are often used to collect information and record the completion of required quality activities. Sufficient records must be kept to provide objective evidence that the quality activities are being carried out.

Phase 4: Working with the registrar

- Pre-assessment

- Site visit (audit)

- Registration or corrective action

- Follow up

Finally, the overall structure of a company-wide ISO 9000 implementation is illustrated in Figure 4.18. This figure not only identifies the individual phases

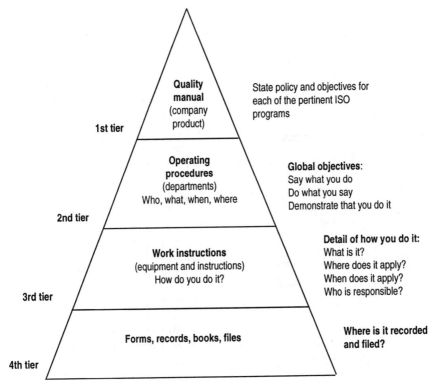

FIGURE 4.17   The ISO 9000 quality pyramid (the four tiers of documentation)

that the implementation process must go through, but in addition identifies the sequence of events that must be followed in the pursuit of certification.

One of the most important steps in Figure 4.18 is registrar selection during Phase 2. This is very important as it may take some time to secure a registrar for the certification process. Be prepared as early as possible.

Because the ISO structure provides for the foundation of quality, it is by definition less stringent than the total philosophy of TQS. To be sure, contrary to public opinion, ISO provides for *continual improvement* in the scope of the standard, the corrective action subsection, and elsewhere. To move from ISO to TQS requires an extension of all the basic quality guidelines as found in ISO and an active initiative in the principles of:

- Measurement
- Customer satisfaction by actively listening to customer needs, wants, and expectations

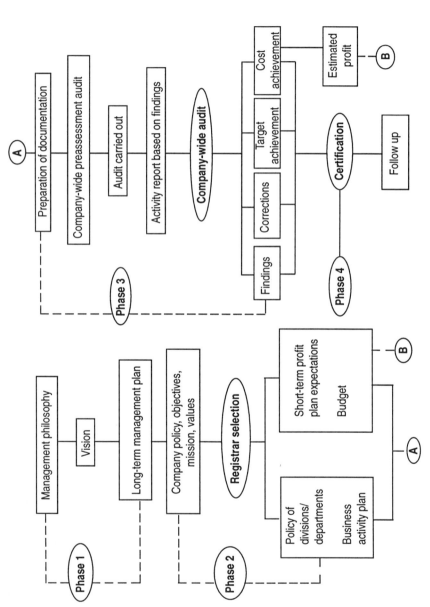

FIGURE 4.18 The structure of a company-wide ISO 9000 implementation

- Continual adaptation to changing market conditions

- The best is yet to come

- Market-driven attitude

The expanded relationship of ISO and TQS is illustrated in Figure 4.14.

THE DEMING MODEL OF IMPLEMENTATION

In the manufacturing and service worlds, W. Edwards Deming is considered to be one of the legends of the 20th century because he defined a way of thinking that indeed can energize any organization. His approach is fundamentally the Fourteen Points, which he calls the fourteen obligations of management. Deming's success story in Japan and throughout U.S. industry is a matter of record. It is this success that makes his approach worth implementing in the service industry at large.

Deming's Fourteen Points

The Fourteen Points are the basis for transformation of American industry. It will not suffice merely to solve problems, large or small. Adoption of and action on the Fourteen Points are a signal that management intends to stay in business and aims to protect investors and jobs. Such a system formed the basis for lessons for top management in Japan in 1950 and in subsequent years.

The Fourteen Points apply anywhere—to small organizations as well as to large ones and to the service industry as well as to manufacturing. They equally apply to divisions within a company. They are as follows:

1. Create constancy of purpose toward improvement of product and service, with the aim to become competitive and to stay in business, and to provide jobs.

2. Adopt the new philosophy. We are in a new economic age. Western management must awaken to the challenge, must learn their responsibilities, and take on leadership for change.

3. Cease dependence on inspection to achieve quality. Eliminate the need for inspection on a mass basis by building quality into the product in the first place.

4. End the practice of awarding business on the basis of price tag. Instead, minimize total cost. Move toward a single supplier for any one item, based on a long-term relationship of loyalty and trust.

5. Improve constantly and forever the system of production and service, to improve quality and productivity, and thus constantly decrease costs.

6. Institute training on the job.

7. Institute leadership. The aim of supervision should be to help people, machines, and gadgets to do a better job. Supervision of management is in need of overhaul, as well as supervision of production workers.

8. Drive out fear, so that everyone may work effectively for the company.

9. Break down barriers between departments. People in research, design, sales, and production must work as a team, to foresee problems of production (and in use) that may be encountered with the product or service.

10. Eliminate slogans, exhortations, and targets for the work force which ask only for zero defects and new levels of productivity. Such exhortations only create adversarial relationships as the bulk of the causes of low quality and low productivity belong to the system and thus lie *beyond* the power of the work force.

11a. Eliminate work standards (quotas) on the factory floor. Substitute leadership.

11b. Eliminate management by objectives. Eliminate management by numbers or numerical goals. Substitute leadership.

12a. Remove barriers that rob the hourly workers of their right to pride of workmanship. The responsibility of supervisors must be changed from sheer numbers to quality.

12b. Remove barriers that rob people in management and in engineering of their right to pride of workmanship. This means, inter alia, abolishment of the annual or merit rating and management by objectives.

13. Institute a vigorous program of education and self-improvement.

14. Put everybody in the company to work to accomplish the transformation. The transformation in everybody's job.

Deming's Seven Deadly Diseases

In contrast to the 14-point philosophy which defines the essence of what Deming is all about, the seven deadly sins provide a counterbalance to management and a warning that if any one of these diseases is part of the organization, the result may be a disaster. Any one of these disease is capable of paralyzing management's goals and can make the organization revert to the "good old days." The seven diseases are:

1. Lack of constancy of purpose to plan product and service that will have a market and keep the company in business and provide jobs.

2. Emphasis on short-term profits—Short-term thinking (just the opposite of constancy of purpose to stay in business), fed by fear of unfriendly takeover and by push from bankers and owners for dividends.

3. Evaluation of performance, merit rating, or annual review—It nourishes short-term performance, annihilates long-term planning, builds fear, demolishes teamwork, and nourishes rivalry and politics. It leaves people bitter, crushed, bruised, battered, desolate, despondent, dejected, feeling inferior, some even depressed, unfit for work for weeks after receipt of rating, unable to comprehend why they are inferior. It is unfair, as it ascribes to the people in a group differences that may be caused totally by the *system* (management) that they work in, and not by anything that they themselves could control.

4. Mobility of management, job hopping, and continuous replacement or exchange of people in leadership positions—This leaves everyone wondering about stability, having to deal with new styles of leadership and changes in direction.

5. Management by the use of only visible figures, with little or no consideration of the figures that are unknown or unknowable—This is peculiar to industry in the United States. ("He that would run his company on visible figures alone will in time have neither company nor figures.") What is the figure for failing to satisfy the customer? Improvement of quality and productivity? Poor leadership? Inept design of a product? Failure to improve processes?

6. Excessive medical costs, unsafe products, unsafe processes, unsafe workplace, and job stress.

7. Excessive costs of liability, swelled by lawyers who work only on contingency fees.

The Implementation Process: Points and Questions

To enumerate 14 principles is one thing. To think that anyone may follow them is quite another, and their implementation requires some planning. To actually implement them requires understanding and commitment by the total organization. What follows is an explanation of Deming's 14 principles, how a service organization can implement them, and some of the pitfalls and obstacles that management may experience in the process of implementation.

1. Create constancy of purpose for service improvement. For Deming, the idea of short-term mentality has not been successful. It is imperative that management create a constancy of purpose with a long-term perspective. This perspective should be anchored in today's problems as well as tomorrow's. Therefore, stating organizational goals and philosophy should be in terms of:

- The beliefs and values of the organization for both the short and long term

- Making long-term decisions easier to make

- Developing a mission statement and operating philosophy that are understood and lived by everyone in the organization

To appreciate this point, it must be related to the overall philosophy. That philosophy reveals that the contribution of this point is in defining the allocation of resources and in minimizing and/or eliminating overreaction to variation. This is done by developing a mission statement that is a living document. It communicates in clear language the roles of senior management and encourages feedback and action based on the feedback. To be successful, participation, either direct or indirect, by all employees is essential, as is communication with stockholders and the board of directors. The following questions pertain to this point:

- What is the aim of the organization five years from now? Do all the top leaders agree? How widely is this aim of the organization shared? What do data from employees suggest?

- If the continual improvement of quality was, in reality, treated as the primary business principle, would anything change in the work now done or in the way it is done in the organization?

In pursuing the constancy of the organization, many obstacles may surface, including:

- Failure to plan for the problems of tomorrow

- Managerial zeal to complete the mission statement

- Behaving as if the mission statement were a faint accomplishment

- Difficulty in writing the mission statement
- Management's inability to prepare a mission statement
- Thinking that the mission statement is cast in stone
- Forgetting the mission statement after it is written
- Belief that the mission statement will dictate behavior in specific situations

2. Adopt the new philosophy. For Deming, change is necessary—but not just any change. What is needed is a change that focuses on customer satisfaction, that pushes for improving quality in a never-ending cycle, that de-emphasizes short-term profits as a goal, and that always looks to define service beyond the needs, wants, and expectations of the customer. This change must address the most common misconception about the relationship between quality and productivity. The idea that increased productivity decreases quality must be diffused by demonstrating that improving quality results in increased productivity.

To be sure, pressure to increase productivity can result in stress, frustration, and fear. However, if the new philosophy takes hold in the organization and continual improvement is the goal, then the benefits of the improved quality will result in increased productivity, lower cost per order, overall lower price, and better morale.

The relationship of this point to Deming's overall philosophy is that the foundation of the entire philosophy is *quality* and that a new attitude will create a ripple effect in the organization and perhaps society. The change in attitude must occur primarily in two areas: (1) improved quality must be the focus of everything and (2) senior management must lead the way in defining quality for the organization, actively seeking to identify and remove any barriers and getting everyone involved. The old adage "If you always do what you always did, you will always get what you always got" (and what you got is not good enough) is an appropriate message that Deming tried to communicate. Some questions that focus on this point are the following:

- What mistakes and defects do we now tolerate in the way we purchase or provide a service in the work we do every day?
- If the rigorous examination of accepted practices is a necessary feature of continuous improvement and better quality, what barriers exist today to open, ready, and willing assessment of present practices in our service delivery?

In pursuing this point, some obstacles may be encountered:

- Continuing to push quantity while espousing a quality philosophy
- An inability to define quality properly
- Inattentiveness to customer feedback
- Becoming overwhelmed by the number of barriers uncovered
- Getting sidetracked by complainers
- Ignoring the bargaining union (if there is one)
- Middle management's fear of change
- Continuing to blame suppliers for poor quality

3. Cease dependence on inspection to achieve quality. Deming's theory on inspection can be summarized as follows: (1) it is always too late and (2) it is not necessarily accurate. To prove the point, try to count the number of times the letter F, in both upper and lower case, appears in the following statement:

> Finished files are the result of years of scientific study combined with the experience of years.

Over the last ten years of using this statement, answers have varied from none to thirty, which illustrates that inspection does not work. In fact, one of the reasons why it does not work is that inspection is often, if not always, performed under some kind of pressure. Deming's alternative to mass inspection minimizes the total cost of incoming materials and final services and works between any two points in the extended process. His alternative is the kp rule, which defines inspection for all or none.

The kp rule states the following:

Let p = the average fraction defective in incoming lots of items

Let k_1 = the cost to inspect one item

Let k_2 = the cost to correct, rework, and test a final piece of output that is unsatisfactory because a defective piece of input was put into the work

If k_1/k_2 is greater than p, then inspection is not necessary

If k_1/k_2 is less than p, then 100% inspection is necessary

Example: The decision is whether or not to hire an inspector for hotel rooms at a cost of $25,000 per year. The cost to screen out rooms needing rework is

$4.00, with a corrective action cost of $20.00. Historically, the average is 1 in 150 rooms needs rework.

$$p = 1/150 = 0.0067$$

$$k_1/k_2 = 4/20 = 0/2$$

$$0.2 > 0.0067 \ (k_1/k_2 \text{ is greater than } p)$$

Therefore, inspection is not necessary.
If no rooms are inspected, then:

$$\text{average cost} = \$20/150 \text{ per room} = \$0.13 \text{ per room}$$

$$\text{savings} = \$4.00 - 0.13 = \$3.87 \text{ per room}$$

At 200 rooms per day,

$$200 \times 3.87 = \$773.40 \text{ per day}$$

At an annualized rate, this translates into a savings of:

$$\$773.40 \text{ per day} \times 365 \text{ days} = \$282,291.00 \text{ per year}$$

The third point relates to the overall philosophy in at least two ways: (1) mass inspection has to be replaced with never-ending process improvement and (2) mass inspection is managing for failure and, as a consequence, does not offer any means of improvement. To focus on the issues of inspection, the following questions may be helpful:

1. If "waiting for the results of the process" rather than "monitoring the key process elements as they are occurring" is really just another form of inspection, what are the manifestations of that in daily managerial work life in your service organization?

2. What are the manifestations of dependence on mass inspection to foster quality in service organizations today?

3. How does the performance assessment and feedback system that you now use help bring this way of work into practice?

In pursuing this point, some obstacles may be encountered:

- Ignoring the need for a statistician

- Lack of communication with suppliers/vendors

- Continuing to use acceptance sampling

4. End the practice of awarding business on price alone; make partners of vendors.

Many organizations purchase on the basis of price alone, as it is common standard operating procedure to award business to the lowest bidder. With this point, Deming emphasizes the need to look at the total cost. It is the total cost that should drive the purchasing agent in making the ultimate decision. To facilitate this purchase of total cost, the purchasing agent should be familiar with the problems encountered in the use of goods and services purchased, should be able to communicate with suppliers, and should be able to judge quality based on some statistics. The following example illustrates that the lowest cost supplier is not always the best deal:

Supplier 1: $11.00 per unit/(defect rate of one unit per million)

Cost = $11.00/(1 − 0.000001) = $11.00 per unit

Supplier 2: $10.00 per unit/(defect rate of 10%)

Cost = $10.00/(1 − 0.10) = $11.11 per unit

Supplier 3: $9.50 per unit/(unknown defect rate)

Cost = $9.50/(1 − ?) = ?

In this case, the most expensive supplier must be considered, since the total cost (purchase cost and use cost) is indeed the lowest. Supplier 3 is a gamble since the use cost is not known.

How can the cost of suppliers be controlled? Historically, most supplier control was based on multiple sourcing. The rationale for that philosophy was that it protects against disaster (acts of God, strikes, explosions, etc.), price increases, supplier bankruptcy or inventory shortage, failure to meet delivery schedule, inability to provide the required volume, obsolescence in technology, and supplier down time.

While all the reasons given above are of concern, the fact remains that multiple sourcing creates arm's length relationships between buyers and sellers. It creates a win–lose situation. It demands price recognition, and in the process, the relationship is really never developed.

Deming, on the other hand, proposes a revolutionary thought. He suggests single sourcing. His rationale is based on the premise that statistical evidence of quality will reduce the number of possible suppliers (he is a strong advocate of supplier certification). Furthermore, by promoting trust in the customer–supplier relationship, quality will be promoted. Deming is also a strong advocate of open negotiation of contracts to deal with errors made at the time of contract.

Deming's recommendation of a single supplier is based on the notion of win–win. This attitude translates into a cooperative effort between customer and supplier toward never-ending improvement. To accomplish this, Deming's philosophy necessitates three major changes:

1. Select the right supplier. Make sure you have a certification program in place to identify your certified, recommended, and approved supplier. To this end, you may develop a supplier manual with all requirements for your quality system and what is expected of your suppliers. In addition, you may also develop a certification checklist or a formal audit questionnaire to evaluate whether or not the supplier is doing what is expected.

2. Change the job of the purchasing agent. A purchasing agent should be a procurement agent. In other words, the purchasing agent should be able to statistically evaluate incoming quality rather than just shop for price. In addition, the purchasing agent must work cooperatively with the supplier base to provide feedback for both current and future improvement needs.

3. The way contracts are written between buyers and sellers must be changed. The adversarial tone of contracts must stop and, instead, an attitude of cooperation must prevail.

The fourth point relates to the overall Deming philosophy in at least two ways: (1) a *Deming company* buys a supplier's process and service/product and (2) long-term relationships are stressed. Some specific questions that may focus on this long-term relationship for an organization are the following:

1. If long-term relationships with suppliers permit accurate knowledge of each other's processes and improvement of value based on that knowledge, how do service organizations today use the long-term relationships they have with their present suppliers to achieve that?

2. If part of the value of a long-term relationship with a supplier is that we are able to study and reduce variation in the way we work together, what kinds of things might be improved with a supplier that you know and regularly use?

3. If real competitiveness will require that we have these types of supplier partnerships with detailed knowledge of each other's processes, how many supplier relationships for any given supply line will we be able to afford? How might working this way with suppliers help to create competitive advantage for a service organization?

In pursuing the point of ending the practice of awarding business on the basis of price tag, some obstacles may surface:

- Senior management resisting single sourcing
- Not providing adequate training and supervision for purchasing agents
- Purchasing agents resisting their new roles
- Management sending double messages about purchasing rules
- Continuing to use *assignment of risk* type contracts

5. Constantly improve every process for planning, production, and service. This point is the theme of Deming's quality message. He recognizes that responsibility for the system rests with management. As a consequence, improvement of the process is inherently a responsibility of management. The focus ought to be on improving the process. In service industries, that means reduction of rework, improved overall quality, higher customer satisfaction, lower customer complaints, higher profits, improved competitive position, etc. These results are based on the notion that management will lead, coach, direct, and so on, but by the same token everyone in the organization has to understand and use statistical methods in all areas. This is very important, because if the organization establishes a quality assurance/control department, this indicates that quality is not everyone's job. Everyone becomes relaxed, because the quality department will catch any problems.

To appreciate this point, it must be related to the overall philosophy. In that philosophy, we see that the contribution of this point necessitates a long-term perspective and crystallizes the notion that improving the system is indeed managing for success. Some specific questions that may focus on this improvement are:

1. How would we know that "continual improvement" is, in fact, occurring? What measure of improvement of the way work is done have you found helpful in your own job?

2. How might the efforts of employees to make improvements in the processes of planning, operations, and service delivery be assessed and recognized in the context of regular performance assessment and feedback systems?

In pursuing this point, some obstacles may surface:

- Attempting to reach never-ending improvement only through automation and capital investment
- Politicalization of the changes needed for never-ending improvement
- Premature large-scale use of statistical methods by hourly workers
- Separating the *real job* and statistical methods

- The inability to create an atmosphere that is conducive to workers' acceptance of their new tasks

- Attempting to improve the process without the guidance of a competent statistician

- Reluctance to make improvements that reduce management's level of responsibility

- Insensitivity to labor's resistance to using statistical tools

- Using statistical methods as a political tool

6. Institute training and retraining on the job. Deming's commitment to improvement is dovetailed with his commitment to training. He believes that unless appropriate and applicable training is instituted, improvement will not occur. For Deming, the training must be integrated into the new philosophy and not the other way around. It must be guided by a new attitude for all employees (current and new). It must be conducted on an ongoing basis. Above all, the training should include not only the specifics of the job but the organization's goals as well. A typical approach is illustrated in Figure 4.19. On the other hand, Figure 4.20 provides a graphic representation of a generic TQS training implementation program for all employees. Of note in Figure 4.20 is the fact that the training is spread throughout the organization (i.e., executives, implementors, and operators). Of course, the requirements for each group are different and, as illustrated, some indeed overlap.

A cursory generic overview of a training program that meets Deming's requirements is the following:

Set up a training program:

- Identify organizational objectives and goals

- Identify organizational goals that will be met through training

- Analyze what needs to be taught

Requirements for training:

- Planning

- Input from all levels

- Training procedures

Evaluation:

- Statistical methods

- Control charts

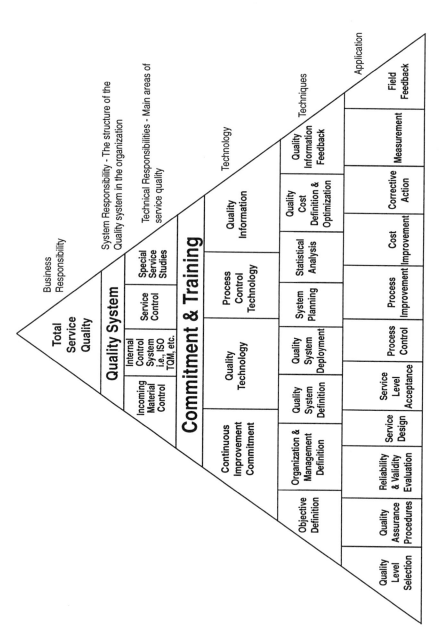

FIGURE 4.19   The pyramid of TQS organizational training needs

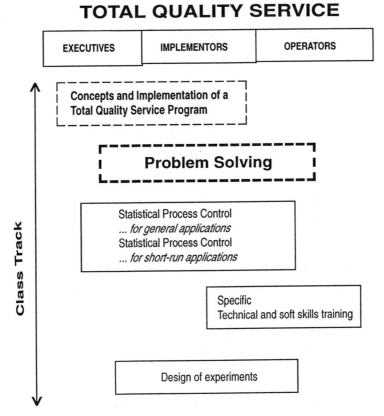

FIGURE 4.20 A generic TQS implementation training program

- Loss of statistical control
- Changing tasks or specifications

Areas of training for teamwork:

- Team organization and development
- Decision making and consensus
- Power struggles within teams
- Developing team objectives
- Conflict resolution
- and so on

The expectations of good (proper) training are that it will:

1. Increase quality awareness and improvement because:
   - Everyone knows the job
   - Everyone is in statistical control
   - Everyone is continually improving
2. Identify whether or not the process is capable
3. Offer security to employees by:
   - Eliminating fear
   - Eliminating rumors
   - Securing jobs
4. Break the barriers between workers
5. Instill or regain a sense of pride in the work produced
6. Decrease stress levels

The sixth point relates to the overall philosophy in several ways. Perhaps the most important relationship of this point to the whole philosophy is that people are the organization's most valuable long-term resource. In addition, it re-emphasizes that training is a process with a long-term perspective and is set up to help the worker succeed. Finally, it contributes to understanding that training helps (but is not a cure-all) in creating a new corporate environment and provides a vehicle for workers to achieve results in statistical control with improved quality. Some questions that may help in defining the role of training in a service organization are the following:

1. How much of the organization's current human resource pool is made up of people who have an incomplete understanding of what their jobs actually are? How much does that cost? Who pays?

2. If training is a management responsibility, what barriers stand in the way of present managers fulfilling those responsibilities?

3. Is most of the significant work that is done in your organization or unit done alone or by working together? In the ways that you now recognize performance, are you able to recognize the work that is done by employees as individuals working alone as well as the work done by employees working together with others? Are the incentives for working effectively together clear and as powerful as those that may exist for individuals working alone?

Some possible pitfalls and obstacles of implementing this point are:

- Using training as a reaction to problems
- Jumping on the bandwagon for every new training fad
- Continuing to rely on on-the-job training
- Using training as a punishment
- Trainers' resistance to the use of statistical training
- Labor's resistance to the new type of training
- Failure to realize that training is a process that requires never-ending improvement
- Delaying implementation of the training
- Experienced workers may not be good teachers
- New workers may have to produce before being ready for further training
- Experienced workers may leave things out
- Employees only learn job tasks

7. Institute leadership for system improvement. Being a boss is not the same as being a leader. A boss may or may not be a leader. A leader may or may not be a boss. It is management's responsibility to find the true leaders, cultivate them, and encourage them to pursue their leadership roles. Deming reminds us that management's responsibility is indeed more than defining the system, finding variation in the process, improving the process, and so on. It is also instituting leadership in the organization with the purpose of improving the system.

In today's world of self-directed teams and empowered employees, it is of paramount importance to recognize that leadership may indeed be shared. Shared leadership encompasses the following:

- Shared responsibility for all members to (1) contribute to the accomplishment of team goals and (2) enhance relationships with team members.
- Different members, with unique talents and experiences, provide leadership at different times. As Will Rogers put it, "We are all stupid; thank God, we are stupid at different things."
- The leadership roles of team members change as the needs and tasks of the team change.

To be effective, shared leadership must meet three conditions:

1. Supervision (group leader) is willing to share responsibility and recognition with team members.

2. Team members are aware of team leadership functions and have developed basic leadership skills.

3. Team members must understand the limits of shared leadership and recognize the point at which the team leader must assume the role of formal leader who is:

   • Responsible for making the final decision

   • Accountable for the actions of the entire team as it completes its task

This is not easy for some leaders, because it means sharing the power and prestige of the leader position while retaining accountability for the team's performance. On the other hand, for team members, it requires a commitment to develop and use their leadership abilities, seek responsibilities, take risks, exchange needed information, and support the leader's final decision.

In a productive teamwork environment, each team member is ready to respond to the emerging situation: to act or to stop action, to give up a position of power or to step into one, to take leadership or to follow. This requires letting go of one's attachment to fixed roles.

Deming's proposal is indeed new and revolutionary in that he proposes a system that dramatically changes the supervisor's job. He makes the supervisor and/or leader responsible for process improvement pushers rather than quantity pushers. To make the transition, appropriate training is necessary. Typical training should cover at least the following:

• The overall philosophy of the organization

• Statistical methods

• Building relationships

• Coaching

• How to create a supportive environment

• Interpersonal communication

• Conflict resolution

The contribution of the seventh point to the whole philosophy is that it presents a different perspective on the way supervisors and leaders are viewed. According to Deming, the new supervision—leadership—concretely demonstrates a long-term perspective and flexibility, through the use of new technology, statistical methods, the amount of time and resources devoted to employees, and unique situations. Some specific questions may help in defining the leadership in an organization:

1. If the job of supervisors and leaders is system improvement, what must they additionally know in order to effectively do that? If the improvement of systems requires a clear knowledge of the actual work flow of the process within which someone works, how often is that level of process knowledge available? What stands in the way of supervisors and managers learning that information?

2. Do the performance assessment and feedback systems reflect the priority of leadership for system improvement? How?

3. There are times that the best of intentions are forgotten, for whatever reason, and some bosses want to show authority at all costs. At that point, the system has failed and you as an individual must remember the two rules of the old style management:

   Rule 1: The boss is ALWAYS right.

   Rule 2: If the boss is not right, see Rule 1

   According to these rules, the boss is the most important customer. However, in today's world, these rules are unacceptable and no one should follow them. Nevertheless, reality being what it is, such rules do exist and you must as an individual learn to accommodate the *status quo* until such time when the organization is ready for the change or you must be willing to leave the organization. The choice is yours.

4. The model of TQS meets Deming's requirements. A typical general model of a quality system is shown in Figure 4.21. The model recognizes the three hierarchical levels of a typical service organization and provides the generic activities within each level. In addition, some tools appropriate for each level in the implementation process are shown. The detailed composition of the model is shown in Figures 4.22, 4.23, and 4.24 for each of the levels of activities.

In pursuing this point in the implementation process, some pitfalls and obstacles may be encountered:

- Believing that a degree in management from a business school prepares someone for supervising employees

- Ignoring concerns about chain of command

FIGURE 4.21   An overall model of TQS

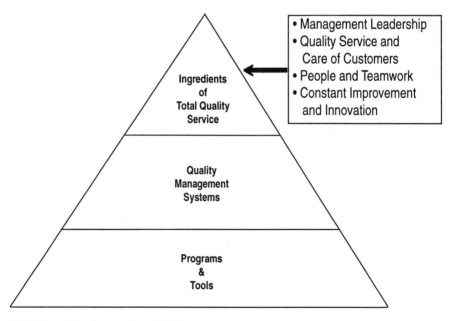

FIGURE 4.22   A model of TQS: strategic activity

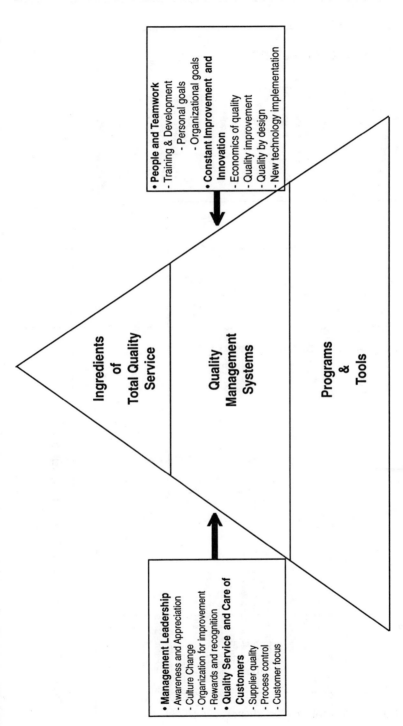

FIGURE 4.23 A model of TQS: managerial activity

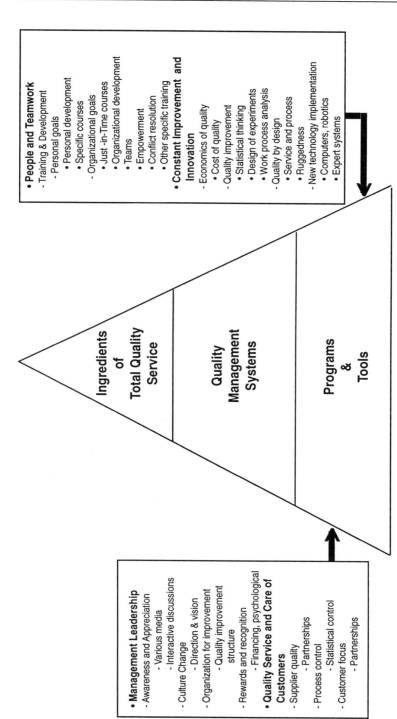

FIGURE 4.24   A model of TQS: operational activity

- Using statistics as a policing tool
- Failing to view the worker as a total human being
- Continuing to reward and punish employees without regard to system variation
- Ignoring the union in the implementation of the new supervision

8. Drive out fear. Fear contributes to a variety of issues, including:

- Physical disorders
- Psychological disorders
- Behavior changes
- Poor morale
- Stifling productivity
- Reduced motivation
- Ineffective communication

According to Deming, it is a moral obligation to eliminate fear because it reduces everyone's ability to participate in improving quality and productivity. Fear can be eliminated through a variety of ways, including the following:

- Physical dangers must be removed
- Training
  - o Ongoing training for everyone in the company's goals and mission
  - o Training in operational definitions, statistical methods, training characteristics, jobs, and specifications
  - o Training in understanding the causes of system variation
- Supervision should stress never-ending improvement
- Supervisors should help workers and listen to their problems
- Eliminate traditional performance appraisals
- Listen to the message rather than the messenger

In the overall Deming philosophy, this point emphasizes that in order to improve quality, people need a consistent, supportive, nonthreatening, secure environment. To focus on this issue, the following questions may be helpful:

1. How do we teach fear to new workers?

2. Does this fear cost the organization or the customers of the organization anything? If so, what? How much?

3. What are the effects of "driving out fear" that we might be able to discover and measure? Does the present performance assessment and feedback system measure those effects when assessing the performance of the managers responsible for creating this environment? How?

Some pitfalls and obstacles in pursuing this point include the following:

• Avoiding the problems of people

• Believing that fear has been eliminated when it still exists

• Not planning for the new fears that the new philosophy will create

9. Break down barriers between staff areas.   Whether we like it or not, the fact is that barriers exist in all organizations. They are primarily the result of poor and/or lack of communication, ignorance of the organization's mission and goals, internal competition, interpretive resolutions, fear, and so on. As a consequence, organizations find themselves in situations where quality and customer satisfaction are decreased, rework and costs are increased, and the smooth flow of the process is impeded.

The overall philosophy is supported by this point by reemphasizing that breaking down barriers is a long-term undertaking, and never-ending improvement can only be pursued if the organization works as an integrated whole. Finally, it reconfirms the need for training throughout the organization as an aid in breaking down barriers. How do you go about formalizing this training? Start with the attitudes of the organization. Attitudes can be changed in at least five ways:

1. **Identify with specialized departmental goals:**   The goal here is to unify the goals as an organization and have one focus. Try to optimize rather than suboptimize.

2. **See the company as an isolated entity:**   The goal in here is to understand the company's place in the extended process. Once identified, then work to improve it.

3. **Individualize work:**   The goal here is to create a team atmosphere and empower individuals to do what is required for customer satisfaction.

4. **Open communication:**   The goal here is to have open communication both vertically and horizontally. All communication lines must be open.

5. **Form teams:**   The goal here is to have an empowered team organized and structured in such a way that positive results are the way of life rather than the exception.

The following questions may help in focusing on the barriers:

1. Where might you find barriers within the operations of your organization that have the effect of increasing your costs and simultaneously reducing your quality?

2. How does the performance assessment and feedback system help you make this concern clear to the people who work for you?

In pursuing implementation of this point, the following may be encountered as obstacles and pitfalls:

• Fear of losing the chain of command

• Denial that barriers exist

• Failure to eliminate special facilities and/or privileges

• Assuming that the training department is free from barriers

• Continuing to view an area as different or special

• Perpetuating the belief that an area is second-string

• Failing to deal with people's fears

• Ignoring turf protection

• Reluctance to expend the energy needed to remove barriers

• Emphasis on specialization in business schools

10. Eliminate slogans, exhortations, and targets for the work force.   The idea of arbitrary numerical goals, exhortations, or meaningless slogans is totally unacceptable to Deming. The reason for this is that arbitrary numerical goals contribute to, if not outright cause, frustration and resentment in employees. They certainly lower quality and productivity as the focus becomes the target rather than the quality. They encourage lying or cheating so that the quota is met. They destroy morale, and they depend on random variation to meet the set goals.

A better way to approach arbitrary slogans, exhortations, and targets is to emphasize the progress that management is making in never-ending improvement. This can be communicated with posters and slogans. An organization can approach this point by removing **all** meaningless posters and slogans, by establishing meaningful goals which are as specific as possible, by getting rid of management by objectives (MBO), and by introducing bottom-up financial planning based on processes in control.

The contribution of this point to the total philosophy is that it focuses once again on training, without actually mentioning it. It is through training that management will be educated to the fact that slogans, posters, and the like seem ludicrous to employees. The following concerns and questions may help focus on eliminating arbitrary numerical goals:

1. Itemize the ways in which you currently recognize the work of individuals. Itemize the ways in which you currently recognize the work of people who have worked collaboratively. Indicate the frequency with which you have used both methods recently. Does your description and analysis correspond to your sense of the relative contribution that individuals working alone and together make to the actual work and accomplishments of the organization?

2. What might be done to assure a stronger correlation between the methods and practices of recognition and the actual way in which valuable work gets done?

In pursuing this point, some pitfalls and obstacles may surface:

• An inability to trust the *new* goals

• Using numerical goals for evaluation

• Continued reliance on posters and slogans

11. Eliminate numerical quotas for the work force and numerical goals for management. If the initial focus is on quantity, it will not be on quality. Therefore, quality will suffer. When management sends the message that quantity is most important, employees will deliver quantity. As a consequence, frustration and resentment will be the result. What can be done about it? According to Deming, the answer is simple. Work standards must go. The reason for this is that they do not provide a road map for improvement. In addition, they prohibit good supervision and training. Workers are blamed for problems of the system. Work standards are psychologically self-limiting. They can be the subject of union negotiation and have nothing to do with process capability, and they do not reflect the current system because they remain fixed. On the other hand, if the message is concern about quality first, employees likewise will respond with more productivity and quality work. The message must be substantiated with statistical methods and a road map for never-ending improvement. The result of this approach will be processes that are stable, in control, and predictable.

The contribution of this point to the whole philosophy centers around the theme of (1) eliminating work standards and quotas and replacing them with statistical methods and/or tools and a commitment to a long-term perspective and (2) getting rid of quotas and providing a road map for improvement as a means of managing for success.

The following questions may be helpful in the elimination of quotas:

1. What are the manifestations of a lack of process knowledge (the processes that produce the results) that might inadvertently characterize presently used numerical goal-setting processes for managers?

2. As a manager, what are examples of ways that you react to the "natural variation" in a process and inadvertently cause someone who reports to you to spend wasted time explaining the variation? How much cost might that represent throughout the organization?

Some pitfalls and obstacles may be encountered in pursuing this point:

- Clinging to a short-term view

- Eliminating standards and quotas at the wrong time

- Accepting current work standards as "the best we can do."

12. Remove barriers to pride of workmanship. Losing pride in one's workmanship may be a symptom of many things in an organization. Some of the sources may be due to poor treatment of employees by management or not understanding the direction of the company. Communication channels may not be open and employees may not even be aware of a quality mission, let alone understand it. Blaming workers or inadequate training may cause inferiority complexes in employees. However, one of the most significant and the surest item that can indeed contribute to barriers to pride is requiring employees to act as automatons.

What can be done to regain the employees' pride? First and foremost, management needs to be made aware of the problem and act accordingly. The areas where management can have tremendous input are defining job descriptions, encouraging employees to report problems (no matter how bad they may be), and supplying employees with the proper tools, materials, and methods to do the job. Second, management must involve all employees in areas where their opinions may make a difference. Third, it is imperative for management to be aware of what is going on by conducting frequent surveys and implementing the results. Finally, management must stress the importance of each employee and his or her contribution to the process.

Why is it so important to regain employee pride? The answer is complex. However, the benefits may include the following:

- Loyalty, excitement, interest, and team spirit
- Empowerment may be easier to implement
- The employees themselves become ambassadors for the organization
- Employees will grow and develop to their maximum potential
- Morale will be restored
- Stress will be reduced
- A team spirit will be created

This point contributes to the overall philosophy by reiterating that restoring pride to employees involves a long-term perspective and is definitely worth the effort. The following questions may be helpful in assessing this point for your organization:

1. How might insufficient supervisory knowledge contribute to decreased pride in work?

2. What are the ways by which managers and leaders can recognize a "job well done" to build and foster pride in workmanship? What methods of current performance assessment and feedback do the most to promote this?

Possible pitfalls and obstacles in pursuing this point include:

- Senior management's isolation from employees
- Trying to instill pride by inappropriate methods
- Establishing a quality control department
- Failure to follow through on employees' suggestions

13. Institute a vigorous program of education and self-improvement for everyone. It is only a matter of time before everyone becomes obsolete in their knowledge and experience. Deming quite appropriately identified this point as part of his overall quality. It is indeed through education and retraining that we learn the jobs of tomorrow. However, in addition to that learning process for the future, education and retraining help to motivate employees, avoid burnout on the job, and provide a smooth transition to a changed organization.

Depending on the service organization, the training requirements may vary. However, some generic training for all service organizations is necessary. Deming's philosophy is that, first, senior and middle managers and then everyone should receive training in:

- Basic statistical techniques

- Basic skills as required

- Job-related subjects as required

- Personal improvement training as requested

This point supports the overall Deming philosophy by recognizing that (1) education and retraining are dependent on a long-term perspective and recognition of the employees' contribution to the survival of the organization and (2) education and retraining provide the tools to manage for success, work toward never-ending improvement, and prepare for the problems of tomorrow.

The following questions may be helpful in instituting a vigorous program of education and retraining:

1. What measurable effects might we look for in the environment of service organizations that would help us know that we have been successful in creating an environment in which it would be clear that we have developed a vigorous program of education and self-improvement for everyone?

2. Does the current performance assessment and feedback system reinforce this point effectively? How? Could it be improved? How?

Possible pitfalls and obstacles in pursuing this point include:

- Management's reluctance to get involved in the training

- Management's misconceptions about the length of time necessary for retraining

- Employee resistance to getting involved with statistical methods

- Lack of adequate internal resources for training

14. Put everyone to work on the transformation. The amount of work that will be necessary to bring about this transformation is so great that resources cannot be wasted. Everyone's help is needed. As important as everyone's contribution is, we must not forget or underestimate the contribution of senior management. It is senior management who must carry the burning desire for change. Without their strength, vision, and true commitment, nothing will happen. For starters, senior management must:

- Begin by creating a critical mass of people who understand the philosophy and want to change the corporate culture as much as they do

- Understand that the total transformation will take years of struggling before any benefits are realized

Practicing and demanding participation means making sure that visions are created and that people are aligned around the vision and are empowered. Another key management function that is often overlooked is managing the learning of the organization. It is imperative that senior management ensure that learning, both at individual and team levels, continually improve over time.

It is senior management's job to encourage teams to develop visions that endure and a commitment to team goals over individual goals. These qualities help teams act cohesively; however, they take time to develop. Senior management must see that conflicts are successfully resolved, but healthy conflict should not be feared, since the clash of differing perspectives is why teams offer better solutions than do individuals.

Worth noting here is the reminder that management is not necessarily the same as leadership. Management tasks include making sure that plans are deployed and progress is measured and reported. Management means providing the resources. By insisting on fact-based management and using statistical methods and problem-solving techniques, management can keep the change on course.

Ultimately, senior management's role in continuous improvement is to sustain an unwavering commitment to change. The organization will take on the characteristics of the leadership. If the leadership wants continuous improvement to happen, the leader must walk the talk. However, once started, you have to do it forever.

The relationship between this point and the overall philosophy may be seen through two points: (1) accept responsibility for never-ending improvement of quality and (2) understand that short-term effects may be unsettling. However, no matter how it is perceived, one thing is for sure. If your organization is committed to apply this change model process, it does not end with a consultant's visit to your organization. It does not end with the most technologically advanced training. It does not end with training everyone in the organization. It does not end with senior management causing something to happen and then walking away. The only way this model will work is for senior management to keep pounding the idea home. Pounding means taking a sincere interest, asking for appropriate reporting, and providing feedback on a continual basis. That is the only way. Asking a basic question will help assess the situation in your organization:

- How will service leaders know that everyone's energies are being tapped in the transformational effort?

Some possible pitfalls and obstacles in pursuing this point are:

- Insulation surrounding top management

- Lack of constancy of purpose

- Expecting immediate results
- Creating a structure without a competent statistician
- Basing managerial decisions only on visible figures
- Too busy to provide feedback
- Reporting seems cumbersome and therefore is dropped

QUESTIONS FOR SERVICE QUALITY LEADERS

When the organization is ready to implement TQS, the management and/or leaders may want to review the following checklist to ensure that the critical characteristics of the program are covered and everyone (both internal and external to the organization) knows about the pending changes.

- Is the definition of quality in your organization clear?
- Does it relate your mission to your customers?
- Is it measurable?
- Does everyone in your organization:
    o Know the purpose of your organization?
    o Know the definition of quality?
    o Know how you measure quality?
    o Know his or her role in improving quality?
    o Know the tools necessary to measure and improve quality?
- How do you know they know?
- Are you committed to the continuous improvement of quality?
- What information do you use to know that you are making continuous improvement in quality?
- Do you know who your customers are?
- Does everyone in the organization know who his or her customers are (internal/external)?
- How do you know you are meeting your customers' needs/expectations?
- Do your systems of performance evaluation and compensation support your efforts in the continuous improvement of quality?

- Do you understand the relation between quality improvement and cost reduction?

- Do the people/institutions/entities who are your suppliers:

  o Know your concern/commitment to the continuous improvement of quality?

  o Understand—and can demonstrate—their role in helping you improve quality?

  o Understand that they could be your long-term partners?

- Does the continued learning that you support for your leaders help them measure and improve the quality of their work?

EXAMPLES OF THE IMPLEMENTATION STRATEGY

The following are examples of the TQS implementation steps that some successful organizations have used in pursuing continual improvement. Each company used a variation of the philosophies of Deming, Juran, and Crosby. Even though the goal is the same for all the companies sampled, note that the actual implementation steps are somewhat different in that they are personalized.

- A national retailer used the following steps:

  1. Define corporate mission and strategy

  2. Define targeted customer

  3. Perform customer communications audit

  4. Perform competitive audit

  5. Determine customer needs, wants, and expectations

  6. Define service delivery

  7. Define what service is *for us*

  8. Provide the appropriate culture and philosophy for TQS for both employees and management

  9. Provide the tools for change

- A financial and leasing company used the following steps to implement TQS as well as ISO:

1. Define the quality mission

2. Define the corporate mission

3. Define the customer base and act accordingly

4. Define a system for problem solving

5. Define and practice quality values

6. Define a program for recognition and rewards

7. Provide an environment that fosters teamwork and empowerment

8. Provide the tools for change

- An international hotel company used the following steps to implement TQS. Note that the way in which this company decided to define TQS is more of a customer satisfaction program than a total quality program.

1. Assess the situation

2. Search for causes

3. Agree on and target solutions

4. Take action

5. Measure results

6. Provide an environment that empowers employees

7. Provide appropriate training at all levels of the organization

8. Demonstrate management's commitment, as much as possible

To facilitate these eight steps, the company identified six principles (key characteristics) of excellent service:

- Warmly greet and acknowledge every guest encountered

- Take care of every guest's request quickly and in a friendly manner

- Project a professional image through appearance and conduct

- Be committed to guest comfort, safety, and security

- Provide reliable information about the services available in the hotel and the local area

- Work to make everything right for the guest

- A health care facility in New York used the PDCA approach with much success:

    1. Executive management TQS awareness training

    2. Employee training

    3. Selection of quality improvement council

    4. Planning and brainstorming

    5. Develop mission statement

    6. Activity assessment and process mapping

    7. Develop and deploy policies and procedures

    8. Develop measurement system criteria

    9. Develop employee suggestion, recognition, and reward system

    10. Quality improvement action team projects

    11. Internal assessment system

    12. Customer-driven continuous improvement

    13. Long-term cultural change

    14. Do it all over again

- A construction company in Detroit, Michigan used the following steps as part of its TQS implementation process:

    1. Top management leadership

    2. Create corporate framework for quality

    3. Transform the corporate culture

    4. Customer focus

    5. Process focus

    6. Collaborative approach to process improvement

    7. Employee education and training

    8. Learning by practice and teaching

    9. Benchmarking

    10. Recognition and reward

    11. Management integration

REFERENCES

Berwick, D. M., Godfrey, A. B., and Roessner, J. (1990). *Curing Health Care*. Jossey-Bass, San Francisco.

Bradford, L. P. (1976). *Making Meetings Work: A Guide for Leaders and Group Members*. University Associates, San Diego.

Clemens, R. R. (September 21–24, 1987). "A Report Case on SPC: The Role of Management on Quality and Its Future." in *TMI: Innovations in Quality, Concepts and Applications—Proceedings* (Vol. 1). ESD, Detroit.

Deming, W. Edwards (1986). *Out of the Crisis*. Massachusetts Institute of Technology, Cambridge, Mass.

English, R. and Josh, E. (September 21–24, 1987). "Teaching SPC Using a Computer Simulated Process Model." *TMI: Innovations in Quality, Concepts and Applications—Proceedings* (Vol 2). ESD, Detroit.

Griffiths, D. N. (1990). *Implementing Quality: With a Customer Focus*. Quality Press, Milwaukee.

Hall, S. S. (1990). *Quality Assurance in the Hospitality Industry*. Quality Press, Milwaukee.

Hausmann, R. C. (September 21–24, 1987). "Initiating Quality Management System in the Construction Industry." in *TMI: Innovations in Quality, Concepts and Applications—Proceedings* (Vol. 1). ESD, Detroit.

Kerzner, H. (1992). *Project Management: A Systems Approach to Planning, Scheduling and Controlling* (4th Ed.). Van Nostrand Reinhold, New York.

Lamprecht, J. L. (1992). *ISO 9000: Preparing for Registration*. Quality Press, Milwaukee.

Latzko, W. J. (1986). *Quality and Productivity for Bankers and Financial Managers*. Quality Press, Milwaukee.

Lipscomb, J. R. (October 14–16, 1991). "Managing the Transition to Continuous Improvement." in *Quality Concepts: Conference Proceedings*. ESD, Detroit.

Nader, G. J. (September 21–24, 1987). "Optimizing Quality Control, People, Performance and Profit." *TMI: Innovations in Quality, Concepts and Applications—Proceeding* (Vol. 2). ESD, Detroit.

Peach, R. W. (Ed.) (1992). *The ISO 9000 Handbook*. CEEM Information Services, Fairfax, Va.

Schein, E. (1985). *Organizational Culture and Leadership*. Jossey-Bass, San Francisco.

Stamatis, D. H. (1991). "TQM Implementation." in *Concepts in Quality 1991*. ESD, Detroit.

Stamatis, D. H. (1992a). *Total Quality Management: From Theory to Execution.* Contemporary Consultants, Southgate, Mich.

Stamatis, D. H. (August 1992b). "ISO 9000 Standards: Are They for Real?" *ESD Technology.*

Stamatis, D. H. (1992c). "TQM and Project Management." Speech given to the Detroit chapter of Project Management.

Stamatis, D. H. (September 1994). "TQM and PM." *Project Management Journal.*

5

TEAMS AND EMPOWERMENT

This chapter focuses on teams and empowerment as they relate to quality. Specifically, what a team is, how a team is formed, and what is expected from a team will be discussed. In addition, the issues of education/training, rewards, and empowerment and its ramifications to the organization are explored. The intent is to provide an overview of the topic rather than an exhaustive discussion of teams and their mechanics and empowerment. For additional information, see Harris (1986), Baird et al. (1988), McCann and Margerison (1989), Mackay (1992), Cusimano (1993), Hoevemeyer (1993), Stamatis (1993), Burns (1994), Donovan and Bond (1994), and Paton (1994).

OVERVIEW

People in the United States are motivated by individual achievement and individual excellence. This self-centered mentality among American employees makes it more difficult for U.S. companies to implement new ideas, develop more efficient processes, and apply better technology to compete globally. People seem to "look out for number one."

From kindergarten through college, students are discouraged from sharing information or ideas, which is often considered cheating. Even in sports, children are taught to find out what they do well, excel at it, and compete against their peers to be number one. The result of all this attention often is that the high achiever captures the limelight and gains more recognition than the entire group that made the achievement possible. Examples are everywhere: in a choir, it is the soloist; in a movie, it is the leading man or woman; in the operating room, it is the surgeon; in sports, it is the pitcher or the quarterback.

Likewise, in the corporate ranks, employees are usually reviewed and evaluated individually, like cakes in a bake-off at a state fair. We all have been conditioned to think that competition among individuals brings out the best in people, but it also keeps people from cooperating. The results of this lack of cooperation show up in subtle ways, as the "me" culture becomes *my department, my group, my division,* and so on in companies.

In the traditional organization, the creative people develop a design and then pass it on to the engineers, who do development and testing and pass it on to the next department. Problems are created when work groups do not cooperate. The process becomes much more expensive because problems are not detected early; work has to be redone, which is time consuming. The result is many quality problems, which result in higher costs.

The message is clear. Cooperation, collaboration, and trust are needed. "I" must be replaced with "we." Accomplishing this goal will require reeducation in both the individual and corporate domains. Part of this education must deal with trust. However, trust is often a cultural barrier. People in the United States do not share a common heritage. They come from different ethnic groups, ancestries, and religions and do not share a single set of values about how they should treat each other. People feel justified in "doing their own thing." Lack of trust and the need for personal recognition keep the flow of information, strategies, and ideas from being shared by others in the same company.

Investing in high technology and expensive information systems cannot overcome the cultural barrier of individualism that U.S. companies face. Many assume that technology is the best solution to the problem and underestimate the role of people by failing to recognize that there are human barriers which technology cannot overcome (Opper and Fersko-Weiss 1992). That is why companies devote considerable resources to new information technology, hardware, and software yet do not get the payoff they expect.

There is a way to overcome the culture clash between technology, communication, and individualism and to cultivate trust. The answer is to operate in teams and to empower workers.

TEAMS

A team has been defined in many different ways (Scholtes 1989; Opper and Fersko-Weiss 1992; Stamatis 1992, 1995). However, for our purposes, a team is defined as a group of people working together toward a common goal, who

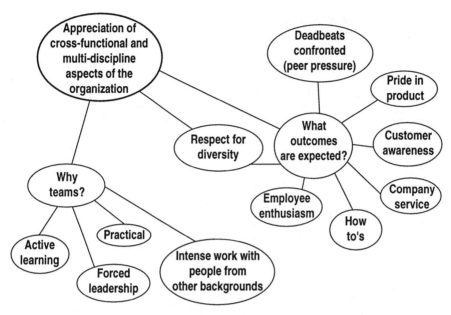

FIGURE 5.1 Teams and great expectations

meet regularly to identify and solve problems and improve process, who work together and interact openly and effectively, and who produce desired economic and motivational results for the organization. This relationship is illustrated in Figure 5.1.

The following factors influence the performance and productivity of a team:

The organization as a whole (culture):

- Philosophy of the organization
- Rewards and how they are handled
- Expectations
- Norms

The team itself:

- Meeting management
- Roles and responsibilities
- Conflict management
- Operating procedures
- Mission statement

Individual team members:

- Self-awareness
- Appreciation of individual differences
- Empathy
- Caring

An overview of the interrelationship of these factors can be illustrated as follows:

It is obvious that in order for a team to work effectively, the individual, the team, and the organization must work in tandem and have the same goals and expectations. Everyone in the organization must work in a synergistic manner. A simple definition of a team is represented by the following acronym:

Together

Everyone

Achieves

More

The theory that encourages team formation as opposed to working individually is *synergy*. Synergy is defined as the sum of the total being greater than the sum of the individual parts. What make the sum greater are the authority and responsibility that the team has been given through delegation by management. Effective delegation requires:

1. **Clarifying responsibilities:** The first step in managing a team of people is to make sure that each person understands his or her responsibilities. Often, in many organizations, responsibilities overlap or are

unclear. Responsibilities should be tailored to the individual, as each person has different abilities, skills, and experiences. Responsibilities should be adjusted as people gain more skills and experience.

2. **Prioritizing responsibilities and projects:** One of the most important things an individual can do to become more effective is learning how to prioritize tasks both for himself or herself and for the people he or she manages. Managers and their subordinates must learn how to organize their tasks into different categories of importance. A good rule for prioritizing is the Pareto principle (80–20 rule).

3. **Setting both short-term and long-term objectives *correctly* for both individuals and units:** Many people and organizations set objectives; few, however, do it *correctly*. This is of paramount importance if objectives are to help managers and their organizations. If a manager sets objectives incorrectly, many problems can result, including higher turnover, lower motivation, and lower productivity. It is also important for managers and organizations to have long-term goals.

4. **Granting specific, clear-cut authority for each responsibility:** One of the reasons why objectives are not met is because authority is granted in a very general way (i.e., you have all the authority you need for this project). This is too vague and causes all kinds of problems for the delegatee.

5. **Allowing people the freedom to achieve their objectives:** As people work toward their objectives, they should be allowed the freedom to devise their own methods. They may develop ways to achieve their objectives that the manager never thought of. People should be evaluated based on the results they achieve instead of how they achieved those results. This approach results in better motivation and more creative solutions to problems.

6. **Developing controls over delegated tasks correctly:** Delegation is not loss of control over delegated tasks. Many people think they are delegating when they are really "dumping" (assigning projects and not checking on them until they are due for completion). Effective delegation includes setting controls over delegated tasks. It also includes setting those controls *correctly*.

7. **Participating with people in determining their responsibilities, priorities, objectives, and authority:** *Effective* delegation is not giving orders and dictating to people. It involves soliciting ideas from people about their assignments, including their priorities, objectives,

and authority, and then checking back on their progress. A participatory approach to management results in better performance and motivation.

8. **Developing people and groups to make increasingly complex decisions.** Managers and supervisors who delegate *correctly* develop their people and units to handle more complex assignments. By keeping responsibilities flexible, setting challenging but achievable objectives for both their people and their units, controlling delegation properly, and training both their people and teams to handle more complex assignments, managers and supervisors allow both their people and teams to grow in their jobs and handle more difficult responsibilities. Teamwork will improve. Managers and supervisors should expand the number and difficulty of responsibilities gradually, building successes upon successes.

9. **Coaching, training, and supporting people and teams as they work toward their objectives:** *Effective* delegation requires managers and supervisors to help their people and units achieve their objectives. Managers and supervisors should provide their people and teams with the coaching, training, and support (proper tools, equipment, working conditions, and so on) they need in order to succeed. Effective delegation means helping people and teams improve their current performance. It does not mean "keeping score" and telling people and units at the end of the year what they did well and what mistakes they made throughout the year.

Effective delegation requires managers and supervisors to appraise the performance of their people and teams frequently throughout the year in order to improve their current performance. By doing so, people and teams will stay on track and increase productivity. Effective delegation requires managers and supervisors to try to improve the behaviors that prevent their people and teams from achieving their objectives.

10. **Selecting capable people to delegate to:** An important part of effective delegation is selecting the right people. It has been said that Andrew Carnegie once remarked, "Take away my plant and equipment but leave me my people, and I will rebuild in three years." Managers must be able to work effectively with existing staff in order to be successful.

11. **Rewarding individuals and groups based on performance:** In order to change the behavior of subordinates who are poor performers

and to maintain the level of performance of the highest achievers, managers must provide rewards based on performance. Positive reinforcement of good behavior is important in sustaining that performance. Different types of reinforcement can be used, most of which are not monetary.

TEAMS AND QUALITY

A vital part of the quality improvement effort is establishing a formal organization of teams to effectively implement and maintain the quality management system. These teams are responsible for managing the quality effort at all locations and within all functions. This may sound simple, but it involves a great deal of work. It is important to consider the entire organizational structure when establishing these teams. In a typical service organization, the various types of teams that will function at the different management levels must be defined. For example, the management committee sets the policy for the organization. This committee is assisted in this effort by the director of quality, who reports to the management committee. Advice is provided to the management committee by the quality council. The council is chaired by the director of quality. It is the responsibility of these two bodies to provide overall direction and guidance to the organization. This includes providing resources, scheduling and coordination of education, and other areas as the need arises. (In some organizations, there is no management committee and the quality council is the same as the steering committee.)

The next level in the formation of teams in typical service organizations is the steering committee. This group should be created to provide similar guidance and direction and to maintain consistency of purpose within the organization. It is important that the members of these committees do not normally interact functionally in their day-to-day operations but are a part of the same business group. An administrative group in the banking industry may serve as an example. This team would be comprised of legal, personnel, control, treasury, communications, development, and planning. The leaders of each of these functions would comprise the steering committee.

Whereas the quality council and steering committee address general problems within the entire organization, the divisional quality improvement team, the location and functional quality improvement team, and the business quality improvement team focus on more specific areas of the organization.

The divisional quality improvement team is a typical staff-level team which is responsible for implementing the quality system in the staff functions and support areas of the division. This team also provides guidance and support to the location and functional quality improvement team as well as the business quality improvement team.

The location and functional quality improvement team is, as the name implies, responsible for implementing the quality system in a given location or function. A branch site is a good example of a location and a commercial loan department is a good example of where a functional team is needed.

A business team may be created in service organizations that have a matrix-type management structure. These organizations are organized around service types, and the teams have the same responsibility as the location and functional quality improvement team. Service industries that may have a need for business teams are the hospitality industry, health care, legal, and construction.

Membership of any of the quality improvement teams (QITs) should represent every function involved. These functions normally interact with each other in order to accomplish their tasks. This interface is where many of the problems arise and are *thrown over the imaginary wall* within the organizational structure.

The first time through the quality system, the QIT members should be from the highest level possible for that entity. At a branch site, for example, the staff reporting to the branch manager should form the QIT. This gives the QIT the authority and decision-making power that it needs and emphasizes the importance of the program to the rest of the supervisors and employees.

Each QIT must have a chairperson (sometimes called a leader), either appointed or elected. Caution must be exercised here, particularly if a senior executive or the quality manager is being considered. If the quality manager is chosen, the quality management system (QMS) could be perceived to be "just another quality program." If an executive is chosen, he or she may dominate discussions and totally control the direction of the process. The intent of the QMS is to get people involved and participating so they will own the system. If the leader dominates the action, this may not happen.

When selecting a chairperson, there are several other characteristics to consider. The chairperson should be well respected and must also understand and firmly believe in the system. This person should be open minded, objective, and results oriented.

The next organizing activity that must be accomplished is the selection of a QIT administrator. This position requires a person with many of the same characteristics as the chairperson. In addition, he or she should be a good organizer. The person should also be somewhat "thick skinned," as some of the duties of the position could be discouraging.

The administrator (sometimes called the secretary) is the support person for the chairperson. It is this person's job to handle the administrative details of the QIT's activities. The administrator should be in charge of minutes and agendas for meetings, should be an information resource for the QIT, and should be responsible for the support needs of the QIT. For example, if the QIT decided on a procedure and measurement chart format, it would be the administrator's duty to have the procedures printed and distributed and the charts ordered and available. The administrator would also help the chairperson follow up on any action items prior to meetings. The duties of the administrator may require a full-time position. On the other hand, the position of the chairperson may not.

Once the QIT has been formed, its first agenda item should be to ensure that all members are educated. Then, the team can proceed to develop its charter and plan the program. The charter should define the structure and membership of the QIT, define the authority and responsibilities (duties) of the QIT and its members, and provide for the records that will be maintained.

Among the responsibilities that might be addressed in the charter is the need to develop and implement the quality system, including schedules for the action items. Members represent their functions to the QIT and represent the QIT to their functions. They are responsible for carrying out the decisions of the QIT in their departments. That is, they are responsible for implementing the QMS actions in their departments. The QIT must also monitor the effectiveness of the system and report to management on its progress. Member participation in training will demonstrate both commitment to and the importance of the quality system.

As the QIT starts developing the plan, it should distribute responsibility for each action to the members, who act as sponsors. This allows them to concentrate on the details for implementing the intent of the action. They will provide the preliminary plan for the action to the QIT for approval. If the action is complex, they may choose to establish a subcommittee to assist in the effort. This will spread the workload to other members of the organization and let others participate in the quality system at an early stage, which assures ownership and facilitates implementation. Typically, the sponsor assists in instructing the management QIT and supervisors in the proper method of implementing the actions and monitors progress in all departments.

At first, QIT meetings should be held every week to speed up the initial implementation. Meetings should not normally exceed one hour in length, and most of the "leg work" should be done between meetings. This will allow the members to deal with decisions at the meetings and assign action as necessary. The meetings should be carefully planned. An agenda should be established for each meeting with a time schedule assigned. Minutes must be kept and should include action assignments with names and dates.

Finally, planning for the QIT in any service organization should provide for the flow of information throughout the organization. Minutes of meetings, data, successes, and problems should be shared with other QITs. This will assist them in solving the same or similar problems that may have already been solved by the originating QIT. A forum should be provided for the QIT chairpersons, administrators, and quality managers to meet quarterly to share these ideas. This would be in addition to the normal vertical paper communication flow in the organization.

Typical Implementation Steps

1. Conduct first organizational meeting (review policy, principles, and quality management action system)

2. Select chairperson

3. Select administrator

4. Educate team members

5. Write team charter

6. Assign element sponsorship

7. Appoint subcommittees

8. Develop implementation plan

9. Hold meetings routinely to implement the plan and monitor the results

Intent of the Action Is Met When

- Quality improvement teams are in place and functioning

- Plans and objectives have been documented

- Formal implementation plans have been developed

- Regular meetings are held and formal minutes are issued to monitor progress

EDUCATION/TRAINING

In its simplest definition, education is the process whereby one learns the whys of something, or knowledge. Training, on the other hand, is the process whereby one transfers the whys into hows. The desired outcome of any formal training is for the participants to learn and later use what has been taught. They must understand what has been presented and use this information in their jobs. All employees, therefore, must be educated in the principles of quality management and the role that each must play in the system. However, the quality education/

training needs of employees vary depending on their position in the company framework. As a consequence, training needs will vary accordingly.

To address these different needs, planning for education must be viewed from four different perspectives. Looking at these, we see that the responsibilities of the individuals in the QMS are very distinct. For example, the responsibility of senior management (chairman down to manager level) is to support the system, as discussed in the commitment action. The responsibility of the QITs is to implement and manage the system, and the other managers must communicate the objectives and current events of the quality system and implement the individual actions in their groups. Finally, the remainder of the employees need to be educated in the principles and understand their role in improving the quality of their work.

Who should be educated, what information they need to understand, the objectives of the education, and how the information is to be conveyed are the issues which will guide the QITs in preparing their quality education plans. A generic training program and model is presented in Table 5.1 and Figure 5.2, respectively. Sample recommendations, focus, and action steps for an effective training campaign are provided in Table 5.1. Figure 5.2 presents a conceptualization of training. The essence of the model is that it provides a continual feed of participants for training based on the specific need(s) of the organization and/or the individual. The model also provides for evaluation at the point of return, to find out whether or not it was a positive investment. In the lower left corner, the model shows graphically the relationship between training and facility implementation over time. It is a reminder that as time passes, the need for classroom training (education) decreases, whereas the need for facility implementation training increases.

Senior management. It is important to note that quality education, as in all education, is a continuous process, starting with the commitment action. As a matter of course, commitment of senior management is the key to achieving improvement goals. This lays the foundation for the attitudes and work standards of individual employees, whether in engineering, sales, accounting, production, management information systems, and so on. Therefore, senior management must be given primary consideration in the education timetable when laying out the program. Education, then, is essential to ensure that senior management properly understands the principles and can support the QMS.

Teams. Members of the QITs that will be responsible for the implementation and management of the quality system must also receive education and/or training in greater detail. Implementation of the actions rests on their shoulders. They must maintain lines of communications in every direction so that all employees are aware of the progress of the quality system. Implementation of

TABLE 5.1   Generic Training Program

Recommendation	Focus	Action Steps
Provide employees with better overall product and process orientation.	A near universal desire exists for greater product and process information. This expressed desire is especially strong on the part of operators/set-up personnel, skill trades, and supervisors. An expression of strong positive motivation increases awareness and understanding so that a larger contribution can be made to production. It offers a window for expanding employee participation.	• Design and install an ongoing orientation process that builds upon the success of the initial orientation. • Utilize graphics and visuals to a far greater degree than is customary to communicate the process to be used and the form of the final product. • Schedule employees for tours of and visits to different service areas. • Capitalize on the natural desire to talk about the work a person does by having a regular process wherein employees brief one another on how they contribute to service production.
Continue to improve management and union cooperation and collaboration.	Throughout the service industry, notable gains have been made in recent years in management and union relations. However, there is a need to move the relationship to a new, higher level that is built upon trust, acknowledges the needs of both management and union employees, and is fully collaborative. It is important that "continuous improvement" extend to management/union relations as well as products and that precious gains not be taken for granted or allowed to languish.	• Explore areas of concern and contention between management and the union as they relate to proposed alternatives. • Gradually move toward more joint leadership positions between task forces, committees, and employees. • Investigate means to extend problem solving and consensus building to avoid "taking stands." • Identify and proceed to work on areas where a collaborative management/union approach can be experimented with.

Make greater use of the knowledge and expertise of technical employees and specialists in the process.	Technical employees and specialists have valuable practical knowledge of and skills in their process. In the past, they have not always been fully consulted. The results have been poor process design and purchase actions which have led to serious but potentially avoidable process and maintenance problems. A strong need exists to provide for input from technical employees and specialists before process/service design is finalized, machines are purchased, or service is implemented.	• Ensure that new work processes are reviewed by the appropriate personnel and have a systematic sign-off procedure by the employee for adequate service responsiveness. • Implement special and appropriate technical and "soft" skills training. • Establish "pools" of employees and specialists, rather than a single specialist, who can offer input process questions. • Establish a task force to explore the means to provide for a more proactive training approach that anticipates the needs of the organization. • Organize meetings of appropriate personnel to review and discuss areas of mutual need and concern.
Initiate changes in the design and management of the Equipment Advisory Team (EAT).	EATS are organized with the sole purpose of providing appropriate input from experienced operators, set-up personnel, supervisors, and skilled trades under the leadership of manufacturing process engineers for each of the different work process. Early meetings are encouraged.	• Obtain top-level management and union support. • Assign responsibility for the effective functioning of the teams. • Develop guidelines for effective team functioning and introduce the use of performance criteria to assess this effectiveness. • Provide team leadership and meeting management training. • Encourage everyone to use group process to negotiate member roles and responsibilities. • Provide regular feedback. • Analyze the possibility of introducing major and new innovations.

TABLE 5.1 Generic Training Program (continued)

Recommendation	Focus	Action Steps
Create a role for employees that includes design and purchase of equipment, EAT facilitation, contributions to training programs, and extended involvement in new work processes including service/production capability.	Many employees currently in the service industry play a very large role in the design of the process and the purchase of equipment. As such, they have a comprehensive view of equipment training needs. However, their involvement and contribution typically end after the design/purchase phase. The result is a loss to the program of their valuable insights and knowledge of the new work processes. There is a clear need to find ways to extend their involvement in the new work processes which they were instrumental in developing.	• Consider the assignment of employees to teams and training on a cross-functional basis. • Designate appropriate facilitators throughout the organization. • Involve all appropriate personnel in the decision-making process. • Establish closer working and communication links between design, purchasing, manufacturing engineers, operators, and supervisors on the floor to promote more effective machine use and provide feedback to the engineers in their decisions.
Utilize a dynamic training model.	An overall model for the training program has been developed (see Figure 5.2) which is dynamic in that it (1) is driven by a vision of what the training should be, (2) uses evaluation of results on preset intervals, (3) emphasizes the identification of training problems as a source of strength, and (4) recycles the training based upon the results of the evaluation.	• Design a method of evaluation which provides comprehensive and diagnostic information as to how well the training program is functioning. • Ensure that the training is relevant to the needs, presented at an appropriate level, and at times/locations suitable for those who will receive it. • Ensure systematic communication to potential trainees regarding the content and utility of the training and teaching methods to be used in the different training experiences. • Provide clear and direct information on how completion of different training sequences will impact and benefit the individual trainee now and in the future.

Extend and expand the culture of retraining and personal renewal.

Basic to the future of all organizations is the training and retraining of employees in basic, generic, and service-specific skills, as well as problem-solving techniques and team dynamics. The critical elements for all training are the following: (1) job relevance, (2) well conceived and presented, (3) appropriate to the educational level and needs of those who will receive it, and (4) experienced as personally rewarding for those who go through it.

- Investigate new ways of communicating information about the training opportunities.
- Explore ways of reducing the threat and anxiety associated with "returning to school" for older adults who have not had recent training.
- Identify ways to minimize the opportunities to apply and relate classroom experiences to current work activities.
- Provide assistance to employees through life/career counseling to determine how the different training experiences will promote their future at the organization and further their career opportunities.

Support/life career planning.

Employees everywhere, including the service industry, must be retrained for the years to come. However, this retraining must be done in a way that builds, not distracts, from their self-esteem and gives them confidence and hope for the future.

- Design program(s) that will assist employees in constructing life plans that will direct and support their efforts toward better managing their development into interpersonally proficient and technically competent employees.
- Develop linkages between existing and new programs.
- Conduct a systematic survey of employees to assess their greatest survival needs and the self-held tools and resources they need to adequately respond to the challenges and opportunities ahead.
- Investigate ways to use the working groups as a self-development resource that contributes to an individual's self-reliance and self-management.

TABLE 5.1 Generic Training Program (continued)

Recommendation	Focus	Action Steps
Avoid broad generalizations about the work processes.	In the service industry, so much of the daily work is so specialized both by functions and products that the need for continual training is essential. For best results, provide the training on an as-needed basis.	• Wherever possible, training should be designed for specific work processes. • Before training begins, make sure all the particular characteristics have been accounted for. • Utilize uniquenesses and differences in work processes as much as similarities in determining training needs and programs.
Emphasize the importance of listening and other interpersonal soft skills.	Effective performance requires a person to be technically competent (e.g., SPC, machine-specific skills, DOE, FMEA, QFD, etc.), but also interpersonally proficient (e.g., listening, team skills, conflict resolution, project management, etc.). Since the emphasis of training as a general rule has been on the technical skills, soft skills are frequently overlooked as important criteria of job performance. A strong need exists for soft skills training, particularly in the communication area.	• Assess the job relevance of an array of soft skills for different work processes. • Identify areas within the current work structure and in training where employees can practice the soft skills they have learned and reinforce their proficiency in them through use. • Establish an effective means for determining the current level of soft skills among employees. • Undertake a study to evaluate the impact of communication and listening skills on job performance.
Extend collaborative planning and decision making.	It has been known for a long time that in the service industry people wear many hats, sometimes at the same time. This provides an infinite advantage in decision making. The broad involvement of persons in diverse positions	• Review decisions and plans to assess how they can be delegated to diffuse responsibility among teams of key players. • Give attention not only to what plans and decisions need to be made, but by whom and how people with

	and with different experience can lead to improved planning and decision making. Properly structured and used at appropriate times, collaborative planning and decision making can result in synergistic outcomes, improve management, and enhance the role of the participant.	diverse backgrounds, positions, and viewpoints can be brought together to act on the issue. • Undertake a review of best-case and worst-case decision making and planning and identify how synergism was promoted in these scenarios.
Combine technical and interpersonal training.	When training is highly compartmentalized, the broad benefits of the training are lost. Employees may not be able to use their technical skills with the same effectiveness as they would if they had learned and applied technical and interpersonal skills together. The challenge is to provide opportunities for applying and using newly learned soft skills in technical situations.	• Sensitize all employees before any specific training. • Provide for extended visitation to other work areas to learn how they respond to stress, handle conflicts, make changes, and so on. • Provide for discussion of soft skills issues and topics in technical training sessions. • Whenever possible, use a brief period at the beginning of each shift to review progress and problems and discuss how difficulties can be alleviated.

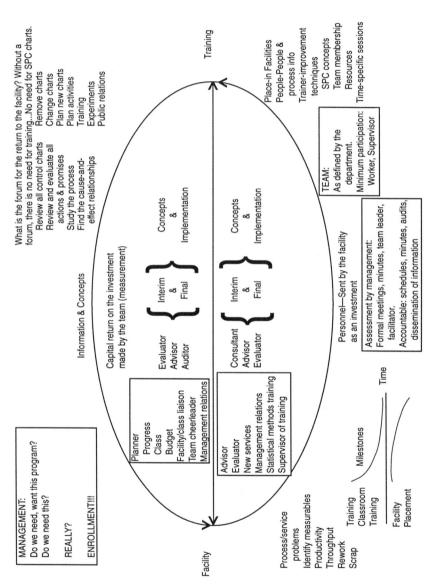

FIGURE 5.2 Training model

the communication actions will help in accomplishing this task. The QIT members must feel that they properly understand and can implement each of the quality management actions. They must also understand the principles and that the actions are meant to communicate the principles.

Other managers. It is particularly important for other managers to understand the principles and be able to explain them to their subordinates. Their attitudes will strongly influence the attitudes of their subordinates. They must also know about current events within the company, for they are the connecting link between senior management and other employees. Their information must be accurate and to the point. In order to achieve and maintain this level of knowledge, training for managers needs to be conducted at different times during the QMS implementation.

Upon implementing the QMS, managers should be given instructions on the principles and the method of explaining them to their people. Also, they should have the policy explained to them and should carry it forward. The need should be understood, and the action should be introduced early. As the actions progress, the managers will need explanations covering the measure/display action, the cost of quality calculations, and the corrective action system. This instruction should, as much as possible, be formalized and well planned.

Prior to the event action, the managers should receive a complete briefing on what to share with their employees. This includes success stories coupled with examples of management's attitude changes and employee involvement. It is extremely important for managers to be able to answer the questions of their subordinates.

Employees. Last but not least, the education/training of the remainder of the work force must be planned and executed in an organized manner. Consideration must also be given to the education/training of new employees joining the company. Since the formal education/training may take several years, a periodic quality communication session must be planned and executed. This session should include:

- Progress of QMS to date

- Explanation of the principles

- Review of the objectives of each action

- Evaluation of education/training in the workplace

A typical example of an education/training program is shown in Table 5.2. The table shows a completely developed education/training program for a health care facility for the entire implementation process and beyond. Of note is the fact

TABLE 5.2   An Example of Quality Education Plan for Health Care

	Quality Council	*Board of Trustees*	*Medical Exec. Medical Directors*
Content	• Facilitating • Teamwork • Articulating vision and management commitment • Leadership • Goals	• Philosophy of CQI • Leadership • Culture • Values	• Leadership • Collaboration • Clinical pathways
Format	Retreat workshop (min. 2 days)	Retreat workshop (min. 1 day)	Retreat workshop (min. 8 hrs)
Basic Quality		No	No
Time Frame	ASAP	ASAP	ASAP
Resources	Workshop Facilitators Instructors	Workshop Facilitators Instructors	Workshop Facilitators Instructors
Outcome	• Skills to monitor and facilitate the continued growth of QIT • Customer FOCUS • Empowerment • Culture • Accountability for process • Daily reinforcement	• Strategic planning • Quality/cost customer satisfaction • Resources • Commitment	Involvement in resolving institutional systems problems

Management	Staff	Vol/Aux	External Suppliers	Patients/ Customers
Basic quality Tools Techniques Processes Methodologies Measurement Prioritizing Facilitating Group/leadership skills	(10–15 employees) • Facilitating • Educating	• Leadership • CQI culture	• PR • PR • Involvement	• PR • Surveys
Retreat workshop (Min. 12 hrs and off-site)	On-site workshop (min. 12 hrs)	Retreat workshop	Daily reinforcement	• PR • Involvement
Yes	Yes			
ASAP	Ongoing	Within reasonable time		• Daily reinforcement • *Select processes*
• Quality Ed coordinator	• Quality Ed coordinator	Workshop Facilitators Educators		
• Team process • Statistical Process Control (SPC) • Survey • Measurement • Customer satisfaction *Daily reinforcement Interdepartmental Team formation Lead transformation*	• Facilitate • Instruct • Teach others • Intra- departmental team • Rollout of program		Involvement in prudent equipment, product, facility redesign Eliminate/ reduce variation	

that all levels of the health care facility are accounted for in the training process. In addition, note that plans for patient as well as voluntary help are accounted for.

Typical Implementation Steps

1. Plan and identify the employees to receive education/training

2. Select trainers

3. Review all programs for appropriate training opportunities

4. Develop materials for the classes

5. Prepare material for the communications sessions

6. Formalize the schedule for these strategy steps

Intent of the Action Is Met When

A formal education/training plan has been generated and approved. Since this action is continuous, plans must be continuously updated.

REWARDS

It is important to ensure that a reward system within a company—whether large or small—is consistent. This is a difficult effort to coordinate. Therefore, this action needs to be addressed by a subcommittee of the QIT with approval of the steering committee for that QIT. Corporate policy for employee recognition, once established, should be communicated as much as possible throughout the organization.

The focus of any reward program should be recognition. Recognition, however, should be part of the QMS, as well as measurable accomplishments. It is important to consider how employees are selected for recognition. Avoid a selection process that may give the perception of favoritism by management. QIT members and members of key subcommittees must not be forgotten in the recognition program (Curley 1994).

Groups and individuals who meet or exceed goals should be properly recognized for their accomplishments. It is important to take advantage of documented successes to reinforce the communication effort. Recognition of such achievements can provide the individual with satisfaction as well as provide a positive influence on the QMS as a whole.

In time, employee behavior and attitudes will change due to the credibility which management develops in supporting the efforts of all employees. Recognizing accomplishment is just one significant management action that will build this credibility. Actions by management must be sincere in order to build this credibility. Employees are not easily fooled, and they will soon see through any actions that are not sincere. An example of a reward program for participation in submitting problems might be to give the employee a preferred parking place for a week or lunch with the boss. Nothing elaborate is necessary to show sincere appreciation. What is really necessary is that the form of the rewards must be meaningful and consistently applied.

For significant accomplishment, a more permanent form of a reward, such as the medals awarded to military personnel or an Eagle Scout award for Boy Scouts, should be considered. These are memorable items that last and can be displayed for everyone to see. Be careful with cash awards. They should not be overemphasized, since cash rewards are, at best, short-term motivators. What employees really want and need is the opportunity to contribute, to make their jobs easier by eliminating problems, and to be appreciated for it. They understand the long-range benefits which they and the company will experience as a result.

An example of an award system is as follows:

Type of Recognition	Nominated by	Selection Process	Frequency	Award
President's award	Plant manager and group V.P.	Corporate committee	Annual	Sterling silver pin
Plant manager's	Any one employee	Plant committee	Maximum 2 per year	Award certificate and personalized nameplate
Individual achievement	Plant manager or group V.P.	Plant manager approved by president	Once per quarter	Personal framed letter of recognition
Special group award	Any employee	Approved by quality council	Twice per year	Group plaque and individual gift

Typical Implementation Steps

1. Assign subcommittee

2. Prepare and approve plan

3. Ensure consistency within company

4. Other recognition awards

5. Educate supervisors on the system

6. Start as soon as there is something to recognize

7. Publicize successes

Intent of the Action Is Met When

- A reward program is approved by the QIT and the local steering committee

- The plan is being used

- Public recognition is routine in most operations

EMPOWERMENT

Most management books tell us that the most important asset any organization has is its people. Yet in the real-world environment, we find that people are mistreated and not given the opportunity to either grow or perform at their optimum level. The saddest part of the situation is where management and employees mistrust one another, and the results are low morale, low productivity, apathy, and so on (Burns 1994).

Is there anything that can be done to reverse this situation? The answer is a categorical yes. Over the years, we have learned much about the human psyche and how humans behave in organizations. The answer, of course, is in empowerment. To empower or enable is to provide people with the knowledge, resources, and opportunities to achieve something, usually something new. It is precisely this definition that allows the employee to seek the authority and responsibility to satisfy his or her personal needs. The result, from what we know so far, is that people are happier, enthusiastic about their work, morale is positive, and generally speaking everyone is satisfied with the results within the organization (Cusimano 1993; Ludeman 1993; Mann 1994).

In pursuing this personal satisfaction, we must be careful to balance what is being asked for and what the organization really needs. To help in this distinction between employee and corporate need, we must become cognizant of the term empowerment in its totality. For example, in most organizations where empowerment is used, a team is assigned a problem. The team members share the responsibility for achieving the agreed-upon objectives. This sharing and responsibility have been delegated by the organization to empower them to plan, control, coordinate, and continuously improve their work. But herein lies the problem. Whereas in theory many organizations try to unlock employees' creative potential, through empowerment as well as team involvement, the reality is that there are employees who indeed find the opportunity exciting but there are also those employees who are threatened by it. Empowerment confuses many people and leaves others uncertain about how to achieve it.

To combat this dichotomy (the willingness to self-govern versus fear of the unknown), empowerment has to be viewed from two perspectives. The first is empowerment with a "small e," which empowers people to do their work, make decisions needed to satisfy their customers' requirements, and operate with little or no supervision. An example of this kind of empowerment is the customer service representative who approves the return of an item costing up to $100.00 without the intervention of a supervisor.

This kind of empowerment enables the team members to do their work effectively by having the ability, means, and authority to resolve problems or delays that might occur. Management has empowered the team to do what is necessary to complete the required task.

The second perspective of empowerment is empowerment with an "uppercase E," which empowers the team members to manage the unit's performance by planning, controlling, coordinating, or improving the work in addition to doing it. An example of this kind of empowerment is a health care team that defines the characteristics for triage in an emergency environment.

This kind of empowerment expands the team's work to include the planning, controlling, coordinating, and improvement functions that were performed by supervisors and/or staff specialists. This new notion of managing and doing your own work is indeed frightening to some people, and unless appropriate training is given to these individuals, they will fail.

Empowerment does not come first when creating a self-managing team; it comes last. The transition begins with organizational readiness for self-management, followed by team building, an empowerment plan, and continual training of supervisors to act as coaches and ready to empower their teams. The ingredients of work force empowerment are:

1. Must be selected

2. Must be educated and trained

3. Must be led

4. Must be coached

5. Must be directed

6. Must be given authority and responsibility

7. Must be rewarded

HOW TO EMPOWER YOUR EMPLOYEES

Stamatis (1992) has identified ten tasks that management must identify and do in order for individual employees to be empowered to do the things that are necessary for process improvement and employee satisfaction:

1. Understand that there is a need for change. Change is a process with a beginning and without an end. As a consequence, the organization must effectively communicate why the company needs to change for continual growth.

2. Provide a clear role to play. Unless specific roles of authority and responsibility are defined, the individual will lose interest. The participant must know where he or she is going before the plan is made.

3. Provide for appropriate education and training. Education provides the *whys,* whereas training provides the *hows.* Both are important. However, make sure that the combination is not at the expense of one or the other.

4. Provide the resources to get the job done. No amount of delegated authority or responsibility can guarantee success, unless applicable resources are within the jurisdiction of the empowered team.

5. Allow the freedom to be creative and innovative. In the process of taking this freedom, mistakes may happen. Do not hold it against the team's career path or retaliate with a demotion or withholding a merit increase. Instead, look at the failures and mistakes as learning experiences and incorporate them in your experiences.

6. Allow and encourage the freedom to "rock the boat" without fear. The days of labeling someone a troublemaker or a person with an attitude problem must be gone in the days of empowerment. The person who challenges the status quo without fear of any kind is truly practicing empowerment. It is through this challenge that different and/or improvement events will happen. Remember the old saying: If you always do what you always did, you will always get what you always got. Unless something changes, you will never change. Rocking the boat is one way to bring about change.

7. Give people the authority to exercise their best judgment. Again, without fear of retaliation of any kind, members must be allowed to exercise their judgment. To be sure, this judgment may not meet the organization's expectations; however, always make it part of the learning process.

8. Give people the responsibility to improve continuously. If the delegated authority does not include the responsibility, nothing will happen. In order for the process to improve continuously, team members must be allowed to experiment and must be given the responsibility of owning that process.

9. Give people the recognition they deserve. As long as the task is completed, regardless of the level of success, recognition should be part of the closure. Recognition does not have to be monetary; rather, it can be acknowledgment of a job well done, a token of appreciation, a thank-you note, a letter in the personnel file, and so on.

10. Give people a sense of ownership. Be prepared to answer the question: What's in it for me? Once employees recognize that the process is their own, and there is a personal interest in the improvement, then they will be able to take reasonable risks for improvement. To give a sense of ownership, you must be willing to let go.

REFERENCES

Baird. L. S., Beatty, R. W., and Schneier, C. E. (March 1988). "What Performance Management Can Do for TQI." *Quality Progress.*

Burns, G. (February 1994). "The Trouble with Empowerment." *Quality Digest.*

Curley, J. P. (January 1994). "Awarding Quality with Quality." *Quality Digest.*

Cusimano, J. M. (March 1993). "Creating Leaders through Employee Empowerment." *Quality Digest.*

Donovan, M. and Bond, D. (March 1994). "Empowering Self-Managing Work Teams." *Quality Digest.*

Harris, P. R. (April 1986). "Building a High-Performance Team." *Training and Development Journal.*

Hoevemeyer, V. A. (September 1993). "How Effective Is Your Team?" *Training & Development Journal.*

Ludeman, K. (December 1993). "Helping Managers: Walk the Empowerment Talk." *Quality Digest.*

Mackay, H. (March 1992). "Team Work." *Successful Meetings.*

Mann, B. (January 1994). "Empowerment: An Enabling Process." *Quality Progress.*

McCann, D. and Margerison, C. (November 1989). "Managing High-Performance Teams." *Training & Development Journal.*

Opper, S. and Fersko-Weiss, H. (1992). *Technology for Teams*. Van Nostrand Reinhold, New York.

Paton, S. M. (February 1994). "Implementing Self-Directed Work Teams at USG." *Quality Digest*.

Scholtes, P. R. (1989). *The Team Handbook*. Joiner Associates, Madison, Wisc.

Stamatis, D. H. (1992). *Team Building and Development*. Contemporary Consultants, Southgate, Mich.

Stamatis, D. H. (1993). *TQM & ISO Facilitator: Skills Training Course*. Contemporary Consultants, Southgate, Mich.

Stamatis, D. H. (1995). *Failure Mode and Effect Analysis: FMEA from Theory to Execution*. Quality Press, Milwaukee, Chapter 6.

6

CONFLICT RESOLUTION

This chapter covers the issue of conflict from a quality perspective. Specifically, it addresses what conflict is, what makes conflict possible, and what we can do about it.

OVERVIEW

In any service organization, conflict may arise in a variety of ways, including at the point of purchase (wrong tag on merchandise, an employee who does not know his or her job) or the customer service counter (person not empowered to handle complaints, does not know the procedure for returned merchandise, does not know how to use the cash register to issue credit). It may also simply be a misunderstanding of some sort.

How we handle conflict may be the difference between a satisfied and a dissatisfied customer. Generally speaking, the resolution of any conflict is an opportunity to improve both employee and customer relationships and communication, to lessen levels of friction and tension in the workplace, and to eliminate longstanding problems. While these are admirable goals, unfortunately conflict is not seen in such a positive light. Consider, for example, the following typical definition of conflict.

Conflict occurs when two or more parties in an organization have to interact to accomplish a task, make a decision, meet an objective, or solve a problem and (a) the parties' interests clash, (b) one party's actions cause a negative reaction by the other party, or (c) parties who are unable to resolve a controversy lash out at each other. Productivity suffers as long as the conflict remains unresolved. The parties in conflict influence co-workers, who begin to take sides or withdraw from the situation. In the end, conflict adversely affects the productivity and working relationships of not only those directly involved, but the whole work group.

The following scenario presents conflict in a somewhat different vein. July 17, 1994 was a very important day. That was the day of the final match of the 1994 World Cup of soccer, indeed a very important day for any serious soccer fan. This particular Sunday was also a very important day for my wife, who is not a serious soccer fan. Sunday is the day that she cleans the house and takes care of the houseplants. She works during the week, and Sunday is her day to clean. During the penalty portion of the game, she decided to vacuum around the TV and take care of the plants. In the process, the TV was moved and... That is my definition of conflict: two or more important things interfering with one another.

These definitions, as different as they are from each other, share a common bias: conflict is an evil and has a negative impact on individuals and organizations. (While the second situation does not spell out the results of the conflict with my wife, we can easily foresee what they will be.)

In fact, there are two kinds of conflict: conflict that costs very little and that which costs a great deal. Both conflicts described above have high costs. They cause disruption and loss of productivity in an organization. Low-cost conflict, in contrast, may be considered constructive controversy, and new ideas and improvements arise out of such controversy.

To resolve conflict, one must follow a certain path of development (see Figure 6.1) and use certain skills. These skills have been identified by Blake and Mouton (1964) to be avoidance, accommodation, competition, compromise, and collaboration.

Avoidance is withdrawal from a conflict or failure to take a position on it. The employees involved make no attempt to understand or correct the cause of a conflict. Management, when asked to help resolve it, denies its existence.

In accommodation, employees overlook their own concerns and allow the other employees involved in a conflict to obtain what is important to them. Differences are downplayed in the attempt to reach an agreement. The accommodating management, concerned with a quick fix for the problem, rolls the issues together and decides what will be the best, most quickly achievable solution.

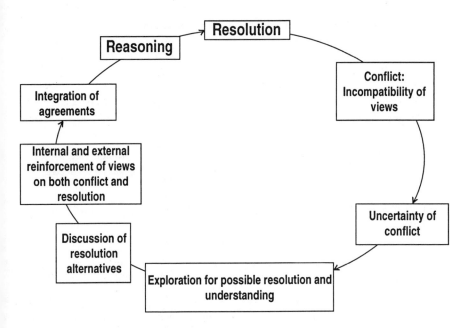

FIGURE 6.1 The cycle of conflict

In the competitive mode, a simple "win–lose" mentality prevails. Each employee strives to obtain his or her objectives and win even at the expense of other employee(s). The competitive manager called in to resolve a conflict chooses an employee he or she believes should win and works to achieve a victory for that employee.

Employees using the compromise method are willing to give up part of their own objectives in order to resolve the conflict. Compromising managers obtain concessions from each employee and guide the negotiations until a settlement is reached. This settlement may not fully satisfy either employee, but both agree that it is the best resolution of the conflict.

During collaboration, a mutual problem is resolved. Each employee accepts the other's objectives and they work together to achieve the best outcome for both. During the collaboration process, trust and openness are required because attempts are made to identify and resolve concerns that underlie the conflict. Trust and openness, in turn, are increased through the process. The manager involved in a collaboration works along with the employees to find the best possible solution.

Before selecting a method for resolving a particular conflict, the manager must consider the nature of the conflict and the likely consequences of the solution. Again, keep in mind that successful conflict resolution, especially in

TABLE 6.1   Selecting a Conflict Resolution Approach

Use the interpersonal facilitator approach when:	Use the interface conflict solving approach when:
Only representatives of the organization and not organization members are meeting	Presence of group members at meetings will strengthen implementation of any change
Personal chemistry blocks direct discussions between the principals	Personal chemistry problems are not sufficient to prevent cooperation between group leaders
Group members will not reject their representatives for agreeing to change or compromise	Group members will not allow their leaders to agree to change or compromise without their say-so
The representatives understand the depth and scope of the problem	The leaders do not understand the depth and scope of the problem
The change can be implemented successfully without group members' agreement about its soundness	Successful implementation of the change requires that the group agree to its soundness
A deadline is near and quick decisions, even though imperfect, are necessary to prevent a total breakdown	Sufficient time is available to develop the best possible solution
A multiplicity of views exists within each group and members are not unified	Each group's members are united in their stance

service organizations, almost always benefits the organization. In general, collaboration and accommodation are desirable methods because they promote employee cooperation and harmony. However, because such methods may be time consuming and may produce results that are not entirely satisfying to any of the employees involved, these methods are inappropriate in some cases. The selection process is summarized in Table 6.1.

Like conflict, confrontation is also a word with a bad reputation. It conjures up images of one person shouting at another or telling another person that "this is the last straw" and stomping away. However, confrontation is also a learned, step-by-step process or sequence of events that is used by two parties who are in conflict and who are trying to resolve their differences. Stamatis (1987) has identified certain conditions that contribute to a successful confrontation:

- At least one of the parties is aware that a conflict exists.

- One of the parties is willing to start the confrontation process.

- Both parties are willing to use a clearly defined confrontation process and problem-solving framework (i.e., collaboration, compromise, etc.).

- Both parties expect, or at least hope, that this process will resolve their differences.

The process of confronting a conflict involves six major steps.

Step 1. Awareness. During the awareness step, the parties involved recognize that a conflict exists.

Step 2. The decision to confront. The alternatives to conflict are measured and the decision is made that a confrontation is preferred to avoiding the concern.

Step 3. The confrontation. In this step, both parties in the confrontation, more often than not, decide to use the collaboration or compromise model. In most cases, the conflict is resolved here.

Step 4. Determining the cause of the conflict. In this step, the parties should try to describe their own feelings, opinions, reactions, and fears in relation to the conflict. A key objective of this step is determining the root cause of the conflict. If the parties involved cannot agree on the cause of the conflict, then the confrontation has failed.

Step 5. Determining the outcome and further steps. Up to this point, both parties have been involved in defining the problem and sharing information. In Step 5, the parties attempt to devise specific means of reducing or eliminating the root cause of the conflict. If both parties agree on a solution, then the confrontation has been successful.

Step 6. Follow-through. After the solution has been implemented, both parties should plan regular checks at specific times in the future to ensure that their agreement is being kept.

A successful confrontation can have many positive outcomes for the parties involved and the organization, including a good solution to a problem, increased work productivity, a raised level of commitment to decisions by both parties, a willingness to take greater risks in the future, increased customer satisfaction, and a more open and trusting relationship between the parties.

The collaboration process, as well as the methods of conflict resolution described above, is primarily for use in solving conflicts between individuals or small groups. Conflicts also arise between much larger organizations, but that issue is beyond the scope of this chapter.

Conflict is indeed an inevitable part of life in the workplace and is generally regarded as a negative force that creates tension, lowers productivity, and disrupts employee relationships. As a result, employees who are frequently called upon to resolve conflicts within the domain of their jurisdictional task often regard them with dread. For the employee who learns to resolve conflict skillfully, however, conflict instead becomes a welcome opportunity to improve and benefit the workplace and provide an increased level of customer satisfaction.

HOW TO DEAL WITH DIFFICULT PEOPLE

Bramson (1981) identified several types of difficult people, as follows.

Hostile-aggressives. These are the people who bully and overwhelm by bombarding others, making cutting remarks, or throwing tantrums when situations don't go the way such people are certain they should.

Complainers. These people gripe incessantly but never do anything to resolve what they complain about.

Silent and unresponsives. They are the types who respond to every question and every plea for help with a yes, a no, or a grunt.

Super-agreeables. These are the type who are very reasonable, sincere, and supportive in the presence of others but do not produce what they say they will or act contrary to the way they have led others to expect.

Negativists. These are the people who always claim and/or proclaim to the rest of us "it won't work" or "it's impossible" every time something new is proposed. All too often, they deflate any optimism others might have.

Know-it-all experts. These are the type who are "superior" people. They believe and want others to recognize that they know everything there is to know about anything worth knowing. Such people are condescending, imposing (if they really do know what they are talking about) or pompous (if they don't), and they often make others feel like idiots.

Indecisives. These are the type who stall major decisions until the decisions are made for them. They can't let go of anything until it is perfect, which means never.

Whereas Bramson categorizes and labels people, Monroe et al. (1989) address difficult behavior as what people do despite corrective feedback from employers and/or third parties. After all, everyone does some things that irk other people. To change the behavior, Stamatis (1987), Monroe et al. (1989), Friedman (1991), and Kerzner (1992) recommend the following.

Bridging the gap. The discrepancy between what is occurring now (the current situation) and what is preferred (the target) by devising a plan to facilitate that change.

Separate relationship issues from substantive issues. When people at work disagree, two outcomes are in doubt: (1) what decision will be reached and (2) how the individuals will feel about working together in the future. The first question involves a substantive issue: how the content of the dispute will be resolved. The second involves a relationship issue: how the individuals will deal with each other as people.

You can win at one level and lose at the other. In other words, you can get what you want substantively yet make an enemy; on the other hand, you may not obtain what you want substantively but you may strengthen a working relationship. To disentangle the two issues, explicitly separate your working relationship with the other person from whether you agree with or approve of his or her viewpoint. That means thinking, "I will treat this person well whether or not I like what he or she thinks or does."

Be unconditionally constructive. Many people deal with difficult people in the same way those people treat them, by reciprocating what they receive. This may be called an "eye for an eye" policy. If the other person yells at them, they yell back. If the other person insults them, they insult that person right back. If the other person cheats them, they cheat the other person.

The eye for an eye policy is based on a traditional approach to justice. Unfortunately, in a modern organization, it is largely ineffectual and even dangerous, because the "victim" often is harmed as much as the perpetrator. Reciprocation sets off a negative spiral and does not resolve anything.

Be aware of partisan perceptions. Each of us sees the events in our own lives and other people's behavior from our own vantage point. Thus, we see only "part" of the whole. We tend to think, nevertheless, that our perspective is accurate and representative of what is occurring.

Unfortunately, there are at least two sides to every story and many ways to view every incident. At the end of a hard week, for example, a boss and a subordinate may reflect on life in their organization, but each sees things a little differently.

Balance reason with emotion. We all know that in some instances too much emotion can diminish performance. The person who is very agitated when taking a test or giving a speech performs poorly. A person who becomes furious at a child who commits a minor transgression hurts rather than helps the child. A person who fears going to the dentist feels the pain from a toothache escalate.

On the other hand, an organization with little or no emotion is dull and lifeless. Some experts tell us that the most effective leaders are extremely emotional—and even act as cheerleaders—about the goals they are trying to achieve. Parents who coolly lecture their children and rarely hug them or show emotion are doing them a disservice. An appropriate amount of emotion helps a speaker be energetic and vital.

Responding impulsively and emotionally to a difficult person usually only worsens the relationship, especially if the person is making you angry. A good working relationship with a difficult person requires a reasonable approach. What can you do to balance emotional and rational reactions to behavior that upsets you? Fisher and Brown (1988) have several suggestions:

1. Take a break.

2. Count to ten if an official break is not possible.

3. Consult a third party.

4. Acknowledge and talk about your emotions.

5. Accept responsibility and apologize if an argument erupts.

6. Prepare yourself when you know an emotional situation is likely.

Inquire, listen, and understand. Every year in this country, thousands of companies merge with or are acquired by other companies. A shockingly high percentage of these mergers fall far short of their financial goals. The predominant reason is that people in the acquiring company do not really understand the people, processes, or culture of their new partner. We cannot deal effectively with difficult people unless we understand them. However, people usually overestimate their understanding of others.

When you feel that someone is being difficult, it is always best to assume that there is a good reason for their behavior which you do not as yet understand. In an interview with *Psychologist Today*, psychologist George Miller said, "In order to understand what another person is saying, you must assume it is true, and try to imagine what it's true of." Unfortunately, most people assume that what other people say is absurd or untrue and try to imagine what could be wrong with them to make them say something so ridiculous.

The Japanese have an apt story that illustrates how important it is to be open to inquiry, to listen, and to understand. An American tourist visited a Zen monastery and asked the abbot to explain Zen philosophy to him. The abbot could tell from the American's manner that he already thought Zen to be merely a quaint, archaic, bizarre way of life, so he asked the visitor to join him for a cup of tea. The American was annoyed by this delay, but agreed to it nonetheless. The abbot set out two cups. He poured tea into the American's cup until it was full and then continued pouring. The American shouted, "Stop, you can't fit any more tea in there—it's spilling over the side!" The abbot smiled and replied, "Ah, and that's what would happen if I tried to explain Zen to you. Your mind is already full of preconceptions. You have no space to receive what I would say. My words would simply pour over the sides. Empty your mind. Become open to learning, and then we can speak meaningfully."

Consult before deciding. When people work closely together, what one person does usually affects the other. (This interdependence certainly applies to members of a family.) Yet we often make decisions or take actions that affect other people without consulting them or even notifying them in advance. Doing so, unfortunately, usually upsets the people who are kept in the dark and destroys good working relationships.

Why do we sometimes neglect to consult those affected by our actions? Usually, it simply doesn't occur to us, or we assume there is no need to. Perhaps we think we already know what the other person will say, or we are sure we have made the right decision and feel we have the authority to do so, so we just "tell" the other person what we have done and expect that person to accept it.

People do not like being controlled by others, even if what is decided is substantively in their own best interests. People like to participate in decision making, even if they would have made the same decision anyway. Therefore, it is always best to consult anyone who will be affected by any of your decisions. This does not mean giving up your right to decide.

Be trustworthy. Working relationships are better among trusting people. People who can be counted on to keep their word are trustworthy. Trustworthiness is not an objective measure of honesty and reliability. It is a qualitative measure. If I believe you will do what you say, then I perceive you as trustworthy. If I suspect you will not, your credibility with me is low.

Faith in people is fragile. Once broken, it is difficult to restore. You may think, "I have good intentions; I usually come through with most things I promise; I'm not trying to hurt anyone; I should be trusted." However, being trustworthy in three out of five instances does not earn you trust. Every breach of trust diminishes people's confidence in you. Even if you keep your word nine out of ten times, others will remember the one time you did not and wonder when you will disappoint them next. (Many people's trust is as disproportional as the man who told the dictionary author, "You're disgusting. I've read your book and there are at least ten instances of profanity in it!")

Use persuasion, not coercion. When people are being difficult and you have more authority than they do, it is tempting to force or coerce them to do as you wish. However, compliance through coercion (such as threatening harm) provides only short-term gains and long-term losses. People resent being coerced and eventually express that resentment in angry outbursts or acts of revenge. Coercion creates competition to see who will win, as methods to create win/win solutions are overlooked. Rather than resolve difficulties, coercion usually just perpetuates or escalates them.

A difficulty should be seen as a problem that both parties wish to solve through cooperation. Both should be on the same side of the line, attacking the problem instead of each other. Managing difficult behavior is not a contest. It is a challenge to invent a solution both people support and feel committed to implementing.

To do this, neither party can afford to adhere to only one way of handling the problem. An either or, take it or leave it approach usually creates a standoff or results in one party coercing the other or giving up in despair.

The story of two frogs thrown into the center of a huge vat of milk is applicable here. One looked around, could not see the rim, gave up on survival, sank to the bottom, and drowned. The other, thinking there had to be a way out of the predicament, kept swimming. By morning, he was standing safety atop a pile of butter his churning had created.

Accept and deal seriously with difficult people. It is tempting to scorn and reject people who do not fulfill our expectations. When disappointed, we become critical and disdainful. We slam the door on communication and give up on problem solving.

We have to remember, however, that the action that upsets us is only a small part of the difficult person's constellation of behavior. Consider, for example, the advertising executive who mishandled an account and had to report it to his board of directors. He started his talk by posting in front of the room a large sheet of white paper with a small black dot on it. He asked the board members to tell him what they saw. They all said, "A small black dot."

The executive said, "Yes, and there's also a large white sheet of paper." Notice that when something is blemished, we attend to that small blemish and overlook the broad background on which it is placed.

The difficult behavior of many people is simply a small dot on a large background. Be sure to keep that background in mind. Let the offending person know you are aware of his or her positive qualities. Whether a support worker or an executive, each person is equally a human being and worthy of basic respect. Treating people with acceptance and respect, even if their behavior is difficult at times, provides the framework for improvement.

HOW TO MANAGE NEGATIVE THINKING

The issue of negativity is a very real one in everyday life. However, in service organizations, it seems that it always comes up at the wrong time. To manage the negative thinking, we must understand it. To understand it, we must look at its foundations. Conceptually, negativity is based on nine basic concepts:

1. Negativity is destructive to morale and productivity in the workplace. It is contagious. It may start with one or two individuals, but it can attract unwitting participants and hangers-on. It can become firmly entrenched.

2. Negativity may be a reflection of personal problems or institutional vulnerability, or both. It may show up in one-to-one transactions or may involve group conflicts.

3. All negative individuals have some things in common. They are basically alienated and insecure. They feel cut off from the positive aspects of life. When confronted with their negativity, they usually argue that their attitude is realistic, given the circumstances.

4. Negativity may be expressed in many ways: sexism, racism, put-down, sarcasm, and so on. Passive-aggressive behavior, gossip, and backstabbing are more covert forms.

5. All negativity represents an attempt to solve what these individuals experience as real problems in either their own lives or in the organizations they work for.

6. In order to deal with negativity effectively, everyone involved has to acknowledge three things:

   a. That it exists

   b. That it is a symptom of possibly serious personal or organizational problems

   c. That even if individuals are not negative themselves, they may unwittingly facilitate negativity

7. The goal of reducing negativity is to channel the wasted energy of negativity into productive activity. This is accomplished by finding better

ways to solve the sometimes real, sometimes imagined underlying problems that are the origins of the negativity.

8. Combating negativity can be difficult. Negativity combines elements of pessimism and paranoia. There is almost always some basis for it. If an organization is downsizing, it is understandable if individuals begin to worry about keeping their jobs. This is a good example of negativity as the symptom of an underlying problem that needs to be dealt with.

9. Combating negativity can be dangerous in some settings. It may be deeply entrenched, especially in the hands of powerful, insecure individuals. Seeking employment elsewhere may be the only reasonable alternative.

Often we ask the question: Since we all know negative individuals, is there a negative organization? The answer is yes, there is. In fact, Carter-Scott (1989) identified the characteristics of the negative organization as:

Rumor	Powerlessness	Sarcasm
Dissatisfaction	Hesitation	Lack of ownership
Impatience	Lack of dignity	Anger
Lack of trust	Rustout	Lack of respect
Burnout	Lack of commitment	Unhappiness
Lack of mission	Sullenness	Lack of goals
Sluggishness	Backbiting	Worry
Sabotage	Pessimism	Withdrawal

Dellinger (1989) suggests that in order for us to understand negativity and its impact, we must also define its two components. These two components are the verbals and behaviors. Now that we know the components of negativity, we can use a formula to determine its negative impact:

$$V + B = NI$$

where V = verbals, B = behaviors, and NI = negative impact.

For example (observations):

$$\text{Sarcasm} + \text{Tardiness} = NI$$

$$\text{Expressing doubt} + \text{Sulking} = NI$$

Low-level expectations + Lack of participation = NI

Expectations:

Nondamaging humor + Punctuality = Team Player

Expressing concern + Demonstrating neutrality = Team player

Neutral expectations + Positive participation = Team player

The process of identifying the components of negativity is indeed very simple. However, in its simplicity it also presents the problem of perception. When we talk about negativity in any form, we must understand that we talk about a belief system that can damage and distort a healthy reality base. Yet belief systems form the basis for what we think we know is true.

Therefore, how we perform on the job is the result of how we see (perception) our input into the organization. Our level of input is determined by a number of significant factors that we ourselves define. They may be correct, but then again they may not be. Our focus, then, is to neutralize our emotions and perceptions as much as possible. Table 6.2 shows that relationship.

By emotionalizing our response, we weaken our probability of success, since our response, more often than not, will be made in haste. On the other hand, if we neutralize the input before our response, we increase the probability of success, since our response will be well thought out. We can increase this probability of success even more by utilizing the team and/or empowerment concepts.

In deciding to change negative thinking (manage it) into a more neutral perception in our lives, we must take a different view of the issue of responsibility. It is true that responsibility and accountability will indeed manage pro-

TABLE 6.2 Emotionalize versus Neutralize

Emotionalize	*Neutralize*
Anger	1. Analysis
Stress	2. Reality check
Anxiety	3. Options
Resentment	4. Flexibility
Frustration	5. Decision
Limitation	

gressively all negativity. The application to the service industry, of course, is that we must always remain cool and in control when handling any conflict because, as someone (author unknown) has said,

It is not easy...

to apologize,
to begin over,
to be unselfish,
to take advice,
to admit error,
to face a sneer
to be charitable,
to keep trying,
to be considerate,
to avoid mistakes,
to endure success,
to profit by mistakes,
to forgive and forget,
to think and then act,
to keep out of a rut,
to make the best of little,
to subdue an unruly temper,
to shoulder a deserved blame,
to recognize the silver lining—

But it always pays.

We use conflict resolution in everyday situations within the organization and almost always in customer service environments. The organization can apply conflict resolution effectively by allowing employees to form teams and delegating (authorizing) true empowerment throughout the organization. Of course, true delegation and empowerment are dependent upon the authority and responsibility that one has been given.

REFERENCES

Blake, R. R. and Mouton, J. S. (1964). *The Managerial Grid.* Gulf Publishing, Houston.

Bramson, R. M. (1981). *Coping with Difficult People.* Ballantine Books, New York.

Carter-Scott, C. (1989). *Negaholics.* Ballantine Books, Chicago.

Dellinger, S. (1989). *Psycho-Geometrics.* Prentice-Hall, Englewood Cliffs, N.J.

Fisher, R. and Brown, S. (1988). *Getting Together: Building a Relationship that Gets to Yes.* Houghton-Mifflin, Boston.

Friedman, P. (1991). *How to Deal with Difficult People.* Skill Path Publications, Mission, Kans.

Kerzner, H. (1992). *Project Management: A Systems Approach to Planning, Scheduling and Controlling* (4th Ed.). Van Nostrand Reinhold, New York, Chapter 7.

Miller, G. A. (January 1980). "Giving Away Psychology in the 80's." *Psychology Today.*

Monroe, G., Borzoi, M., and DiSalvo, V. (April 1989). "Conflict Behaviors of Difficult Subordinates." *The Southern Communication Journal 54.*

Stamatis, D. H. (December 1987). "Conflict: You've Got to Accentuate the Positive." *Personnel.*

7

CUSTOMER SERVICE AND SATISFACTION

Much has been written about customer service and customer satisfaction (Butterfield 1987; Sarazen 1987; Blume 1988; Chandler 1989; Goodman 1989; Goizueta 1989; Wells 1989; Vanocur 1989; Graham 1991; Lovelock 1989; Test 1990; Hunt 1990; Tague 1990; Sheridan 1993; Shoemaker 1994; Janson 1994; Wargo 1994; Weiner 1994; Griffin 1994; Powers 1994; Trabue 1994; Zemke 1994; Pyzdek 1994; London 1994; Berwick 1994; Silverstein 1991 and many others). However, it may be summarized as follows: know thy customer (Albrecht and Zemke 1985), and in order to win on perceived quality, you need to have more refined data than your competitors (know more about evolving customer needs by segment and more about changing competitive performance) and you need to use this information from quality-directed research in a strategic framework (Buzzell and Gale 1987).

To optimize customer service and satisfaction, that service must be understood before asking your customers what they want. In order to do that, you must have data. The data may be qualitative and/or quantitative. Contrary to what most people think, service is not as mushy and touchy-feely as it has been made out to be. To be understood, it requires hard work from management and nonmanagement alike, in addition to measuring what is important.

This chapter addresses the following issues: what a customer is, what customer service is, what customer satisfaction is, measurement, the levels of customer satisfaction, and surveys.

OVERVIEW

When we talk about customer service and/or satisfaction, we talk about creativity. Creativity allows us to handle or diffuse problems at hand or later on in the process of conducting everyday business. We talk about how or rather what the organization has to do to gain not only the sale but also the loyalty of the customer. We want to know the payoff of the transaction both in the short and long term. We want to know what our customers want (Hutchens 1989). We want to know if our customers are satisfied. Satisfaction, of course, means that what we delivered to a customer met his or her approval. We want to know if the customer is delighted and is willing to come back. Fleiss (1989) and Feldman (1991) have written examples of precisely that delight in their examples. Fleiss has written about Ben and Jerry's ice cream and Feldman has written about excellence in a cab ride.

As important as delightfulness is, some of us minimize it, if not disregard it altogether. At this point, of course, we fail. Some of the issues that will guarantee failure in sales, satisfaction, and loyalty are:

- Employees are required to adhere to a rigid chain of command

- Employees are closely supervised

- Conflict—in whatever form—is not allowed

- Rewards are based on "carrot and stick" principles

On the other hand, we increase our chance for success if we allow employees to take personal responsibility for their actions in the areas of communication, performance, and customer satisfaction. How do we go about sensitizing employees to all these issues? First, we must identify how we define the customer. Second, we must understand the levels of customer expectations about quality. Third, we must understand the strategy for customer service quality. Fourth, we must understand the measurement and feedback cycles of customer satisfaction.

In the case of customer definition, we have defined a customer as the person or unit receiving the output of a process of the system. In fact, earlier we emphasized the fact that the customer may be an immediate, intermediate, or the ultimate customer. It may be a person or a process.

Customer satisfaction, on the other hand, is when the customer is satisfied with the service and it meets his or her needs, wants, and expectations. To further understand customer satisfaction, we must also look deeper into the levels of specific satisfaction. To understand the notion of the levels of customer satisfaction, we must also recognize that there are levels of customer satisfaction which in a sense define the basic ingredients of quality. There are at least three levels of customer expectations about quality.

Level 1.   The expectations are very simple and take the form of *assumptions, must have,* or *take it for granted.* For example: (1) I expect the airline to take off, fly to my destination and land safely; (2) I expect to get the correct blood for my blood transfusion; and (3) I expect the bank to deposit my money into my account and to keep a correct balance for me.

Level 2.   The expectations are a step higher than in Level 1, and they require some form of *satisfaction* through meeting *requirements* and/or *specifications.* For example: (1) I expect to be treated courteously by all airline personnel; (2) I went to the hospital expecting to have my hernia repaired, to hurt some after it was done, to be out on the same day, and to receive a correct bill; and (3) I went to the bank and the bank teller was very friendly, informative, and helpful with my transactions.

Level 3.   The expectations are much higher than in Level 1 or 2, and they require some kind of *delightfulness* or a *service* that is so good, that it *attracts me to it,* as in the following examples. (1) They gave all of the passengers traveling coach class the same superior food service that other airlines provide only for first-class passengers. On one flight, the flight attendants actually baked cookies for us right there on the plane. (2) Everyone who was involved with me treated me with respect and explained things very carefully to me. But what surprised me was that they called me at home the next day to find out how I was doing. (3) At my house closing, the bank officer not only treated me with respect and answered all my questions, but just before we shook hands to close the deal, he gave me a housewarming gift.

The strategy issue is also a very important element of customer satisfaction, primarily because it sets the tone for the appropriate training, behavior, and delivery of the specific service. The strategy for service quality should address the following four items.

1. The Customer Service Attributes

The delivery of the service must by timely, accurate, with concern, and with courtesy. One may ask why these elements are important. The answer is that all services are intangible and are a function of perception. As such, they depend on interpretation. In addition and perhaps more importantly, service by definition is perishable, and if left unattended, it can backfire on the organization.

This relates directly to the acronym COMFORT (introduced earlier) to signify the importance of service. Recall that COMFORT was defined as caring, observant, mindful, friendly, obliging, responsible, and tactful. These characteristics are the most basic attributes of customer service; without them, there can be no true service of any kind. They all depend on interpersonal skills, communication, empowerment, knowledge, sensitivity, understanding, and some kind of external behavior.

Caring shows that indeed you are very much interested in what the customer has to say. You may spend time with the customer to find out what his or her real needs, wants, and expectations are. It is not unusual to even tell the customer that you may not be able to help, at the expense of losing the sale. Furthermore, you may go as far as suggesting someone else or some other company.

You must be observant. In most cases when dealing with service-related items, observations may contribute to satisfying the customer more than direct communication. Pay attention to body language and mannerisms and, if necessary, read between the lines. Always try to be one step ahead of the customer. Anticipate his or her action. Actively listen to what the customer is communicating as well as—and perhaps more importantly—what he or she is not communicating.

You must be mindful. Remember that you and your organization exist to satisfy the customer. Without the customer's need, you do not have a job nor does the organization have a service to provide. The customer has a choice, and as such, if you or the organization does not recognize the urgency, the sensitivity, the uniqueness, the expectations, and the influence that the customer has, you will not be successful in satisfying the customer.

You must be friendly. Friendliness does not mean being a pest. Offer guidance and information, and let the customer know you are there to help. If you have to, provide feedback to help the customer make his or her decision. If you do provide feedback, be truthful. For example, someone comes into your retail clothing store, walks around, picks up some clothing, and tries it on. As a salesperson, you may advise the customer about fit and answer any questions that the customer may have.

You must be obliging. Patience is the key word in customer satisfaction. Sometimes the customer does not know what he or she wants and may be making up his or her mind while talking with you. You are serving as the "guinea pig" for the customer's decision. As such, accommodating the person may make the difference between a satisfied and a dissatisfied customer. It may make the difference between a sale and a walkout. When obliging the customer, do not hesitate to educate the customer as well.

You must be responsible. You are the expert. The customer is looking to you to provide the appropriate information in a clear, concise, and easy-to-understand manner. Don't try to make the sale at all costs. That strategy may backfire.

What you are trying to accomplish is to develop a relationship where your expertise can indeed help the customer.

You must be tactful. In any service organization and in any service delivery, there are going to be problems between you and the customer. Do not panic. Tactfulness is the process through which the conflict may be resolved. Your focus is to satisfy the customer, and as such you should try to identify the problem, analyze it, and then resolve it in the most expedient way. Being tactful does not mean that you have to give in to the customer all the time.

What it does mean is that you act in a professional manner, are composed, and communicate to the customer in a way that is not threatening or demeaning. It means you are willing to listen and exchange information with the intention of resolving the conflict. It means you have a way of presenting the facts and information in a nice and nonintimidating way. It means listening patiently. It means thinking before speaking. It means listening to the customer without interrupting.

Notice that cost is not an attribute that will make or break either service or satisfaction. The reason is that, in service especially, cost is equated with value. This does not suggest that high cost is a prerequisite to good service or vice versa. It simply suggests that you have to continue to generate more value for the customer without "giving away the store." It is indeed a very delicate balance.

2. Approach for Service Quality Improvement

The basic question one must be able to answer is, *why bother with service quality?* The answer is a three-pronged approach. The first is cost, the second is time to implement the program, and the third is the customer service impact. Together, they present a nucleus for understanding and implementing a system that is responsive to both customers and the organization for optimum satisfaction.

For example, the Japanese are working on the notion of a sensuous car. Basically, the car itself gives you a kind of delight and surprise just by opening the door, hearing the sound, and pressing the accelerator. Everything is being thought through "now," almost emotionally.

3. Develop Feedback Systems for Customer Service Quality

The feedback system one chooses will make or break the organization. Make sure not to mix the focus of customer satisfaction and marketing. They are not the same. The focus of customer service and satisfaction is to build loyalty, and the focus of marketing is to meet the needs of the customer profitably. Another way of putting it is that marketing's function is to generate customer value profitably, whereas the purpose of customer service and satisfaction is to generate repeatability, recognition, and overall satisfaction with the transaction.

The concern here is to make sure that a goal exists; a reporting system for measurement is appropriate and useful for the particular service, as is the reward of service quality. The question then becomes how to develop a system that is responsive to the customer's needs, wants, and expectations. To answer these concerns, we must look to the customer. The value of the information must focus on at least the following areas:

1. Know what customers are thinking about you, your service, and your competitors

2. Measure and improve your performance

3. Turn your strongest areas into market differentiators

4. Turn weaknesses into developmental opportunities—before someone else does

5. Develop internal communication tools to let everyone know how they are doing

6. Demonstrate your commitment to quality and your customers

In essence, measurement of the feedback must be of two distinct kinds:

1. Customer satisfaction, which is dependent upon the transaction

2. Service quality, which is dependent upon the actual relationship

4. Implementation

Perhaps the most important strategy is that of implementation. As part of the implementation process, management must define the scope of the service quality as well as the level of customer service as part of the organization's policy. Furthermore, management must also define the plan of implementation. The plan should include the time schedule, task assignment, and the reporting cycle.

MEASUREMENT

Measurement is by far one of the most important ingredients in customer service. We look for items that crystallize the quality service in such a way that the elements become determinants of all our future expectations. (For examples of such items, see Figures 7.1 and 7.2. Figure 7.1 shows some service performance

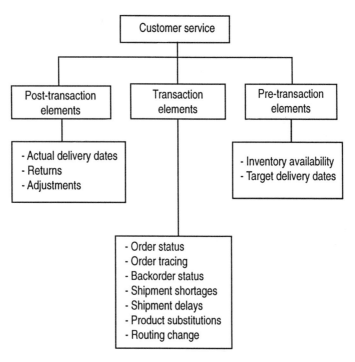

FIGURE 7.1   Possible measures of customer service performance

items and Figure 7.2 identifies some service standards.) Zeithaml et al. (1990) have defined five commitments, to which two have been added here (competition and management leadership).

Reliability.   The ability to provide what was promised, dependably and accurately. Never overpromise and always keep your promises.

Responsiveness.   The willingness to help customers and provide prompt service. Always get the definition of *prompt* from the customer.

Assurance.   The knowledge and courtesy of employees and their ability to convey trust and confidence. Employees need to be empowered to carry out this assurance of both power and knowledge.

Empathy.   The degree of caring and individual attention provided to customers

Tangibles.   The physical facilities and equipment and the appearance of personnel.

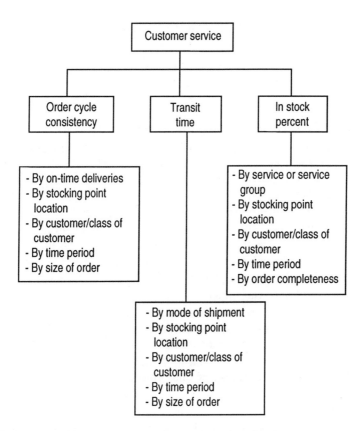

FIGURE 7.2 Examples of customer service standards

Competition. The ability to assess what the competition is doing is of paramount importance. When evaluating or researching the competition, we are interested in the service they provide, the cost of that service, their customers, and opportunity for growth.

Perhaps one of the most important aspects of studying the competition is the notion of *zone of tolerance* (ZOT). A pictorial view of ZOT is shown in Figure 7.3. Competition decreases the zone of tolerance, because as competition increases, the customer is able to find precisely what he or she is looking for, through availability. In essence, through competition analysis, we want to go beyond mere satisfaction of the customer to identify an extremely satisfied customer, a loyal customer, and, of course, a delighted customer.

Management leadership. A very popular general once said, "The definition of leadership is the art of influencing people to progress with cooperation and enthusiasm towards the accomplishment of a mission."

Low   <u>Adequate</u>   **Zone of Tolerance**   <u>Desired</u>

-------   --------------------

FIGURE 7.3   The zone of tolerance

The sole objective of leadership is to accomplish a mission. The objective is not to make everybody happy, nor is it to make yourself popular with employees; if that happens, it is a bonus. In fact, you can be a successful leader without happy employees or popularity, provided that is your objective as you transmit and interpret it. The art of obtaining the enthusiastic cooperation of employees is the crux of the leadership problem. The mission objectives as the leader interprets them may not at first seem desirable to your employees. It is up to the leader to make these objectives seem desirable. Through the leader's ability, personality, education, and experience he or she must *inspire* the employees, both individually and collectively, to their best effort. The leader should inspire rather than demand and lead rather than drive.

Leadership is learned by practice and study. People are not born with the ability to lead; it must be acquired and cultivated, just as the pilot has to learn to fly, the teacher to teach, and the athlete to play ball. You cannot become a successful leader just by reading about it. A prerequisite for good leadership is a certain amount of ability, risk taking, and a *burning desire* to become a leader.

Leadership is a position where everything is dynamic. As a consequence, the leader must be able to adjust and improve. In fact, continual improvement is one of the basic essentials of leadership. The leader must develop these abilities until they become natural. Leaders who never progress beyond the mechanics, to paraphrase Wheatley (1992), are poor at best. Normally, a leader will not be successful if he or she rigidly adheres to rules or tries to imitate a successful leader. A leader must develop his or her own techniques which best fit his or her own personality.

The fact that leadership is an art should not discourage anyone from taking the call of becoming a leader. However, the leader must recognize that leadership does not provide specific formulae, rules, or methods that will fit every situation. Leadership is an intangible which cannot be seen, felt, or measured except through its results. Moreover, one cannot predict the results with mathematical accuracy. If you have skill as a leader, however, you can predict results within the limits of the objectives.

Since leadership is a form of human relations, it must take into consideration the changeable and complex personality of man himself. Techniques of leading must keep pace with the changing customs, beliefs, and ideals of the society in which we live. Some techniques that were sound in the past century are worthless today (Rhinesmith et al. 1989).

Especially in service quality, one must not only understand the concept of leadership, but must also practice it. Leadership has become more technical and more in need of measure because organizations have become more complex. As a consequence, the responsibility and accountability of today's leaders have increased. Perfection in leadership, as in any art, will never be realized. No matter how skillful one becomes as a leader, one can always improve.

One of the strongest common tendencies of all people is a desire for successful achievement. An individual usually prefers success in a given field. If that is not forthcoming, a person will usually shift his or her attention to some other field in which he or she may achieve the desired success.

Humans work for many reasons; however, the primary reason is to gain satisfaction of some sort. The nature of this satisfaction may be in any form—advancement, recognition, affection, esteem of others, and so on. If, as a result of his work, a person does not approach his or her desired end, enthusiasm quickly falls, and with it falls the quality of the work he or she is doing. This is where a good leader with responsibility, authority, and love of people helps channel the effort and enthusiasm of all concerned toward a specific goal.

Leadership is essential and is important to all of us. But what does it really take to become a leader, and once we are leaders, what do we have to do to keep this leadership? The following is a composite list of leadership characteristics based on much research and reading:

Learn to get excited about what you are doing. Enthusiasm is contagious. Love the people you work with and the project's progress you represent.

Examine your own motives for wanting a position of leadership. Do you want to serve others, or are you merely serving your own ambitions and boosting your ego?

Avoid arrogance, impatience, irritability, and resentment. Adapt to the group and adhere to a code of ethics (how you play the game). Attitude is important.

Develop sensitivity to the needs of others. Leadership is a guiding force; it is diplomacy instead of demands and delegation instead of dictatorship. These are the basic essentials of good leadership.

Establish goals and evaluate progress toward those goals periodically. If you do not know where you are going, how can you effectively organize available resources to get there?

Responsibilities of many kinds accompany any position of leadership. These include responsibility to yourself, to your family, to your peers, to those you lead, and to the project at hand.

Set the example! Once you become a leader, you are in the spotlight. People watch to see how you act, how you behave, how you dress, and how you speak. Actions do speak more loudly than words.

Have the courage of your convictions. You know what is right. Do it! Do not be persuaded by selfish pressure groups or vocal dissidents. Lead rather than being led.

Is what you are doing in the best interests of the project? This question is a good yardstick for measuring performance in relation to goals. Integrity, initiative, imagination, and indifference to personal gain should characterize your actions.

Pride in your position and organization and those you represent should be reflected in your leadership role and in your personal activities.

It is indeed these characteristics and/or measurement commitments that a leader must demonstrate when decisions regarding the following are made:

1. Attract new customers.   New customers provide growth and new opportunities for the organization.

2. Differentiate the organization from competitors.   Differentiation provides for niches in the market and the opportunity to delight the customer because of much more specialization than would otherwise be provided.

3. Keep customers for the long term.   Loyalty is much more economical than pursuing new customers. Loyalty also creates good will and serves as advertisement through word of mouth. Long-term customers provide the organization with testimonials. Do not overdo it or become complacent with it. Remember, "there is no such thing as loyalty that two cents off won't cure."

4. Improve the organization.   Through the knowledge that the organization may gain from benchmarking, focus groups, surveys, and so on, adjustments can be made in both the delivery of the service and the organizational structure as well as the customer base.

5. Cost of poor quality.   This is the barometer of improvement. By analyzing internal and external costs, the organization has the opportunity to streamline unnecessary costs and focus on improving the service. Appendix G provides a very detailed list (not exhaustive) of service items that cost of quality may address.

6. Customer retention.   It is the business of the organization to know how much customer retention programs cost and how effective they are. How much does it take to retain your customers? How much of your budget goes to customer acquisition as opposed to customer retention? If the cost is very high, then the relationship needs a different kind of measurement or perhaps a different customer base, a different delivery, or even a new service.

7. Lifetime customer cycle. The organization must know the lifetime customer cycle, so that appropriate actions can be taken to secure the vitality of the organization. A typical customer cycle is as follows:

1. **Dissatisfaction (problem):** This is where the first signs of frustration about the service occur.

2. **Anger:** A recurring problem is faced with the customer.

3. **Change:** The person involved with the problem is looking for change. The change of alternatives also provides an opportunity for competition, if indeed there are many dissatisfied customers.

4. **Impact of change:** This is where the customer analyzes the impact of the change. It may be financial, personal, organizational, and/or utilitarian.

5. **Change occurs:** At this point, the customer, after a thorough analysis and evaluation, makes the change.

So far, we have identified some important elements of measurement within customer service. Our focus has been somewhat global in nature without any specific plan. At this point, let's turn our focus to specific measuring steps for customer satisfaction. The steps are as follows.

1. Identify the moment(s) of truth. The moments of truth are the points at which a customer (internal or external) contact is made. The contact may be significant, insignificant, often, irregular, long, short, etc. It may occur at any level of the organization. A pictorial view is provided in Figure 7.4.

FIGURE 7.4 Moment of truth: The relationship between the organization and the customer

2. Identify key personnel. Identify the key players in the customer satisfaction study. Generally, the key personnel are those who will be impacted by the results of a customer satisfaction or service quality study.

3. Identify the focus of the study. You must know the level of the customer and the specific items you are about to analyze.

4. Develop the measurement plan. Develop a plan that will measure the items of interest. As part of the planning, make sure that the people involved with the study are aware of the things that can go wrong, the sampling flow, and the appropriate sample selection. Some of the things that can go wrong are:

1. **Nonresponse error:** This may be a clue that this sector of customers is the least satisfied. You may look at the design of the instrument and review for problem areas. In addition, you may follow up with a random sample of nonrespondents and use data to adjust estimates.

2. **Measurement error:** In this category, you may find that the respondents deliberately lied, misunderstood the question, were careless, and so on. Review the design of the instrument and evaluate it appropriately.

3. **Frame error:** In this category, you may discover that your list of questions is incomplete, biased, etc. Again, you can review and evaluate the questionnaire and take the appropriate corrective action for improvement.

4. **Selection (sampling) error:** In this category, you may find that the sampling plan is not correct, the sample is not random, names are repeated several times, and so on. To make sure that the appropriate sample is drawn, you may want to consult a statistics book. Freund and Williams (1972) have developed a simple formula for sample selection:

$$N = p(1 - p) \left(\frac{Z\alpha}{e}\right)^2$$

where N = Sample size

   Z = Standard score corresponding to a given confidence level (common levels are 1.64, 1.96, and 2.58 for $\alpha = 0.10$, $\alpha = 0.05$, and $\alpha = 0.05$, respectively)

   e = The proportion of sampling error in a given situation; quite often the value used is 0.10

   p = The proportion of cases in the population; quite often the value used is 0.50, since this amount provides the maximum sample size

A typical correct selection sampling flow is:

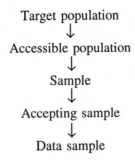

Target population
↓
Accessible population
↓
Sample
↓
Accepting sample
↓
Data sample

There are at least two ways to measure customer satisfaction: quantitative and qualitative. An overview is shown in Table 7.1.

Minimum measurement requirements that all instruments should include are the following:

- Identify the customer(s)

- Identify those impacted

- Identify who you want to focus on

- Identify what you want to measure

- Determine how you are going to measure it

  a. Primary research

    o Complaint tracking

    o Point of contact

    o Gap analysis

TABLE 7.1   Measurement Overview

Type	Qualitative	Quantitative
Goal	Seeks to describe *why* customers believe as they do	Seeks to describe *what* customers believe
Ability to generalize results	Little if any generalizability	May generalize if sample carefully drawn
Example	Interview Focus group Personal	Closed-end survey Mail Telephone

o   Survey

o   Focus group

o   Benchmarking

o   Interviews

o   and so on

b. Secondary research

o   Complaints

o   Customer satisfaction data

o   Surveys

o   Results of past studies

o   and so on

A typical hard-copy measurement plan is shown in Table 7.2.

DEVELOPING A QUESTIONNAIRE

Questionnaires have been used in many applications over the years in many organizations. Their purpose is to gain a variety of information on anything from demographics to quality, to cost, to competition. One of the applications is in the area of customer satisfaction. A questionnaire may be a formal survey, a check-list or outline for a personal interview, or even the script for a phone survey. However, regardless of the specific use or structure of the questionnaire, some crucial points must be always kept in mind:

1. Effective survey design is a complex task requiring research, data analysis, and high-level design skills.

2. Information from a survey is only as good as the quality of the questions asked, the sampling methods used, and the rate of response.

3. People will answer surveys only if it is clear to them that there is a benefit to doing so. If the benefit is clear only to the surveying organization, the response rate will generally be very low.

4. Audits need to be performed regularly. A company that bases its service strategy on an annual audit is begging to be blind-sided. In a very

TABLE 7.2   A Typical Measurement Plan

1. Problem: _____

2. How information will be used: _____

3. Question(s) to be answered: _____

4. Definitions of terms: _____

5. Research method:

    Type: _____

    Sample size: _____

    Control for sampling errors: _____

    Steps to test interviews, questionnaires, etc.: _____

6. Type of data analysis to be used: _____

7. Presentation of results:

To whom?	How?	When?
_____	_____	_____
_____	_____	_____

8. Proposed project plan: _____

9. Resources required:

    People: _____

    Estimated cost: _____

10. Obtain approval. Clear the plan with the key players and seek their approval.

11. Revise as needed. Make all adjustments as needed.

12. Implement the plan. Run the study, collect the data, and analyze.

13. Present the results. The results are presented to management.

14. Develop the action plan for the service improvement. Based on the results, the appropriate action should be planned.

15. Feedback. Evaluate the results of the action plan.

16. Communicate the results. Let your customers know that you heard from them and that their input is guiding your improvements throughout the organization.

competitive market, audits/surveys should be performed more than once a year.

5. With customer audits/surveys, no news is bad news. Your organization is a winner with either one or both. If the results identify deficiencies and/or problems anywhere in the organization, management should target a corrective action plan, so that the quality focus is reestablished as soon as possible in the specific area(s) affected. If the results of the audit or survey are positive, management continues to focus on continual improvement—since whatever they are doing is working.

In addition to these points, when a questionnaire is being designed, consideration of the response is also important. For example, is the response an open-ended question, closed ended, attitude scale, etc.?

Open-ended questions are easy to construct and allow respondents to articulate their answers based on their own vocabulary and experience. However, they present a problem in length and interpretation. For example:

What do you think of the ATM service between 6:00 a.m. and 10:00 a.m. at 1234 Pillar Road in Country Town?

Response:_____

_____

On the other hand, a closed-ended question is very direct and limited. For example:

Do you like our ATM service between 6:00 a.m. and 10:00 a.m. at 1234 Pillar Road in Country Town?   Yes ❑   No ❑

There are several types of attitude scales, each with specific advantages and disadvantages. It is beyond the scope of this book to address each type. For further information on attitude scales, see Kerlinger (1973), Cronbach (1970), Rokeach (1968), Kerlinger (1967), Brown (1958), Edwards (1957), Guilford (1954), Nunnally (1967), and Thurstone and Chave (1929), to name a few. Some of the most commonly used scales in this area are:

1. **Thurstone:** Respondents mark all statements with which they agree.

2. **Likert-type:**

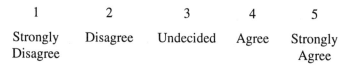

1	2	3	4	5
Strongly Disagree	Disagree	Undecided	Agree	Strongly Agree

3. **Guttman** (forced choice):

I would rather design a desk than build it.   Yes ❑   No ❑

4. **Semantic differential:** Uses a pair of extreme adjectives.

Circle one:

Poor   Excellent

Attitude scale construction involves careful selection and editing of items pertaining to the area of interest. Edwards (1957) has developed a series of techniques and criteria for constructing an attitude scale. However, the following criteria are only a summary for editing attitudinal statements.

1. Avoid statements that refer to the past rather than the present.

2. Avoid statements that are not factual or can be misinterpreted as factual.

3. Avoid statements that can be interpreted in more than one way.

4. Avoid statements that are irrelevant to the psychological object under consideration.

5. Avoid statements that are likely to be endorsed by almost everyone or almost no one.

6. Select statements that are believed to cover the entire range of the affective scale of interest.

7. Keep the language of the statements simple, clear, and direct.

8. Statements should be short, rarely exceeding 20 words.

9. Each statement should contain only one complete thought.

10. Statements containing universals, such as all, always, none, and never, often introduce ambiguity and should be avoided.

11. Words such as only, just, merely, and others of a similar nature should be used with care and moderation in writing statements.

12. Whenever possible, statements should be in the form of a simple sentence rather than in the form of compound or complex sentences.

13. Avoid the use of words that may not be understood by those who will be given the complete scale.

14. Avoid the use of double negatives.

When the study is designed to generate actionable data, avoid an odd-numbered response scale, if possible. The odd scale, more often than not, does not

TABLE 7.3.   A Scale for Generating Actionable Data

Directions: To the right of each service characteristic are two boxes. In the first box, write the number of the word that best describes your view of this department's current service level. In the second box, write the number of the word that best describes the level of importance that you attach to this characteristic. Use the following scale to make your selection for both boxes.

1	*2*	*3*	*4*	*5*	*6*	*7*	*8*
Don't Know		*Never*		*Sometimes*			*Always*

Service Characteristic	*Current Level*	*Importance Level*
In your opinion, to what extent does (name) fulfill a complete phone order?	❑	❑
Bend the rules when necessary to meet your needs?	❑	❑
Listen carefully?	❑	❑
Accept responsibility for solving a problem?	❑	❑
Follow through to make certain the question was answered or the problem resolved?	❑	❑
Seem able to draw quickly upon the organization's resources to help you?	❑	❑
Reflect a thorough knowledge of products and services?	❑	❑

discriminate the response enough to make a sound decision. In such a scale, most people aim for the average, which is the middle number. A template similar to Table 7.3 may be used.

PRELIMINARY STEPS TO AN EFFECTIVE SURVEY

For any organization, it is important to gather information to either find out where the organization is or how to improve to a certain level. The process of finding that information has to be very critical and accurate as well as thought out before even the first question is asked. To develop an effective survey, the following questions should be considered. The list of questions is by no means exhaustive.

1. **What survey is most effective for me: face-to-face, phone, or mailed?**

   • It all depends on the goal, budget, and schedule of the survey.

2. **What sort of response rates can be expected from an effective mailed customer audit?**

   A well-designed, well-targeted, and well-implemented mail survey should get about a 60 to 70% response. If the response rate is lower, it almost always signifies design shortcuts or poor targeting.

3. **What influences response rates?**

   Many factors, including whether or not respondents believe answering the survey will have any social utility. The well-educated tend to respond more readily to surveys. Specialized audiences, if their interests are being surveyed, tend to respond more readily. Length of the survey can influence response. Ten to twelve pages (roughly 125 questions) seems to be the optimum length.

4. **How can a survey designer encourage response rates?**

   a. Reward the respondent by:

      • Showing positive regard

      • Giving verbal appreciation

      • Using a consulting approach

      • Supporting his or her values

      • Offering tangible rewards

      • Making the questionnaire interesting and useful

   b. Reduce costs to the respondent by:

      • Making the task appear brief

      • Reducing the physical and mental effort required

      • Eliminating chances for embarrassment

      • Eliminating any implication of subordination

      • Eliminating any direct monetary cost

c. Establish trust by:

- Providing a token of appreciation in advance

- Identifying with a known organization that has legitimacy

- Building on other exchange relationships

5. Is response rate the crucial indicator of the success of a survey?

Certainly it is one of the crucial factors. However, the obsession with response rates can lead to overlooking barriers to representativeness, such as:

- Sampling—whether each unit of the target population has an equal opportunity to be included

- Selection criteria—determining which person in the target organization is to be surveyed

- Whether the respondent can be located

- How badly the survey will be damaged if the wrong person responds

6. How important is the wording of questions?

Very. Strive for a 6th to 8th grade level of readability. People who do surveys are far more likely to overestimate than underestimate the reading levels of respondents. It is crucial that questions be tested with members of the target group prior to survey mailing. A well-designed, carefully pretested survey could easily go through six to twelve drafts. Everyone underestimates the time and effort required to develop clearly worded questions.

7. How important is the order of questions?

Very. There are guidelines to follow for ordering questions:

- The first question is the most crucial. It has to be compelling and neutral.

- Start with questions that the target group would see as most useful, then work down to the least useful.

- Place ranking questions before detail questions.

- Group questions similar in content together; within content areas, group by type of question.

- Put potentially objectionable questions after unobjectionable questions.

8. **What are the steps in a well-designed implementation plan for a mailed survey?**

   - Mail out introductory letter (optional step).

   - Send out a cover letter which provides a reasonable explanation of the study, its benefit to the group with which the respondent identifies, and the individual importance of the respondent to the success of the study. Make sure this is sent on letterhead with the researcher's real signature. Enclose a stamped self-addressed envelope.

   - Exactly one week after the initial mailing, send a follow-up post-card to all members of the target group. If they have returned the survey, thank them. If not, this is a reminder.

   - Exactly three weeks after the initial mailing, send out a new cover letter and questionnaire to nonrespondents by certified mail.

9. **How long does this implementation plan for a mailed survey take?**

   Figure several weeks for design, eight weeks to implement, and several weeks to analyze and report on the data. This means a minimum of three months, depending on sample size.

10. **Can the mailed survey be used as a basis for a phone survey?**

    Not really. Excellent mailed questionnaires do not make very effective phone surveys. This is so because:

    - The effectiveness of phone surveys depends on verbal, rather than visual, communication.

    - The interviewer, if he or she reads the questions incorrectly, can become a barrier to the respondent's understanding.

    - The phone survey has a far greater need for fast coding and analysis at the end of the survey.

11. **Whose needs have to be met in a phone survey?**

    Three groups:

    - Respondents

- Interviewers

- Coders

12. What are the needs of the respondents?

To know that the survey will not take too much time. This means that surveys must be designed for easy answering. They must subtly force the respondent to stay focused. For example, the survey has to have a clear progression, and the questions must be immediately understandable.

13. What are the needs of interviewers?

- To have a ready and believable explanation if their credibility is questioned.

- To stay in control. It is better not to ask questions that require the interviewer to write long responses, which creates long silent periods during which the respondent's mind can wander. Also, do not ask questions that you have no intention of using or you know the answer to.

- To have an interview format that is easy to read and easy to understand.

- To not interview more than several hours at a stretch. After two or three hours, phone interviewers will start making mistakes and your data will be polluted.

14. What are the needs of coders?

Precoding—that is, identifying the computer card columns and punches for each response category on the questionnaire.

15. What are the special problems in wording questions for telephone questionnaires?

- Questions that are too long

- Too many response categories

- Too many ranking categories

16. Is the ordering of questions in a phone survey as important as in a written survey?

Yes. Usually phone respondents have the greatest difficulty answering when a question entails both topic changes and response format changes from the preceding question. Thus, questions should be grouped by topic and within topic by consistent formats. As was the case with the mail survey, start with items of central importance to the respondent in each section, moving to items of less importance.

17. Should phone surveys be pretested?

Yes—with the target group on the phone.

18. We'll try again. What survey is most effective for me: face-to-face, phone, or mailed?

It all depends on the expectations, goals, budget, and schedule of the survey.

19. What does it take to end the survey with a high and accurate response rate?

A well-designed questionnaire with good follow-up procedures.

20. What are the steps in a well-designed implementation plan for a focus group?

  a. Selection:

   • Focus—The focus is always on a fixed purpose.

   • Group—The group should be between 7 to 15 people. However, in selecting the individual participants, it must be stressed that homogeneity in terms of occupation, education, and/or socioeconomics plays a major role in the outcome of the results. In all cases, the selection process must very carefully identify people with different opinions, who are unfamiliar with each other, and individuals who are outspoken.

   As for the moderator, he or she should be a person who can control the group, is a good listener, has good self-control, and, more importantly, can blend with the group.

   • Interview—The interrogation should be based on questions and responses rather than pencil and paper responses.

   • Location—The location should be neutral.

   • Compensation—The compensation for time spent should be determined ahead of time.

   • Schedule—The participant's schedule should be considered.

  b. Characteristics:

   • Group—7 to 15 participants

- Time—Minimum of $1\frac{1}{2}$ hours but no more than $2\frac{1}{2}$ hours
- Interview—The questions must be asked using a guided—structured—approach, with the following in mind:
  - o Open-ended questions
  - o Frank discussions
  - o Relaxed and informal environment
  - o No threat of humiliation
  - o Goal of discovery

c. Advantages: The advantages that a focus group provides are:
- Additional insight
- More interaction
- Thought-provoking
- Added value of listening
- Relatively inexpensive results
- Relatively fast results

d. Limitations: The limitations inherent in a focus group are:
- Lack of generalizability
- Unwarranted credibility
- Moderator bias
- Dominant member bias

e. Appropriate applications: A focus group may be appropriate for the following applications:
- Collect perceptions/attitudes
- Collect expectations
- Generate hypotheses
- Diagnose potential problems
- Develop questionnaires
- Interpret previous results
- Evaluate programs

f. The process of a focus group:

- Define the purpose
- Define the approximate number of questions
- Emphasize informality
- Explain confidentiality
- Explain tape or video recording (if done)
- Explain ground rules
- Introduce everybody (pass out name tags or placecards with first name only)
- Begin discussion
- Probe for questions and/or answers
- Stop when there are no more questions and/or probing
- Collect and analyze the data
- Report results

A TYPICAL QUESTIONNAIRE EVALUATION FORM

As previously stated (Item 19 above), it is imperative that we devote the time and effort to design a good questionnaire and provide for follow up. In order to be successful, all questionnaires—of any kind—must:

1. Explain the benefits to the customer

2. Have a professional and readable format

3. Have clear directions

4. Provide logical order

5. Provide incentives

6. Provide a postcard sent five days after initial contact

7. Provide a second mailing

8. Provide follow up with a phone call or personal interview

The intent of all questionnaires is to maximize the following characteristics in the customer:

1. Expectations

2. Recognition

3. Altruism

4. Sympathy

5. Catharsis

6. Meaning

7. New experience

To help bring the evaluation into the practical domain and to specifically address the concerns just raised, a generic evaluation of a survey instrument is provided:

1. Is the first question clearly related to the topic?

2. Is the first question clearly applicable to everyone?

3. Will the first question probably be interesting to everyone?

4. Does the first question bias your response in any way?

5. Are questions on a similar topic grouped together (e.g., all questions regarding responsiveness grouped together)?

6. Are questions that use similar scales placed together?

7. Is there a natural flow to the questionnaire?

8. Is every question clear?

9. Is there only one idea to be evaluated in each question?

10. Are questions of a similar nature all on the same page?

11. Are demographics questions (e.g., name, title, buying habits) at the end of the questionnaire?

12. Are the directions brief?

13. Are the directions clear?

14. Are the directions distinct (e.g., in boldface print or all caps)?

15. Do you know what to do with the questionnaire when you have completed it?

16. Does the questionnaire explicitly tell you how the information will be used to help you, the customer?

17. Are there any incentives (e.g., discount coupons, candy, money, etc.) for completing the questionnaire?

18. Is there anything to help you believe your response will be seriously considered?

19. Is the questionnaire aesthetically pleasing?

20. Is there enough white space so the questionnaire is easy to read?

21. Are the questions in lower case?

22. Are the responses in upper case?

23. Are scales placed under a hat (e.g., 1 = little, 2 = some, 3 = much)?

24. Are questions connected to the answer choices by dotted or straight lines?

25. Are directions repeated at the top of every page?

26. Do arrows show you how to skip items?

27. Is it clear that the questionnaire continues on to the next side or page?

28. Does the author avoid the use of the word "questionnaire"?

29. Does the author thank you for your response?

Comments or concerns: _____

_____

_____

The final evaluation of a questionnaire lies in the validity and the reliability of the instrument. Validity determines whether it measures what it was supposed to measure. Face and content validity are measured by the use of expert panels. Reliability measures the consistency of what was supposed to be measured. The usual tools for measuring reliability are pilot tests in similar settings and statistical tests based on the Cronbach Alpha with a Likert scale.

MAKING SENSE OF YOUR DATA

To make sense of the data, you must understand the different kinds of data available to you as an experimenter. Depending on the data, the appropriate analysis has to take place. Four kinds of data are available:

1. Nominal. This kind of data provides some kind of naming. For example: marital status, zip code, telephone number, and so on.

2. Ordinal. This kind of data provides information about ranking, a degree of something, product quality characteristic, and so on. It is more flexible than nominal data in the sense that some mathematical calculations may be performed. In addition to order, ordinal data provide intervals of unequal size and greater than or less than characterization. For example: money, hardness, and so on.

3. Interval (Likert scales). This kind of data provides information that is more powerful than both nominal and ordinal data. It allows for more advanced statistical/mathematical analysis and offers the ability to arbitrarily define an interval as well as the "zero." For example: groupings of population, income, and so on.

4. Ratio. This kind of data is the most powerful of all. It allows the experimenter to use any mathematical and/or statistical tool available. It can utilize all the characteristics that all the other categories use and in addition provides a true "zero." For example: age, weight, and so on.

Regardless of what data are available, by themselves, all data are useless. For data to come alive and be useful, they must be organized, summarized, analyzed, and presented. The process of doing this organization, summarization, analysis, and presentation is the art of statistics. To use statistics effectively, some fundamentals must be understood. It is beyond the purpose of this book to introduce all the basics and analytical tools. Figures 7.5 to 7.7 address some of them in a summary format. For further details, see Rousseeuw and Leroy (1987), Gibbons (1985), Fuller (1987), Cohen and Cohen (1983), and Winkler and Hays (1975).

PRESENTING YOUR RESULTS

Even if you have a beautiful report, whether formal or informal, sooner or later you have to communicate the content of the report to someone else via some medium. The objective of the presentation is to effectively communicate the message of the study and to draw the appropriate conclusion (Harris 1994; Katz 1991). There are three ways to present a study.

1. Formal. The formal report is a bound document. Minimum requirements are:

Title: The title of the study

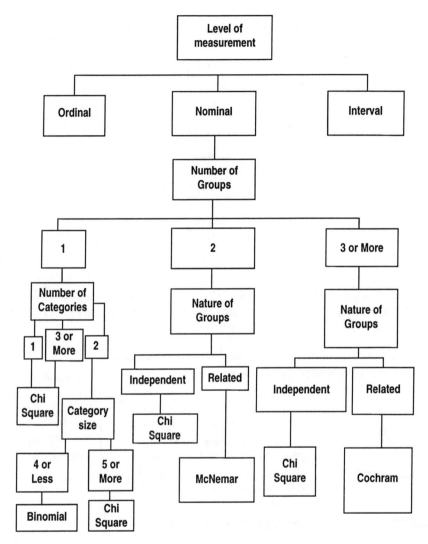

FIGURE 7.5 The road map to statistical analysis

Executive summary (1–2 pages): The summary for executives, indicating the main point of the study.

Introduction: The introduction generally covers four items:

- The need for the study
- The theory behind logic flow

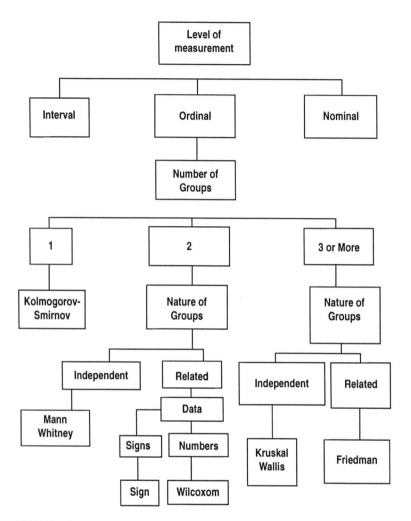

FIGURE 7.6   The road map to statistical analysis

- The research questions
- The assumptions of the study

Methodology: This section covers the following:

- Type of research
- Population sample
- Instrumentation (reliability and validity)

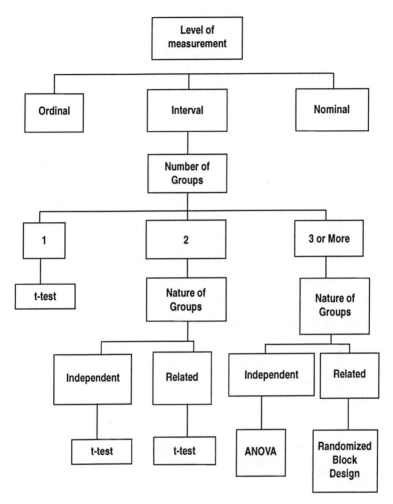

FIGURE 7.7 The road map to statistical analysis

- Process description
- Data analysis

Results: This section contains the results of the study in a very detailed fashion.

Recommendations: The formal report in this section provides for the action steps based on the data analysis and results, as well as the projected cost implications to the organization.

2. Executive overview. This is a summary of the formal report. It covers four basic items without any discussion or documentation. It is indeed the skeleton of the report. The assumption of this report is that if the user is interested in further information, the full report should be read. The four basic items that the executive summary attempts to address are:

- What we are trying to learn
- What we did
- What we found
- What we recommend

3. Informal report. This report is generally called the oral presentation. It is not as detailed as the formal report, but it is very complete and its objective is to disseminate the information to the organization. The assumption again is that the formal report should be read for full details.

To be effective in a presentation, the presenter must decide the following:

- What you can best accomplish in the time allotted
- What message you want to send
- Which concerns bear most directly on your audience
- How you can best visually/graphically support your message

Perhaps one of the most difficult and challenging tasks in defining the presentation is the issue of visuals. To be effective and to communicate the true message, the following are some ideas:

- Determine your message. Make sure you know the message and you have packaged it for your audience.

- Identify the main issues of the presentation. Make sure you know the issues you are addressing and how they relate to the present situation as well as the future.

- Select the appropriate visuals. As a presenter, you must know the advantages and disadvantages of using specific visuals in your presentation. For example, when presenting the results of the study, the presenter should know the reasons for selecting a pie chart as opposed to a dot chart or column chart.

EXAMPLES OF CUSTOMER SERVICE

A Good Example of Customer Service from an Airline Carrier

One of the most spectacular customer service programs in recent years is Southwest Airline. Southwest's policy and execution is to keep passengers happy.

This policy is internalized through a unique interpretation of how customer service ought to be. It focuses first and foremost on the employees, the communication process within the airline, and satisfying the factors that consumers have rated as important. Some of the most important factors that Southwest pays special attention to are:

- Fares

- Baggage handling

- Customer service

- Airplane age

- Accident rate

- Frequent flier plan

The result of this policy is that the airline is the fastest growing and most profitable airline of the 1990s. In addition, it has dominated every market it has entered, and most of the mainstream airlines are following its path of innovation.

What is unique about Southwest and how does it relate to customer service? The answer is simple. It provides reliable transportation without frills. Delivery, however, is based on the concept of happy employees, which is very revolutionary. It is revolutionary because many companies preach it, but very few, if any, practice it. The foundation of customer service for Southwest is based on at least the following six areas:

1. Job descriptions are written very loosely to allow workers to move easily from task to task. Empowerment at work is in all levels. The fact that Southwest is a union shop makes this even more profound and worth studying.

2. Flight delays are analyzed with a very simplified coding system. If there is a problem, Southwest does not spend a lot of time finding someone to blame. It is the entire team's fault and the entire team's responsibility to make sure it does not happen again. (Most other airlines, in contrast, list hundreds of reasons for delays. Individual managers spend hours arguing about why delays were caused by somebody else's department, not theirs.)

3. Workers from different departments, like baggage handlers and ticket agents, are encouraged to talk about and solve problems. "Love" reports express praise. "Irregularity" reports focus on problems. Team-building meetings are called, often without supervisors or union representatives, when things get out of hand.

4. The airline encourages teamwork by the way it selects and trains workers. Southwest does not place a high priority, for example, on hiring

people with prior airline experience. It likes young people just out of high school or college.

Before they are hired, applicants often have to stand in front of a group of Southwest officials and other applicants and tell funny stories about themselves. This gives the company a sense of how comfortable they are interacting with people. Applicants are also tested for teamwork skills. If they are applying for a marketing position, for example, they will be assigned to a group of three people and given a few minutes to organize and present a plan for how Southwest should make an announcement on scheduling flights to a new city.

5. Southwest promotes mostly from within and insists that top officers of the company stay in direct contact with front-line workers. People marvel when top officers show up in coveralls to load suitcases, call them by first name, and return their telephone calls. There is a point to this close contact; it allows two-way communication that is a constant source of new ideas.

6. It pays people in ways that reward strong team performance. Southwest workers also receive profit sharing and are required to invest part of the money back into the company. Workers (as of this writing) own 13% of the airline.

In the final analysis, customer service for Southwest is focused on a common culture and a common language and a communication process that cuts across work groups with the understanding that each other's jobs depend on their livelihood. The result is a company that practically brags about its performance and customer satisfaction since the 1970s, when it was an upstart Texas airline with just three planes.

For Southwest, customer service begins with enthusiastic, dedicated, and knowledgeable workers and ends with satisfied customers and increased business. Its performance is a matter of record. Southwest's philosophy can be summarized as:

1. Know your customer. Southwest has been able to study its customer base to the point where it identified the most important airline quality factors to the customer.

2. Pitch like mad. Back in the 1970s, Southwest committed to be an airline with a future. To that end, it changed the operations, habits, and attitudes of the then-current trends in the airline industry. It has not stopped being innovative.

3. Do more than the competition. Southwest has and is currently forcing other airlines to play by its rules, because it is changing the way people

TABLE 7.4   Airline Quality Ratings

Airline	Turnaround Time	Station Productivity	Overall Productivity
Southwest	39	17.2	0.25
Continental	59	8.8	–0.34
USAir	69	10.5	–0.01
America West	73	13.6	–0.29
TWA	78	6.8	–0.29
American	83	6.6	0.23
Delta	89	8.1	0.08
United	89	8.6	0.18
Northwest	96	8.5	–0.25

Source: Ratings by researchers at Wichita State University and University of Nebraska at Omaha, U.S. Department of Transportation.

work, the way they think about their jobs, and the definitions of service and satisfaction.

4. Use controls to make more controls. Southwest has been able to improve in all major categories (see Table 7.4), including turnaround time (39 minutes), station productivity (17.2 passengers), and overall productivity (0.25), based on close analysis of customer needs, wants, and expectations, as well a close scrutiny of its own system.

A Very Bad Example of Customer Service from a Software Company

DacEasy, Inc. is a software company that produces an accounting and/or payroll program. There were many problems with version 4.0, and as a result the president of the company wrote to each of the users on file to apologize The letter was mailed on DacEasy's stationary with the president's signature and without a date. The content of the letter was as follows:

Dear DacEasy 4.0 Customer:

This letter confirms that you are scheduled to receive a FREE 4.1 version of DacEasy Accounting and/or Payroll. At the present time, this version is being reviewed and tested by many companies such as your own. It now appears version 4.1 will be ready for release the last week in March.

The release of the 4.0 plattorm (sic) has been a difficult time for most of you and for my employees. In the past few months we have demonstrated characteristics unlike the type of company the employees of DacEasy created in 1985. As the original founder, I am extremely disappointed in the delay of the 4.0 platform, the bugs, the feature cuts in the initial release and, most of all, for our inaccessibility during this trying time. I sincerely apologize, if we let you or your company down during these past few months.

Not only have we fixed all outstanding bugs and included the omitted features, but we have made many of the improvements and changes you requested during the past two months. It is faster, less keystroke intensive, and more flexible. We have also revised the manual to answer the most commonly asked questions, made needed corrections to match the new program perfectly and re-indexed so you could find subjects faster. You will also receive a FREE copy of the 4.1 manual with your shipment.

It will take up to two weeks to ship all 4.1 revision orders, at which time they will be shipped UPS (unless you specified otherwise). Please allow 5 to 7 working days for UPS. If you haven't received your order by April 12th, please fax, write or call. Please do not call to check on the status of your order before April 12th. We will contact you if there are any further delays.

Again, please accept my apologies if we failed to serve you properly and thank you for your patience.

Sincerely,

(The president's signature)

The letter is self-explanatory and needs no further comment.

REFERENCES

Albrecht, K. and Zemke, R. (1985). *Service America: Doing Business in the New Economy.* Dow Jones-Irwin, New York.

Berwick, D. M. (April/May 1994). "Kevin Speaks: The Voice of a Customer." *Continuous Journey.*

Blume, E. R. (September 1988). "Customer Service: Giving Companies the Competitive Edge." *Training Development Journal.*

Brown, R. (1958). *Words and Things.* The Free Press, New York.

Butterfield, R. W. (December 1987). "A Quality Strategy for Service Organizations." *Quality Progress.*

Buzzell, R. and Gale, B. (1987). *The PIMS Principles.* The Free Press, New York.

Chandler, C. H. (February 1989). "Beyond Customer Satisfaction." *Quality Progress.*

Cohen, J. and Cohen, P. (1983). *Applied Multiple Regression/Correlation Analysis for the Behavioral Sciences* (2nd Ed.). Lawrence Erlbaum Associates, Hillsdale, N.J.

Cronbach, L. (1970). *Essentials of Psychological Testing* (3rd Ed.). Harper & Row, New York.

Edwards, A. (1957). *Techniques of Attitude Scale Construction.* Appleton, New York.

Feldman, P. D. (August 19, 1991). "I Searched for Excellence and Finally Found It in a Cab." *Marketing News.*

Fleiss, R. (February 1989). "Here's the Scoop on Ben and Jerry's." *Office Systems 89.*

Freund, J. E. and Williams, F. J. (1972). *Elementary Business Statistics: The Modern Approach* (2nd Ed.). Prentice-Hall, Englewood Cliffs, N.J.

Fuller, W. A. (1987). *Measurement Error Models.* John Wiley & Sons, New York.

Gibbons, J. D. (1985). *Nonparametric Statistical Inference* (2nd Ed., revised and expanded). Marcel Dekker, New York.

Goizueta, R. C. (February 1989). "The Business of Customer Satisfaction." *Quality Progress.*

Goodman, J. (February 1989). "The Nature of Customer Satisfaction." *Quality Progress.*

Graham, J. R. (August 19, 1991). "Do It Right the First Time; You May Not Get a Second Chance." *Marketing News.*

Griffin, P. (June/July 1994). "Taking the Mystery Out of Customer Service." *Continuous Journey.*

Guilford, J. (1954). *Psychometric Methods* (2nd Ed.). McGraw-Hill, New York.

Harris, R. M. (July 1994). "Practically Perfect Presentations." *Training and Development Journal.*

Hunt, S. (March 1990). "It's Basic but Necessary: Listen to the Customer." *Marketing News.*

Hutchens, S. (February 1989). "What Customers Want: Results of ASQC/Gallup Survey." *Quality Progress.*

Janson, R. (June/July 1994). "Time to Get Some Satisfaction." *Continuous Journey.*

Katz, S. N. (July 1991). "Power Skills for Effective Meetings." *Training and Development Journal.*

Kerlinger, F. (1967). "Social Attitudes and Their Criterial Referents: A Structural Theory." *Psychological Review.*

Kerlinger, F. (1973). *Foundations of Behavioral Research* (2nd Ed.). Holt, Rinehart and Winston, New York.

London, M. J. (April/May 1994). "Betting Pay on Customer Satisfaction." *Continuous Journey.*

Lovelock, C. H. (January 30, 1989). "Competitive Advantage Lies in Supplementary, Not Core, Services." *Marketing News.*

Nunnally, J. (1967). *Psychometric Theory.* McGraw-Hill, New York.

Powers, V. (June/July 1994). "Can You Read My Mind?" *Continuous Journey.*

Pyzdek, T. (April 1994). "Toward Service Systems Engineering." *Quality Management Journal.*

Rhinesmith, S. H., Williamson, J. N., Ehlen, D. M., and Maxwell, D. S. (April 1989). "Developing Leaders for the Global Enterprise." *Training and Development Journal.*

Rokeach, M. (1968). *Beliefs, Attitudes, and Values.* Jossey-Bass, San Francisco.

Rousseeuw, P. J. and Leroy, A. M. (1987). *Robust Regression and Outlier Detection.* John Wiley & Sons, New York.

Sarazen, J. S. (December 1987). "Customer Satisfaction Is Not Enough." *Quality Progress.*

Sheridan, B. M. (December 1993). "Changing Service Quality in America." *Quality Progress.*

Shoemaker, C. (June 1994). "Higher Bank Fees Don't Equal Value." *Marketing News.*

Silverstein, M. (August 1991). "World-Class Customer Service Builds Consumer Loyalty." *Marketing News.*

Tague, J. P. (March 5, 1990). "Philosophy Lifts Midway to New Heights." *Marketing News.*

Test, A. (March 5, 1990). "Would You Want Yourself as Your Own Customer?" *Marketing News.*

Thurstone, L. and Chave, E. (1929). *The Measurement of Attitude.* University of Chicago Press, Chicago.

Trabue, G. and Jones, P. (June/July 1994). "Exceeding Expectations at Eastman Chemical." *Continuous Journey.*

Vanocur, S. (February 1989). "A Conversation with Sander Vanocur." *Quality Progress.*

Wargo, R. A. (June/July 1994). "How to Avoid the Traps of Benchmarking Customer Satisfaction." *Continuous Journey.*

Weiner, M. B. (June/July 1994). "S.N.U.B.NET: The Crime of Unused Customer Feedback." *Continuous Journey.*

Wells, F. (February 1989). "Marketing Factors and Customer Satisfaction." *Quality Progress.*

Wheatley, M. (1992). *Leadership and the New Science.* Berrett-Koehler, San Francisco.

Winkler, R. L. and Hays, W. L. (1975). *Statistics: Probability, Inference and Decision* (2nd Ed.). Holt, Reinhart and Winston, New York.

Zeithaml, V., Parasuraman, A., and Berry, L. (1990). *Delivering Quality Service: Balancing Customer Perceptions and Expectations.* The Free Press, New York.

Zemke, R. (June/July 1994). "Q&A with Ron Zemke." *Continuous Journey.*

8

BENCHMARKING

The military calls the process of gathering information about the enemy spying, intelligence, and reconnaissance. Industry called it industrial espionage and then industrial intelligence. The modern world, and especially the quality world, calls it benchmarking. Regardless of what one calls it, it is imperative to understand that the foundation of all benchmarking is to gather data—from either internal or external sources, friendly or unfriendly—for some future action. All the above definitions provide for such action. However, from the quality perspective, benchmarking is more systematic, friendlier (in the sense that it is voluntary and is based on cooperation between partners), and provides the goal of and the map for a world-class organization.

In this chapter, the issue of benchmarking is addressed from the service perspective, although the discussion is not exhaustive. For more information on the subject, see Grayson (1994), Prihod (1994), Powers (1994), O'Dell (1994), Chao (1994), Kinni (1993), Swanson (1993), Ford (1993), and others from the selected bibliography.

OVERVIEW

Benchmarking is the process of gathering, analyzing, and evaluating the world outside your organization and comparing it to your own. The results of this process become the cornerstones of your improvement. It is dependent upon your organization's determination to discover and continuously monitor the industry leaders and best practices of business. The process is deceptively simple. However, it requires much time for planning, implementation, and interpretation of the data. Thus, the goal of benchmarking is to make your organization the best it can be based on information from both internal and external sources.

When the concept is applied internally, the focus of the competitive spirit shifts to a cooperative spirit. When the concept is applied externally, more often than not to noncompetitive organizations, the focus is on each other's best practices. The secret to benchmarking is the notion of *best*. The way we define and use "the best" will determine the measuring stick used to define and measure performance. Once this characteristic has been defined and measured by the organization, this knowledge is used to evaluate and/or improve your own processes.

BASIC BENCHMARKING

The focus of benchmarking is to identify and measure the best practices—wherever they are and in whatever organization—and to use this information for improvement. The question is, however, how does one go about benchmarking? The answer is in the following steps.

Preliminary Steps

Before the organization undertakes a study to benchmark specific processes and/or the entire organization, there are some prerequisite steps that should take place.

1. You must know your own organization/process. Unless you know where you are, you will not be able to identify measurable characteristics in the organization. It is imperative that everyone concerned with measurement and improvement be familiar with the subtleties of the organization and how they are going to overcome them. One way to learn about the organization and its processes is to use process flowcharts, storyboards, affinity charts, cause-and-effect diagrams, brainstorming, and so on.

2. You must be committed to continual improvement. Unless the management and in fact the entire organization is committed to the continual improvement process, not much is going to be completed. Commitment is necessary to develop the vision, appropriate the budget, and provide the enthusiasm for the long journey of improvement.

3. You must know the customer and the customer's needs, wants, and expectations. Unless the customer is identified appropriately, the organization may be chasing the wrong item. For example, the needs, wants, and expectation of internal customers differ from those of external customers. The process of satisfying each is different. Therefore, the planning and organization of the studies to identify the customer(s) and their needs, wants, and expectations may have to follow different routes. One of the best tools to define the customer and the customer's needs, wants, and expectations is quality function deployment (QFD).

4. You must be willing to share information. Unless the organization is prepared to share its own best practices, there is no hope for true benchmarking. If the organization shares, the probability that someone else will share their best practices with you increases tremendously. It is this principle of sharing that guides most organizations—and indeed is encouraged—to find noncompetitive partners. By doing so, the threat of confidentiality and proprietary information is diffused, if not completely eliminated.

These four preliminary steps are perhaps the cornerstone or foundation of a good benchmarking study. Once these steps have been accounted for, the organization is ready to move on to the implementation of benchmarking.

Main Steps

5. Decide what to benchmark. Not everything in your organization must be benchmarked. As such, the first step in any formal benchmarking undertaking is to decide *what* and *why* to benchmark. To answer these fundamental questions, you must be prepared to look at your own processes with a fine-tooth comb. You may start looking at:

- Process flowcharts of your operation for any deviations
- Things that leverage success
- Things that cause problems
- Factors that contribute to customer satisfaction
- Problems reported by customers
- Factors that define criticality
- Factors that define performance

- Level of interest (you need to go deep enough so as not to miss key practices but not so deep as to become trivial)

- Factors/characteristics you are willing to share

Example: To say you will benchmark the *service* of your organization is too broad. The reason is that service means different things to different people, and it will be very difficult to homogenize the responses, to say nothing about your questions in pursuing the appropriate definition. On the other hand, time to respond to a request for service is much more specific. In fact, that request can be subdivided into other levels (i.e., request for a message return, request for appointment, request for a refund, and so on). The point is that whereas service is too general, time to respond to a request for service is general enough that it can be benchmarked across many industries and, more importantly, the benchmarking can be subdivided into other more specific areas. Some areas where service benchmarking may be considered are:

- Level of skill of customer service people

- Organization and training of personnel

- Location of supply drops

- Warehousing and distribution practices

- Inventory

- Packaging and unpackaging practices

6. Identify the candidates who are to be your benchmarking partners. The focus of benchmarking is to compare your organization with the best. As such, the second step is to find the industry leaders, the best competitors, or the best practitioners. Your mission in identifying the best is to explore the service characteristics and processes which work and/or delight the customer. Under no circumstances should you try to jeopardize their competitive position. To make sure that does not happen, try to find organizations that perform the same or similar services but in different industries. Where or how do you find candidates for benchmarking? The following may serve as a start:

- Get leads from a business library or database

- Articles in public magazines or industry journals may provide the latest and/or best practices

- Ask around your own company—talk to your own internal experts, customers, suppliers, or even your own industry association

- Attend conferences and trade shows with the intention of always looking for better ways to provide a particular service

- Ask outside consultants

Regardless of how you find your partners, you always need to be honest and upfront with them. That means that you exchange information on an even basis.

Example: Let's suppose you want to benchmark the average delivery time of mail service. The first step is to define what kind of mail service you will focus on and then try to find other organizations that provide the same or similar service. Let's assume we are interested in overnight letter/package delivery. The second step is to identify the best organization and to start collecting data about this particular service, recognizing all along that you have to share some of the same information with that organization. The idea in this step is to generate enough information to be able to compare your tasks, processes, procedures, and policies with theirs.

7. Define how the data will be collected.   The data collection method can be simple (as in the case of secondary data) or difficult (as in the case of primary data). In the first case, library research is necessary, whereas in the second method you must generate the data. Both cases can work for benchmarking and both can be just as effective, provided they are used appropriately. In case you decide to visit your partner in person, remember not to overwhelm your host with a large entourage and a lot of unnecessary questions.

Example: You are starting a new pizza delivery service. First, you may want to gather as much information as possible about the general demographics of the location that interests you. This data will probably come from your local library and will be classified as secondary data.

In addition to this information, you may also be interested in your competition. You may want to know some problems they encounter in the delivery process, some concerns, and so on. Furthermore, you may also want to know something about your customers and how they are reacting to this particular service. This data will more likely come from you, as part of your personal investigation (primary data). In this example, both forms of data collection are necessary, but in some cases it is possible to need only one or the other.

8. Collect the data.   Collection of the data may be performed with questionnaires, personal interviews, phone surveys, and so on. Quite often, more than one technique is used in a given benchmark study. For more details, see Chapter 9.

9. Analyze the data. Analysis of the data will depend on the kind of data you have collected. However, in all cases the analysis should provide answers to the following:

- Where are we in comparison to the best?

- What is the current gap between us and them?

- Why are they better?

- Can we learn anything from their practices?

- Do we want to continue this service?

- What is a reasonable catch-up rate?

- Are appropriate funds available?

At this point for most organizations, including service organizations, the benchmarking process is logically finished (Scheffler 1994). However, if your organization stops here, you will miss an opportunity to improve even more (Feltus 1994). The fact is that once you have reached this point and you know what is out there, you must decide what you are going to do about it. The following steps provide the answer. We call them the advanced steps of benchmarking.

Advanced Steps

As mentioned, the purpose of conducting a benchmark study is not only to find the *best* practices, but to exceed those practices in your organization. Is this a realistic goal? Yes, it is. The reason for this positive attitude is that in pursuing this *best*, you have already answered two of the most troublesome questions: (1) Is this *best* valid? (2) Is this *best* reliable? Obviously, the answers to these two questions have to be in the affirmative, since the *best* practices are already used and indeed provide a competitive challenge. Validity is ensured by the fact that the practices have already been proven to be achievable, and reliability is proved by the fact that these practices are indeed the leading-edge daily practices that contribute to the success of real organizations.

If in conducting the benchmark study you discover that you are the *best* in your industry, you are still not done. Now your focus is to challenge your operations, practices, procedures, etc. to improve even more. The question now becomes: How do we incorporate the *best* practices in our organization or how do we improve our *best*? The following steps provide the minimum requirements.

10. Plan the action plans. At this stage, plans are made for the future of your operations, procedures, practices, and so on. Typical action plans may include:

- QFD
- Customer satisfaction surveys
- Feasibility studies
- Training requirements
- Budget allocation

11. Communicate the results and action plans. This is perhaps one of the most critical stages in the entire process of advanced benchmarking. This is the stage where the communication medium and message must be defined and communicated throughout the organization. Another way of saying this is: Who gets what and by when? Basic questions and concerns in this stage are:

- Is management ready for the results?
- Is our organizational culture ready for the transformation?
- Is our paradigm of quality service on target? If not, how can we change?
- Have we set our objectives with milestones in mind? Remember, our objectives at this stage are attainable.
- Have we identified the most important factors—for us—to achieve the objectives?
- How are we going to *sell* "the best" to our organization?

12. Implement the action plan. At this stage, we do what we said we were going to do, with no surprises. Obviously, depending on what we have decided to do, the implementation process may differ. For example, the requirements for training differ from those for acquiring new equipment.

13. Monitor the implementation. At this stage, monitoring the results and adjusting for any problems that may arise is the focal point. Monitoring is important in this process, because implementing something does not guarantee success. Just because something works someplace else does not necessarily mean it is going to work for you. What we are interested in here is verifying the progress we are making compared to the benchmark track of our plan. If we are not on track, we must investigate the reasons for the deviations and modify accordingly.

14. Start all over again. When all the steps for benchmarking have been completed and the recommendations have been implemented with success, at this point the organization begins the process of continual improvement all over again.

In conducting a benchmark study in a service organization, an additional benefit may be that the results can be used as a differentiation tool to define the image and/or the specific service that your organization offers. It is important, however, to remember that the goal is not to provide the best possible quality, service, and image to a given organization, but rather only those aspects of differentiation for which the customer is willing to pay.

Although benchmarking differentiation will not give you the answer, it will enable you to identify and focus on competitive differences and to address explicitly the cost/differentiation trade-off. That is the primary value of differentiation benchmarking. Managers who analyze competitive differentiation explicitly and with good competitive data will almost always come to a better decision than those who do not.

EXAMPLE OF DEFINING THE PROCESS OF BENCHMARKING

Situation: We are working for company XYZ, Inc. The company produces a product, but sells both the product and service. We are interested in conducting a benchmark study on cost. What do we do?

The steps for conducting the study are:

1. Identify XYZ's company cost chain

2. Identify the key drivers for each step in the chain

3. Gather the data for the key drivers

4. Gather the data for the best-in-class for the key drivers

5. Model the cost of the best-in-class

6. Compare to your cost to:

   • Determine XYZ's relative cost

   • Identify where XYZ's cost is high and low

   • Identify why the cost is high and low in XYZ, Inc.

To begin the study, try to identify the best characteristics of the cost drivers. In our investigation, the drivers we are focusing on have the following general elements:

- They are defined in a straightforward way, so that they are relatively consistent among companies.

- Data for them is available for the competition as well as our own company.

- They capture most of the cost of a given function.

For example, cost for the sales function is usually largely people cost; therefore, various cost drivers that together reflect people cost capture most of the cost of the function. Those drivers may not capture the cost of the telephone bill or the money spent on office supplies, but those costs are a relatively small part of total cost and are relatively insignificant. The benefit of using the cost drivers is twofold, and both are very powerful:

1. It is really the only way the analysis can be done, for the reasons stated above. (You often cannot get actual cost data from your competitors.)

2. Even more important, modeling costs through use of cost drivers allows us to arrive at a dual result. Not only do we learn how our costs compare to those of our competitors, but we also learn why our costs are higher or lower as a function of the various underlying factors or drivers. This makes the information much more useful for developing recommendations on how to reduce our own cost.

For XYZ, Inc., the cost drivers may be defined from the following areas. The specificity, however, will depend on the particulars of the study and the individual organization.

Cost benchmarks and drivers—raw materials:
- Cost as percent of sales
- Purchase price/unit
- Yearly purchase volume
- Typical purchase lot size
- Source (domestic versus foreign, specific location, suppliers)
- Exchange rate trends (if overseas)
- Freight costs
- Duties

- Applicability of "corporate umbrella" purchasing agreements
- Defect rate, other measures of supply quality
- Yield (unit output per unit input)

Cost benchmarks and drivers—sample direct labor cost:
- Cost as a percent of sales
- Head count
- Hourly wage rates
- Benefits rate
- Exchange rate trends (if overseas)
- Standard weekly hours per worker
- Overtime hours
- Overtime rate
- Unit productivity (product revenues per man-hour)
- Skilled versus unskilled labor
- Education levels
- Union versus nonunion labor
- Age and experience levels

Cost benchmarks and drivers—sample indirect labor cost:
- Overall cost as percent of sales
- Head count—management to direct labor
- Direct labor to support
- Salary levels
- Benefits rates
- Exchange rate trends (if overseas)
- Unit productivity (units produced per man-hour)
- Revenue productivity (product revenues per man-hour)
- Education levels
- Union versus nonunion labor
- Age and experience levels

Cost benchmarks and drivers—sample R&D, marketing and administration:
- Overall cost of each function as percent of sales
- Head count for each organization

- Head count broken down by direct versus management versus support
- Head count broken out by role or specialty of employee
- Salary levels
- Bonus plans
- Benefits rates
- Exchange rate trends (if overseas)
- Revenue productivity (revenue per individual in the function)
- Patents per engineer (R&D)
- Drawings per engineer
- Purchase volume per purchasing agent
- Turnover rate
- Educational levels
- Age and experience levels

Cost benchmarks and drivers—sample sales:
- Overall cost as percent of sales
- Overall sales organization head count
- Revenue productivity (revenues per direct salesperson)
- Types of salespeople (e.g., national accounts, regional, industry specialists)
- Ratio of sales support to direct sales personnel
- Ratio of management to direct sales personnel
- Salary levels
- Compensation/incentive plan
- Benefits rates
- Quotas
- Average number of accounts per salesperson
- Sales calls per day
- Sales calls per account per year
- Turnover rate
- Education levels
- Age and experience levels
- Sales training and recruiting
- Cost of literature and samples

Cost benchmarks and drivers—sample miscellaneous:
- Square feet or rent cost as a percent of sales (or per employee)
- Execution compensation as a percent of sales
- Corporate training costs as a percent of sales
- Bad debt expense as percent of sales
- Warranty expense as percent of sales

Cost benchmarks and drivers—sample capital cost:
- Overall asset turnover (sales/assets)
- Fixed asset turnover
- Fixed asset utilization rates
- Capital expenditures as a percent of net fixed assets (or depreciation)
- Net fixed assets to gross fixed assets
- Depreciation rates
- Yearly lease costs
- Maintenance costs
- Inventory turnover
- Days receivable
- Days payable
- Cost of capital

Note that these cost drivers may indeed be confidential information, and the only way you may get access is to modify your questions by asking for ratios or percentages. Also, since this is an example to identify the applicable drivers, we have tried to give examples of as many drivers as possible throughout the organization. In real situations, your organization will focus on the few critical ones rather than as many as possible.

If the focus of the study is to identify product quality and/or service features, then the characteristics must be based on:

1. Determining the most important set of features to the customer. In some cases you will find that what is important to one customer or group is not the same as what is important to another. In these cases, it may be necessary to identify the most important product features for each customer. Good tools for such an undertaking are QFD, specific questionnaires, and/or focus groups.

2. Comparing our product's features to those of the competitors.

3. Determining our major areas of strength and weakness, keeping in mind the customer's feature preferences and priorities. The key is make sure our product includes those features which are most important to the customer. The goal is not to include all possible features, but rather to incorporate only those features that the customer is willing to pay for.

A variation on this analysis is to compare the range of feature options offered to the customer. The goal of this analysis is to identify value added for the product and/or service.

Benchmark drivers for product quality:

- Production yields (percentage of units determined to be below standard after manufacture)
- Rework rates (percentage of products quality corrected after manufacture)
- Warranty expense/repair costs
- Mean time between product failure (reliability)
- Mean time to repair (serviceability)
- Quality methods such as worker participation, quality controls, and innovative manufacturing processes

To be successful in product quality benchmarking, one of the most informative sources is customer input. XYZ, Inc. may survey its customers' perceptions of the quality of competing products in order to supplement the data listed above.

Benchmark drivers for service:

- Hours of availability of personnel
- Response time
- Repair time
- Measures of speed of delivery, such as "fill rate"
- Order-to-receipt cycle time
- Quality of the personnel interacting with the customer (e.g., level of experience and nature of expertise)
- Order entry systems (e.g., ability to order products quickly via telephone or computer)
- Availability of training and informal "consulting" for the customer
- Customer complaint volume

As product advantages become increasingly difficult to maintain in many industries, benchmarking services as a way to achieve differentiation is becoming increasingly important.

Benchmark drivers for image:

- Awareness levels
- Positive or negative association with various vendors
- Positive or negative association with specific aspects of the image of various suppliers (e.g., quality, responsiveness, integrity)

Competitive inputs may include:

- Level of advertising
- Media selected for advertising
- Message of advertising
- Promotions
- Participation in trade shows
- Public relations efforts
- Actions aimed at influencing opinion leaders

At this point, we continue with developing the measurement instruments, collecting the data, analyzing the data, and so on.

REFERENCES

Chao, J. L. (May 1994). "Benchmarking Service Laboratories." *Quality.*

Feltus, A. (April/May 1994). Exploding the Myths of Benchmarking." *Continuous Journey.*

Ford, D. J. (June 1993). "Benchmarking HRD." *Training and Development.*

Grayson, C. J. (May 1994). "Back to the Basics of Benchmarking." *Quality.*

Kinni, T. B. (November 1993). "Benchmarking: One Measurement in the Continuous Process." *Quality Digest.*

O'Dell, C. (April/May 1994). "Out-of-the-Box Benchmarking." *Continuous Journey.*

Powers, V. J. (April/May 1994). "Go, See, Do." *Continuous Journey.*

Prihod, K. (April/May 1994). "The Land of NIH." *Continuous Journey.*

Scheffler, S. (April/May 1994). "Benchwarming: Despite Its Potential, Benchmarking Sits on the Bench in Many Organizations." *Continuous Journey.*

Swanson, R. (December 1993). "Quality Benchmark Deployment." *Quality Progress.*

9

PROBLEM SOLVING AND
TOOLS USED IN TQS

This chapter provides a brief discussion of problem solving and presents some of the most commonly used tools in service quality. Specifically, this chapter addresses both qualitative and quantitative tools applicable for the service industry. For a more detailed discussion of problem solving and specific tools, see Whiting (1958), Likert (1961), Osborn (1963), Fulmer (1974), Summers and Major (1976), Juran (1979), Grant and Leavenworth (1980), Rowe (1985), Palm (1983), Feldman and Arnold (1983), Ishikawa (1987), Mizuno (1988), Brassard (1989), Tribus (1989), Burr (1989), Duncan (1986), Gitlow et al. (1989), Berwick et al. (1990), Parsaye and Chingnell (1993), and others.

THE SIX STEPS IN THE PROBLEM-SOLVING PROCESS

The ability to solve problems is a central prerequisite for human survival, but the mechanics of the process itself remain a puzzle. Intelligence is generally regarded as a basic attribute of human beings and a main ingredient in problem solving. Yet its meaning continues to be a matter of uncertainty and dispute. To further complicate matters, in addition to intelligence we require the will to solve problems (opportunities). Perhaps more importantly, however, the process of problem solving requires systematic thinking and both personal and organizational enthusiasm.

Many approaches to problem-solving techniques exist, for example, Kepner-Tregoe (1981), the Scientific Method, and the TOPS approach (Ford 1987), among others. This discussion will focus on a six-step approach which is simple and quite appropriate for the service industry. The approach is as follows:

1. Identify and define the problem (What is the problem?)

2. Generate alternative solutions (What are possible solutions?)

3. Evaluate the alternative solutions (How do you evaluate the alternatives?)

4. Decision making (Which solution seems best?)

5. Implement the decision (Who needs to do what by when?)

6. Follow up to evaluate the solution (How do you evaluate the outcome?)

POINTERS ON PROBLEM DEFINITION

Before any problem can be solved, it must be identified. The reason for such identification is twofold:

1. If well stated, the definition will expose the essence of the problem to be dealt with and thereby guide the investigation of the problem.

2. A poor definition tends to confine the mind to a very limited area of search for solutions, whereas a good definition unlocks ideas and enables the mind to examine a number of different directions for finding solutions.

As a consequence, forming a problem definition statement is a very important task. It is so important that, according to common folk wisdom over the years, half of the solution to any problem is defining the problem. Defining the problem requires knowledge and skill. The knowledge may be based on education and/or experience The skill, on the other hand, is learned through guidance and/or coaching. Some guidelines in formulating a problem definition are the following:

1. Define the problem broadly. To test an initial definition to see if it is broad enough, ask *why*. For example, if the definition were "how to make a better paintbrush," asking why could lead to the thought, "to apply paint faster," which could lead to the revised problem definition: "how to apply paint more efficiently." This type of definition opens up such possible solutions as spraying, sponging, or rolling on paint.

2. Question the basic assumption of what the problem is by asking "why do this at all?" Sometimes the problem stated is not the real problem. Force yourself to look for the real root cause.

3. Word the definition concisely, so as to express just the essence of the problem. Eight or ten words should usually be sufficient.

4. Redefine the problem in several ways.

5. Divide the problem into subproblems, and write a definition for each of the subproblems.

6. Give the problem various interpretations. Express definitions in a variety of ways—shift word order, substitute other verbs, change negative statements to positive ones, change active voice to passive, etc.

7. Word the problem in a form that encourages idea generation by beginning the statement with "how to _____" or "ways to _____" or "what to do about _____."

8. Allow time for new perceptions of the problem to develop before settling on a final definition of the problem.

PRINCIPLES OF TEAM PROBLEM SOLVING

All problems can be solved by either an individual and/or a team. However, in this section we will address the principles of problem solving as they relate to the team environment. These principles are:

1. Success in problem solving requires that effort be directed toward overcoming surmountable obstacles.

2. Available facts should be used even when they are inadequate.

3. The starting point of the problem is richest in solution possibilities.

4. Problem-mindedness should be increased, whereas solution-mindedness should be delayed.

5. Disagreement can lead to either hard feelings or innovation, depending on the discussion leadership.

6. The idea generation process should be separated from the idea evaluation process because the latter inhibits the former.

7. Choice situations should be turned into problem situations.

8. Problem situations should be turned into choice situations.

9. Solutions suggested by the leader are improperly evaluated and tend to be either rejected or accepted.

To assist you in listing problems in your area, the following questions may be asked:

1. What specific jobs/items present most of your problems?

2. What jobs/items are held up because of delays or bottlenecks?

3. What jobs/items frequently require overtime?

4. What jobs/items require too many people?

5. What jobs/items require lots of chasing around or walking?

6. What jobs/items are causing a lot of rework?

7. Where do forms, reports, or records require unnecessary information?

8. Where can forms, equipment, or supplies be eliminated?

9. Where can an operation be combined with another operation to save time?

10. What jobs or procedures take too long?

11. What jobs can be rescheduled to eliminate peaks or idle time?

12. Where can better use of space be made?

13. Where is work distributed unevenly among employees in terms of quantity, difficulty, urgency, or importance?

14. On what jobs are too many mistakes being made or is quality or work unsatisfactory?

15. What shortcuts can be employed?

16. Where can wear and tear on equipment be reduced?

17. Where can materials, parts, or supplies be reused?

18. Where can machines or equipment be used to reduce handwork?

19. What jobs require a lot of checking?

20. Where does it take too long to locate records?

21. Do any of the machines you use cause you trouble?

22. What trouble results from these machines?

23. What parts seem to cause more problems in your area?

24. What problems do these parts cause?

PROBLEM-SOLVING TOOLS

So far we have addressed the issue of problem solving from the team point of view and how teams can be used in the problem-solving process. Specific tools and their uses in the service quality area utilizing the team approach are discussed in this section. The list and/or explanation of available tools is not exhaustive. (For a more complete explanation, see the references and selected bibliography.)

Delphi Method

This technique is basically a means of gathering opinions from people by mail. It is used in formulating goals, obtaining consensus, and soliciting undefined information. It is an excellent tool for identifying future trends in service. This method can also be used in conjunction with quality function deployment, especially in the very early stages. The Delphi technique, originally developed by the Rand Corporation, is a conceptually simple innovation which may be used to summarize opinions or judgments obtained through mailed questionnaires. The Delphi method consists of the following steps:

1. A panel is selected, composed of management and employee representatives (or specialist in the area of study).

2. A questionnaire is designed, tested, and mailed to panel members, asking them to list their opinions and judgments about the subject being considered.

3. Recommendations from the panel are refined by recirculating their original responses in a priority format.

4. Items received as responses on the second questionnaire are analyzed and reported. This analysis is returned to the panel for another round of prioritization.

5. This third questionnaire is also analyzed and sent back to the panel for a final opportunity to revise the ratings. It is not unusual for the Delphi method to have more than three iterations if the problem is large scale.

Some of the advantages of the Delphi method are:

1. Permits focused interaction between people who are geographically dispersed

2. Allows people in separate fields to exchange ideas

3. Is relatively inexpensive

4. Requires less time commitment from panel members as compared to a team

5. Provides each panel member with information about the responses of the other panel members

6. Gives panel members time to consider their judgments and to make independent decisions

7. Can be adopted for a wide range of problems

Some of the disadvantages are:

1. Misinterpretation of the issue by panel members

2. Vague statements may lead to ambiguous results

3. Depending on the magnitude of the problem, time considerations may be of concern

4. Lack of interaction through face-to-face discussion

Potential applications may be in the following areas:

1. Evaluate possible budget allocations

2. Determine some of the "customer" concerns for product design

3. Develop causal relationships in some design products

4. Expose priorities of personal values and goals in the corporate culture

5. Delineate the pros and cons associated with potential policy options and/ or changes

6. Plan a total quality program

7. Plan for a training program

8. Plan customer satisfaction

9. Develop customer requirements

Cross-Impact Analysis

This extension of the Delphi technique depicts the interrelatedness between events using a matrix analysis. It examines events in the context of their local setting. The methodology for this technique was developed by Gordon and Helmer at the Institute for the Future. A cross-impact matrix is an array consisting of a list of potential future developments and two kinds of data concerning them. The first is the estimated probabilities that these developments occur within some specified period in the future. The second is estimates of the effect that the occurrence of any one of these events could be expected to have on the likelihood of occurrence of each of the others. In general, the data for such a matrix are obtained by collating expert opinions derived through the use of methods such as the Delphi technique.

The advantages of this technique are:

1. Provides a statistical method for determining the impact of interactions among events on the original probability of occurrence

2. Permits analysis of events within a wide technological context

3. Can be used with a large number of variables

Disadvantages include those listed for the Delphi technique plus the following:

1. Implementation may be complex, requiring either a series of probability calculations and/or computer analysis, especially if there are many variables

2. Events are assumed to influence each other in consistent ways

3. The sequence of events is not considered; yet in reality that sequence may in fact affect the outcome

Uses of this method include those listed for the Delphi technique plus the following:

1. Failure mode and effect analysis

2. Prioritization of variables in a process for further analysis

The Cross-Purpose Matrix

This technique provides for stimulating discussions about various goals advocated in any team activity. It provides a way to prioritize goals without using ratings. Competing goals are displayed in a matrix; then, through discussion and deliberation, the relative value of each with reference to the others is determined. In cross-purpose analysis, a goal is defined as an event that someone intends to occur.

The advantages are:

1. Forces those who advocate a goal to be specific in their strategies

2. Provides an opportunity for individuals to examine their own judgments

3. Calls upon advocates to explain the value of their goals

4. Focuses attention on the worthiness of specific goals in relationship to the whole

5. Identifies goals that may be in opposition to each other

The disadvantages are:

1. Not data based

2. May be time consuming

3. Requires openness on the part of participants

4. May be difficult to understand

Uses of this technique are abundant in the quality field. It may be used as a probing tool, as a specific alternative to prioritize a given problem, or in the early stages of any team effort to identify the problem.

Simulation/Gaming

This technique allows possible future events to be generated by means of a speculative game. It provides an opportunity to simulate in order to consider possible problems and the effect of a suggested program implementation before actually trying it. In all applications of gaming/simulation, certain common elements (characteristics) can be found, some of which are the following:

1. Roles do not necessarily correspond to those assumed in the real-life situation

2. A scenario defining a problem area or a given state of the system

3. An accounting system designed to record such decisions and events, together with their consequences that occur during the simulation

4. Algorithm(s) (implicit or explicit) which indicate operating procedures for playing and controlling the exercise

Advantages of simulation/gaming are as follows:

1. Provides an interactive learning situation

2. May be used to help clarify values

3. Allows the testing of a plan before it is put into action

4. Allows planners to consider their actions in relation to the total context

Disadvantages are:

1. May be considered no more than play by participants

2. The high-level mathematical background needed may discourage people from using it

Uses of this technique are increasing every day, especially in the quality field. Gaming may be used in particular where there is a need for teamwork as opposed to individual effort. Many commercial exercises are available, such as the "Human Synergistics" programs on "Desert Survival Situation," "Desert Survival Problem II," "Project Planning," "Par Excellence," "T.E.A.M.S.," and others.

Simulation, such as the Monte Carlo technique, may be used with excellent results in areas for optimum production schedules, just-in-time deliveries, all phases of design, queuing processes, and customer satisfaction.

Trend Extrapolation

This technique uses past and present trends to predict future trends. The technique assumes that what has happened in the past will likely continue in the future. Trend extrapolation uses statistical data that have been plotted along a time line to observe emerging patterns or trends.

Advantages of this technique are:

1. The method is well defined based on the accuracy of the database

2. It may be an accurate predictor is there stability in the process

Disadvantages are:

1. It does not analyze underlying causes of trends

2. Predictions may be erroneous if there are other problems in the process, such as cycles and/or other erratic elements

Uses of this technique can be seen in control charting analysis.

Scenario Writing

This technique calls for the generation of possible futures by speculating about what might or could be. It is generally used to stimulate thinking about positive changes in regard to system goals and priorities. Its focus is to show how a certain chain of events will lead to a desirable or undesirable outcome in the future.

Advantages of scenario writing are:

1. Forces people to look at possibilities they may never have considered by generating alternatives that could occur

2. Takes people out of the present and forces them to focus on the future

3. Provides a view which shows the interaction of psychological and technological elements

Disadvantages are:

1. May be controlling in that it suggests possible alternative futures

2. Is nondata based

Uses applicable for scenario writing are:

1. Design phase of a service

2. Performing a quality function deployment

3. Writing a failure mode and effect analysis

4. Writing a control plan

5. Plan for a total quality program (training and implementation)

Historical Analogy

In this approach, key events from the past are related to the present and the future. The technique may be used to determine if past pitfalls can be recognized and avoided in future planning. This technique requires a parallelism in history, an essential similarity of key variables. This similarity must extend to those factors that are meaningful and important rather than peripheral. History may repeat itself in some essential respects, but such repetition is not inevitable.

Advantages of historical analogy are:

1. May be used to project the future as an extension of the past

2. Allows for reflective view of conflict

Disadvantages are:

1. May be risky

2. Has no defined procedure

Uses of this technique are:

1. Utilization in control charting analysis

2. Utilization in cost of quality reporting and analysis

3. Limited use in a failure mode and effect analysis

4. Limited use in service design

Brainstorming

This technique stimulates uninhibited input of ideas by a team. As many creative solutions to problems as possible are generated.

Brainstorming is a relatively simple procedure that can provide a wealth of ideas in all areas of quality including problem identification. Steering committees as well as employee teams have used it to generate ideas about unique ways to collect data on particular projects, to identify goals, and to list different ways of implementing a program. Through brainstorming, one can consider approaches to individual problems as well as implementation strategies to those problems. Some ideas for improving the results of the technique are:

1. The problem on which the brainstorming session focuses should be specific rather than general. If the problem is too large, then break it down.

2. Brainstorming participants should be selected with care. Persons with a wide range of expertise as well as some who have no knowledge of the area should be included. The latter group more often than not introduces ideas and perspectives that the experts have taken for granted and therefore excluded from the discussion process.

3. An appropriate group size for brainstorming is 8 to 20 people. The group/team should be large enough to generate a range of ideas but not so large as to be unmanageable. A few individuals who can and will provide some starting ideas should be in the group, and the members in general should be able to provide ideas on anything and everything relating to the question (problem) introduced. The make-up of such a group stimulates thinking and gets sessions off to a good start. It should be noted that power figures tend to inhibit participants. They and visitors should be included *only* with the approval of the organizers.

Prior to the first session, the participants should be briefed on the problem they will be brainstorming. A letter reminding them of the date, time, place, and topics to be considered allows for a period of individual thinking. If this is not feasible, the problem should be posed at the beginning of the session and then participants should be given five minutes to think and make individual notes before beginning the process.

Actual sessions should be conducted in accordance with four minimum "ground rules" of brainstorming, with the assistance of a facilitator. The ground rules are:

1. No criticism allowed

2. Encourage unrestricted thinking

3. Seek as many ideas from different people as possible

4. Combine ideas offered by different people

Advantages of the brainstorming technique are:

1. Generates a wide range of creative ideas

2. Provides an environment in which individuals do not feel threatened

3. May uncover new ways to solve old problems

Disadvantages are:

1. Possible difficulty in pinpointing problems

2. Reluctance of participants—fear of humiliation

3. Criticism during the session

4. Preclusion of problems requiring value judgments

5. Difficulty in selecting "kinds of problems"

Uses of the brainstorming technique in the quality area are abundant. Specifically, it can be used to identify critical characteristics of a process or narrow the field of quality issues in control charting, failure mode and effect analysis, quality function deployment, and other areas.

Buzz Session

This technique is used in a meeting or conference by dividing members into subgroups to discuss a topic and to share their reactions with the total group. It tends to eliminate the domination of a group by a few individuals and to stimulate participation by everyone. This technique was originally developed by

J. Donald Philips to encourage audience-wide participation in discussion. His concept of the technique was that groups of six persons would discuss a problem or assigned topic for six minutes. The technique is particularly effective when larger audience thinking and input into the process is desired. The basic goal of this technique is to encourage *democratic* participation in a meeting or conference and to limit the influence of a small but vocal minority who tend to inhibit wider participation. It can be used during the traditional question-and-answer period following a presentation, as the basis for an entire meeting, or in conjunction with other standard discussion and participation devices.

The buzz session is designed around a carefully prepared question on a specific point and has both a stated objective (the answer to the question, suggestion(s) for action, or recommendation) and a limited time to reach that objective.

To begin a buzz session, the audience should be divided into groups of six using any convenient method. Each group is asked to select a facilitator and a recorder. The facilitator ensures that everyone has an opportunity to participate and that the group keeps moving toward its objective to reach a definite conclusion. The recorder takes notes pertinent to the subject and makes a list of the ideas produced. The notes (or a sample of them) are reported to the total audience. Members of an audience are more satisfied when the leadership sends strong signals to them that they have been heard, that what they said is important, and that it will be acted on.

Advantages of the buzz session are:

1. Encourages individual participation in a group process

2. Prevents a vocal minority from controlling a meeting

3. Allows a wide representation of community views

Disadvantages are:

1. Requires that the facilitator be proficient in organization and diplomatic in guiding a large group

2. May not generate any useful information

3. May be noisy and distracting

Uses of buzz session in the quality area are:

1. Allows fair representation in the implementation of a total quality program in a specific department

2. Encourages different points of view in the design stage of a product

Fishbowl

Four to six people discuss a topic or problem while others surround them and listen and ask questions. This technique is useful for eliciting ideas from a particular group or for presenting ideas from a committee.

In its simplest form, the team of six persons is placed in the center of the group and begins discussing the problem or issue at hand. Those on the outside may look and listen but may not participate in the discussion. In a variation, a person on the periphery may put himself or herself in the center in order to participate. In another variation, the outside group may ask questions for clarification but may not make any statements.

Advantages of the fishbowl are:

1. Stimulates interaction among a group of experts while others listen

2. Allows nonparticipants to observe the roles individuals play in the team process

3. Brings a topic and its discussion before the team

A major disadvantage is that it may be threatening to some people.

The uses of the fishbowl in the quality area are numerous. Role groups can be placed in the fishbowl to discuss the concept of quality as they see it. Suppliers and customers may participate in a fishbowl environment to find the problems that each has in relation to each other. Management and nonmanagement may participate in role reversal and/or discuss issues of concern. A classic application of the fishbowl technique is when management uses it to present a plan to the employees. While in the fishbowl, management presents and discusses the plan and their decisions. The context of this strategy permits the audience to feel that the plan is more open, and often questions are raised (and a buzz session employed). This technique can also be used internally when problems are raised between departments. Some specific areas of use in quality are:

1. Failure mode and effect analysis

2. Quality function deployment

3. Effects of streamlining a process

4. Effects of interaction of variables in a process

Force Field Analysis

This procedure analyzes problems by considering a goal and listing the factors either for or against accomplishing it. It helps to identify the strategies that would enhance goal attainment and diminish the importance of factors that would inhibit implementation. The procedure for this technique is as follows. A statement of the problem is written at the top of the force field format sheet:

Problem Statement:

Forces for →	Now	← Forces Against	Goal
Forces that would assist goal attainment are listed in this column	Statement of conditions as they currently exist	Forces that are against achieving the goal are listed in this column	

A statement of current conditions is written within the vertical column in the middle of the diagram. The column on the right side of the format sheet is used to write a description of the way things will be when the problem is solved or, more explicitly, the goal of the analysis. Two major columns are reserved for listing "forces for" and "forces against" achievement of this goal. Forces for achieving the goal are events that will move things from where they are now to where they ought to be. Likewise, forces that might work against solving the problem are recorded in the column labeled "forces against." The arrows are used cryptically to denote the forces.

After completing the force field, an analysis of individual items is made. The forces that cannot be changed are deleted before deciding which forces to work on. Forces against are ranked in order of difficulty of changing. The forces for are prioritized. Each is then considered in turn. Two companion questions are asked: "What can be done to minimize the forces against goal achievement?" and "What can be done to enhance the forces for goal achievement?" The strategies ultimately selected draw on responses to both of these questions.

Advantages of force field analysis are:

1. Forces issues into the open

2. Recognizes unchangeable circumstances

3. Provides means for analyzing ways to eliminate those things which prevent goal accomplishment

Disadvantages are:

1. Is subjective in nature

2. May not define all aspects of a problem

3. May oversimplify relationships in the problem

Uses in the quality area are:

1. Failure mode and effect analysis
2. Quality function deployment
3. Identify key characteristics
4. May be used by a team to identify goals in a given department and to analyze specific needs with respect to those goals

The 8D Approach

Ford Motor Company has developed an approach to problem solving that is based on eight disciplines (thus the name 8D). The basics of the technique are as follows.

1. Use a team approach. Organize a team of people. Find the people who have the:

- Time
- Knowledge of the product and process
- Authority and responsibility
- Technical skill

The team may include nonproduction personnel and must choose a leader who can plan and drive the improvement process.

2. Describe the problem. Draw a picture of the manufacturing process, preferably with a process flowchart. This will show where the problem is seen. It may show where and how it started. Also, it may identify the places where sampling ought to be done. Some of the activities performed in this stage are:

- Brainstorm ideas
- Discuss causal factors
- Utilize fishbone diagram
- Put the problem into measurable terms
- Measure significance (priority) with a Pareto chart
- Utilize control charts

3. Start and check interim actions. This stage is unique in that it recognizes the problem "right now" and tries to plan and take appropriate steps to contain the problem and its repercussions. Once the problem has been recognized and the team is in this stage, it is imperative that nonconforming parts *not* be sent to the customer. The team *must* be alerted to this and should check the process and its environment often. This alertness and checking may also be enhanced by reviewing the customer's control charts and Pareto charts. In all efforts, the goal of this stage is to contain the problem.

4. Define and check root causes. True problem solving is more than reacting to problems. The reality of "true" problem solving is to find and prevent the root causes. It is more than treating the symptoms with a band-aid. It is prevention. To facilitate prevention, in this stage we use:

- Fishbone diagram

- Experiments and distribution analysis

- Isolation of causal factors

- Planning of corrective actions

5. Check corrective action. In this stage, progress is checked via sampling before and after corrections. The team's intent is to check the data and the effect that the specific actions have had on the process so that a resolution can be made. This is done via experimentation and statistical analyses. One of the foremost analyses in this stage is to analyze the distribution and to use control charts (preferably with variable data) to plot data before and after the correction. When all this is completed, the team or a representative of the team contacts the customer to determine the status of the problem and whether or not their concerns were solved. Finally, in this stage the team or whoever is responsible must make sure that the corrective action did not cause other problems.

6. Start permanent corrective action. If the actions taken in Step 6 were successful, then the team must try to make them a permanent part of the process. To make sure that these are positive results, use ongoing control charts to study the long-term effects of the solution.

7. Stop future problems. Use the input from 4D to avoid the problem again. Act on the process elements before problems start.

8. Congratulate your team. Improvements happen only because many people work together. Everyone deserves credit.

Focus Group

The focus group approach is to select 7 to 15 participants with the purpose of collecting perceptions, attitudes, and expectations about current and/or future services and/or products. Through the interaction of the group, more insightful information is gained at a relatively low cost. A typical focus group may be selected for:

- Generating hypotheses

- Diagnosing potential problems

- Developing/validating questionnaires

- Interpreting previous evaluations

- Evaluating programs

Storyboard

The storyboard approach uses the steps of the FOCUS and PDCA strategy to help teams organize their work and their presentations so others can more readily learn from them. The focus of this approach is to reduce variation in the process by emphasizing the content as opposed to the telling (presenting). One of the strongest advantages of using the storyboard is that the process forms a permanent record of a team's actions and achievements and all the data generated may serve as the working minutes of a team at a later date.

Nominal Group Process

The nominal group process method utilizes a group that does not verbally interact; therefore, the group is labeled nominal (in name only). A typical approach to the nominal process is:

- Without direct interaction, group members write down their ideas concerning the problem.

- Individuals' written lists of ideas may be categorized according to emotions or according to organization dimensions.

- Each person reads his or her entire list of ideas. Copies of each list are passed out to all participants.

- The highest priority items may be identified by a voting system.

GRAPHIC REPRESENTATION

While the preceding tools provide for employee and/or customer interaction in problem-solving analysis, they all depend on good understanding of the problem as well as communicating the problem verbally. In this section, our focus is on communicating the problem and/or solution with some form of graphic representation.

A graph is a drawing that uses lines and shapes to represent numbers and concepts. Charts are the lines and shapes combined into forms. Common forms are bar charts, column charts, pie charts, line charts, organizational charts, flowcharts, time charts, control charts, and others.

Graphs serve as a powerful aid in communication and in our perceptions of the world. This is done through gathering information and processing that information. In general, graphs are ways to:

- Increase the effectiveness and efficacy of transmitting information in quantitative and qualitative form

- Give meaning to information by showing relationships, trends, and comparisons

- Distinguish numbers and ideas of importance

These factors are accomplished by the experimenter (designer) of the graph by making the best and most appropriate decision about the type of graph that will be most effective to present the data. Historically, the lines and shapes used in graphs have been standardized by convention and have been given specific meaning which is easily translated. Graphs are influential modes of persuasion. Translations for a few symbols are:

○	Unity
→	Direction/flow/attraction
□	Area/mass

It is important to recognize that the goal of the graph is to communicate as simply as possible to the audience to which the graph is being displayed the information desired. To do this, the audience must be able to distinguish the shapes from words. Therefore, shapes used in graphs differ from the shapes of letters.

Four key characteristics are critical to the thought process in determining the type of graph and/or chart to be used.

Unity.   All the individual components of the graph must give the impression that they belong together. A good graph requires the establishment of coherent relationships among each component in the design of the graph. However, there are no steadfast rules for designing a particular chart except that the size, proportion, position, and composition of the graph must be given serious consideration.

Size. A chart designed for exhibits or lectures should be larger than a chart designed for reproduction/publication. The dimensions of the chart should relate to visibility and perceptibility, ease of construction, and harmony of components. The thickness of lines and lettering and shading percentages also contribute to the size element as well as to the aesthetics of the chart.

Proportion. Proportion refers to the sense of equal weight among the components of the graph. This necessitates planning and controlling the location, size, and arrangement of lines, shapes, symbols, shadings, scale, and labels incorporated in the chart. Proportion may be determined by:

- Locating the center of the graph by visualizing it and/or mapping it out using mathematical techniques

- The lines and shapes of the graph are more or less balanced to the right or left or above or below the center of the graph

Contrast. Contrast is the variation in size, shape, shading, and location of lines and symbols. In order for contrast to exist, there must be some visual differences in the graph recognizable to the audience. For example, using various shading techniques, the designer of the graph can convey a different sense of importance and size. Shading creates a sense of increased volume and/or size; at the same time, the object seems closer and as a consequence gives the impression of an illusionary image of importance.

The effect of variation created in designing a graph is critical to the interpretation of that graph, since the designer has the ability to deliver several messages with one set of data using different contrast techniques.

Meaning. Meaning is a combination of unity, proportion, and contrast. The audience focuses attention on one item as more important than another and comes to understand the relationships, trends, and patterns displayed in the graph.

The audience's understanding of the graph is accomplished through the use of the sizes and shapes displayed in the graph. That is:

- Positioning of the graphic lines

- Degree of shading

- Use of scale measurements

- Use of word labeling of the forms

Even though graphs provide an easy way of presenting information, there are many types and variations of charts in the world of quality today to facilitate this information process. The most popular, however, share several characteristics:

- **Clarity:** The identification of a specific point and grasping the significance of the point being conveyed

- **Simplification:** The ability to break down a complex thought into smaller components while still maintaining the integrity of the thought in the totality of the graph

- **Interest:** The ability to break the monotony through the use of symbols and shading techniques

- **Reinforcement:** The understanding that various interpretations may result from one point of communication; as a result, it may be necessary to repeat or represent that point via some other vehicle of communication

- **Summarization:** The ability to collect key points while at the same time maximize comprehension of those same points

- **Impact:** The ability to create and communicate the immediate key points given with any form of presentation gets attention

Bar/column chart. This chart is the most widely used in quality assurance/control. Bars displayed horizontally are called bar charts. Bars displayed vertically are called column (histogram) charts. Bar and column charts are extremely useful in emphasizing quantitative information. This type of chart may also be used to effectively demonstrate comparisons between two or more items.

Pie chart. A pie chart is a circle chart segmented into slices, proportional to the area of concern. The circle in its entirety represents the total amount. Pie charts are used to compare various components to each other in relationship to the whole. To facilitate the "right" choice of the proper graph, the following questions may be asked:

- Are you comparing components in relationship to a whole?—If the answer is yes, a pie chart is appropriate.

- Are you comparing one component to another component?—If the answer is yes, a bar/column chart is appropriate.

Line charts. Frequency distribution, frequency polygons, step charts, normal curves, ogives, scattergrams, and surface charts are commonly known as line charts. Line charts show trends, distribution relationships, and comparisons of both trends and relationships. In general, line charts have the capability of containing a greater information load as opposed to bar/column and pie charts. In addition, the impact and credibility created by this type of graph are also greater.

Organizational chart. An organizational chart is a description of how departments, divisions, and staff functions are structured within a given corporation. It is a qualitative chart representing:

- Various staff positions, indicating their structural relationships and span of control
- Different units and how they are arranged and relate to one another
- Various functions and how they are related and organized

Organizational charts specifically make the distinction between staff, units, and functions. Staff positions are indicated by titles and are connected to the line authority via a dotted line. Units refer to the formal subdivisions of a corporation and are connected via a solid line. Functions refer to the manner in which different activities, duties, and responsibilities are related.

Flowchart. A flowchart shows a series of step-by-step activities for a given process of a particular function. Flowcharts show the sequence or "flow" of the steps involved from beginning to end. Flowcharts are another form of qualitative charts as opposed to bar/column, pie, and line charts. The flowchart provides a condensed and concise description of a process even though that process may be extremely complex.

Table chart. A table chart is a word chart divided into rows and columns. The focus of this chart is simplicity and a description of an item indicated by a numerical factor.

Text chart. A text chart is a word chart. Very short phrases or two- to three-word clauses are used to emphasize a key point. To highlight these phrases and/or clauses, symbols are used. Some of the symbols used are:

- Bullet point
- ☐ Box
- → Arrow

Shading, italics, and bold lettering are used in conjunction with symbols to add emphasis and interest for the audience.

Time chart. A time chart is one of the most frequent applications of line charts. Close attention is given to the X and Y axes of the grid where scales are constructed so that absolute numbers are allocated to designated time periods and respective amounts.

PERT chart. The Program Evaluation and Review Technique (PERT) is one of the latest charts that has entered the quality field, especially in the tooling, fixtures, and jigs industries. This chart is designed to provide multiple pieces of information on a project. It is used primarily for very complex projects, although simple projects may benefit from its application. Specifically, this chart shows the relationship of all scheduled events and activities of a given project. It also illustrates how each step in the process interrelates to the project in its entirety. Some information gained from this chart is in the area of:

- Cost

- Early time

- Late time

- Slack time

- Optimistic time

- Pessimistic time

- Sequence of activities and events

In addition to the variety of charts and the information they provide, some basic techniques may enhance the individual charts:

- **Shading:** Shading techniques should be used for a specific purpose and not for decoration. Two reasons to use shading are:

  1. To emphasize one component of a pie or one segment of a bar or column

  2. To distinguish actual from projected with different sets of bars or columns

- **Colors:** Color, like shading, should be used for a purpose and not for decoration. Three reasons to use color are:

  1. To emphasize one segment of a bar or column, trend line, or row of figures

  2. To identify a recurring theme (e.g., show customer-related data in the same color throughout the presentation)

  3. To symbolize (i.e., red for losses or stop, yellow for marginal or caution, green for profit or go)

- **Lines:** The thickness of lines should be drawn with a purpose in mind. Three general rules apply:

1. Thin lines should be used for scale rulings, scale ticks, pies, bars, and columns

2. Medium lines should be used for baselines

3. Thick lines should be used for trends, averages, and border lines

Because of the abundance of charts available in the field of quality, only some of the most common graphic tools are addressed here, as follows.

Process Flowcharts

A process flowchart diagram provides an overall process flow definition and a step-by-step description of each operation in a process. In manufacturing, as in any service, a process flow is a graphic presentation of the flow and sources of variation of machines, materials, methods, operators, environment, and measurement from the start to the end of the process.

Standard symbols have been developed to show the flow in a graphic form:

Symbol	Name	Meaning
○	Operations	Object is changed at the workplace
→	Transportation	Object is moved
□	Inspection	Object is examined
D	Delay	Object is waiting for next operation
◇	Decision	If acceptable, continue If not, repair, scrap, etc.
▽	Storage	Object is retained and protected against unauthorized removal

Using these symbols, the detail of the process can be varied based on the needs and goals at hand. A "macro" process flowchart is used to show a very basic process from raw material to finished goods. On the other hand, a "micro" process flowchart is used to show all the details and operations (steps) in a process. Figures 9.1 and 9.2 are examples of macro and micro flowcharts.

Through a flowchart, the operator may be able to identify the points in the process where more information may be collected. As a general rule, there are three such points in any process.

Incoming material.   Although this check is more expensive than good supplier/vendor quality, the order should be checked for completeness and quality.

Supplier   **Customer**

Patient -------------------- information about condition ------------------Physician

Physician ---------------- order to test ---------------------------------- EW secretary
                                                                            Phlebotomist
                                                                            Lab technician

EW secretary ----------- information about patient & test ---------- Dispatcher

Dispatcher --------------- information about --------------------------- Phlebotomist

Phlebotomist ----------- blood sample -------------------------------- EW secretary

FIGURE 9.1   Sample of a descriptive flowchart (macro): lab test in emergency ward (EW)

In process. This is the focus of statistical process control. It is important for at least three reasons:

1. Expensive operations

2. Irreversible operations

3. Assembly or finishing operations

It is these three reasons that become the impetus for good quality in the process. As a consequence, the process must be checked during operations to make sure that it produces acceptable products.

Finished goods/service. Inspecting *only* at this point is a waste. The service/goods at this point are very expensive and serve no other reason than to identify what the customer will see when the product/service is delivered. If it is used as a sorting mechanism, then a lot of money is wasted before a solution is found.

People have different ideas about a process based on *how, when,* and *what* they do in that process. It is imperative, then, to use the process flowchart as a tool to show the relationship between the different process parts. By using this chart, ideal settings of the process, differences between shifts and/or operators, and process streams may be discovered. (A process stream may be a multiple cavity, different fixtures or pallets, several machines producing the same part,

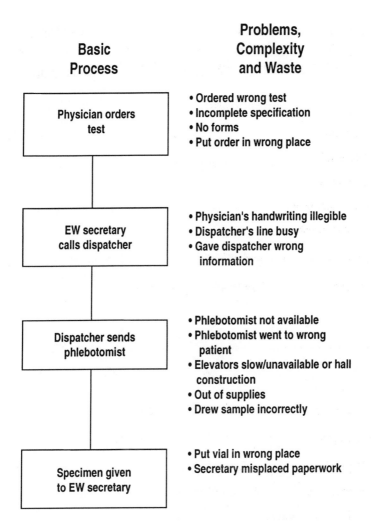

Basic Process

Problems, Complexity and Waste

| Physician orders test | • Ordered wrong test
• Incomplete specification
• No forms
• Put order in wrong place |

| EW secretary calls dispatcher | • Physician's handwriting illegible
• Dispatcher's line busy
• Gave dispatcher wrong information |

| Dispatcher sends phlebotomist | • Phlebotomist not available
• Phlebotomist went to wrong patient
• Elevators slow/unavailable or hall construction
• Out of supplies
• Drew sample incorrectly |

| Specimen given to EW secretary | • Put vial in wrong place
• Secretary misplaced paperwork |

FIGURE 9.2   Sample of a flowchart (micro): process for lab tests in emergency ward (EW)

or teams using different settings and/or procedures). In general, the team's effort will be improved.

Cause-and-Effect Diagram

This is also known as a fishbone diagram because it looks like the skeleton of a fish. It is also known as the Ishikawa diagram, after the person who developed it. This diagram is a problem-solving technique that helps identify the root of a problem. It does so by putting the problem (effect) on the right side and by listing contributing factors (causes) on the left side. The major contributing factors are:

- Machine
- Method
- Material
- Manpower
- Measurement
- Environment

The following is an overview of a cause-and effect-diagram:

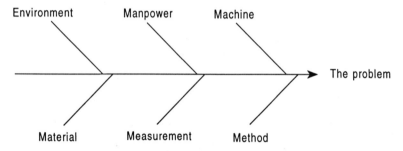

Advantages of the cause-and-effect diagram are:

- It provides a chance to learn
- It makes use of technical expertise
- It is a team activity
- It provides interaction of people with different backgrounds
- It complements the brainstorming technique and process flowchart
- It provides an unbiased base for discussion
- It focuses the discussion
- It provides the beginning of data collection
- It may be used as a checklist
- It is a good presentation as well as an organization tool

- It is very flexible and can be used for both administrative and manufacturing problems

- It provides the team with a benchmark of current knowledge about the process

Disadvantages are:

- A simplistic diagram may show little understanding of the problem at hand

- The problem may not be solved due to lack of real team effort

- The process itself is qualitative in nature

Steps in constructing the diagram are:

1. Gather a problem-solving team. Find people who know the problem well.

2. Use a large sheet of paper (flip chart). Draw a box on the right side and an arrow from the left. Point the arrow toward the box. Write the problem in the box.

3. Write the major causes around the arrow.

4. List the parts adding to each of the major factors.

5. Repeat Step 4 as necessary. Ask the following questions: "Why does this cause happen?" "What adds to this factor?" Speak frankly and **do not evaluate or criticize** until the diagram is complete.

6. Talk about the listed causes. Decide on the main factors as they become priority items. Look for factors that are repeated in different parts of the diagram.

7. Make an agenda. List actions needed to correct the major factors and assign someone to work on each task.

Check Sheet

A check sheet (tally sheet) is a simple systematic way to collect and organize data. Check sheets come in various forms, depending on the specific application for which they are used. Most often, they are used to facilitate the data collection process and to simplify data analysis. A check sheet will sort the data as the data are collected and provide for the construction of a histogram at the same time.

It is important to recognize that the check sheet provides a "picture in time" (which is also true of a histogram) rather than changes over time. For example:

Date:	Number of defects:		Observer:		
Process	*Mon*	*Tues*	*Wed*	*Thur*	*Fri*
A					
B					
C					
D					
E					

Designing a check sheet. Each individual need for data will require a specifically designed data gathering sheet. However, some general rules apply:

1. Decide how the data are to be collected and organized. Think of combinations of headings that will give the most useful information for the problem at hand. Headings to consider may be of the form:

   • Frequency of occurrence

   • Places the problem occurs

   • Shift and/or operator

   • Defect

   • Department

   • Machine

2. Specify the time period.

   • Think of factors which might affect the process, such as start up, job change, or seasonal differences

   • May range from several minutes (lunch break) to several months (seasonal)

3. Lay out the check sheet on paper and modify if necessary. It is important to recognize that how the data are organized is not based on the easiest method of collection; rather, it is based on presenting the data in the most realistic way and solving the problem in an efficient manner.

Histogram

A histogram is a pictorial representation of the distribution of measured or counted items. It is a quick way to establish the average, middle, mode (most frequent), and capability of a distribution. It is also a tool that will show the dispersion as well as the shape of the distribution. A histogram is a data collection technique that usually follows the check sheet. The steps in drawing a histogram are:

- Make a frequency distribution (tally)

- Draw two axes on grid paper

- Use grouped or ungrouped measurements from the frequency distribution on the horizontal axis

- Draw a vertical rectangle as tall as the frequency for those measurements

How narrow or wide the spaces are on the horizontal axis is not important, as long as they are the same for each of the groupings. Also, it does not matter how large the increment (scale) of measure is on the vertical axis, as long as it is the same for all groupings. The bars on a histogram are usually shaded or colored to show better contrast on paper.

Frequency Polygon

This graph is a line curve which can be used in place of a histogram. A frequency polygon is constructed the same as a histogram except that the midpoints of the groupings are connected in the polygon.

Pareto Chart

This chart ranks the causes of a problem. The Pareto principle was developed by the Italian economist by the same name to emphasize the "vital few" as opposed to the "trivial many." The uses of the diagram in the course of problem solving can be extensive. Some applications are:

- Identify the priority of problems

- Clarify the problem in a pictorial form

- Make management presentations

- Track a problem over time to see progress

- Easy to display progress so others can see it

- Used in conjunction with a p chart, it helps to explain the signals generated by the control chart

Unlike the histogram, the Pareto chart may also show the relative (cumulative) percentage of each of the groupings depicted in the diagram.

Steps in creating a Pareto chart:

1. Choose the main factors causing the problem. Usually this can be done from the data collected on a check sheet or histogram.

2. Measure each factor as it adds to the problem. Use a standard measure (scale). Some commonly used measures are:

   - Cost

   - Time

   - Frequency

   If it is important for the problem identification process, more than one Pareto chart can be developed, depending on the measure of concern.

3. Choose a time interval for collecting data. Use a standard time interval. This interval should be long enough to show differences between causes.

4. Make a table. List the causes by the size of their contribution. Place the biggest cause at the top and the smallest at the bottom.

5. Calculate the cumulative number for the factors.

6. Construct a Pareto chart. List the causes on the horizontal axis. Each cause should have equal space. The left vertical axis is the measure (scale). Scale this axis in such a way that there is enough room to plot the total number of observed defects. Draw the vertical line (bar) about each causal factor so that the contribution of that factor is shown.

7. Calculate the ratio and percent number each factor adds to the total. A percent is calculated by first dividing the number of defects by the total number of defects. This ratio is multiplied by 100 to calculate the percentage. At this point, the answer may be rounded off to two decimal places.

8. Calculate the cumulative percent number for each factor. The cumulative percent for the first defect is the percentage for that defect. The cumulative percent for the next defect equals the percentage for that defect plus the previous cumulative percentage.

9. Add a right vertical axis to the Pareto chart. Use this for the percent contribution. Its greatest value is 100%. It is important to use the same height as for the left vertical axis.

10. Put a dot above each vertical bar to show the cumulative numbers. Draw a line between each dot.

11. Label each vertical bar and dot with the correct percentage.

Stem and Leaf Plot

A somewhat unusual type of diagram, the stem and leaf diagram combines the features of an ordered array of numbers and a frequency histogram. The advantage of this technique over the histogram is that it preserves the actual data values (Ryan et al. 1985).

Dotplot

The display of the dotplot is very similar to a histogram with many small intervals which has been turned on its side. Histograms tend to be more useful with large data sets and dotplots with small data sets. The reason for this is that the histogram groups the data while the dotplot groups the data as little as possible. Histograms show the shape of a sample; dotplots do not. Dotplots are very useful to compare two or more sets of data (Ryan 1985).

Box and Whisker Diagram

The box plot is a simple and powerful tool for exploratory data analysis. It may be used as a means of displaying and informally analyzing the results of a design factorial experiment, including detection of interactions among predictor variables. The box plot enables estimating (quickly) the range, median, and any tendency for skew in a data set. The box covers the middle 50% of the data values, between the upper and lower quartiles. The "whiskers" extend out to the maximum and minimum values. Any differences in length of the whiskers, which generally extend $1\frac{1}{2}$ times the length of the box, may indicate skew. The central line is at the median value. Data points that behave differently from the batch of data are labeled outliers (Hays 1981).

Scatter Plot

A scatter diagram is a plot between two variables to illustrate a possible relationship between them. The pattern that the points of the two variables form indicates whether or not there is a relationship. The expected relationship is shown

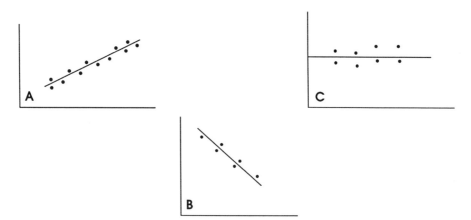

FIGURE 9.3   Scatter plots: (A) positive relationship; (B) negative relationship; (C) no relationship

as (1) positive, (2) negative, and (3) no relationship, as in Figures 9.3A, 9.3B, and 9.3C, respectively.

The scatter diagram may be used to show a correlation between a suspected cause and effect being investigated. Caution should be exercised, however, since correlation alone does not imply causation. To construct a scatter diagram, the following steps are necessary:

1. Select two variables that seem (or are expected) to be related.

2. Construct a vertical axis that will encompass all the values that you have obtained from one of the variables. The horizontal axis will represent all the measurements of the other variable.

3. Plot all the measured values for the two variables.

Relations Diagram

This diagram clarifies the interrelations in a complex situation involving many interrelated factors.

Affinity Diagram

This is essentially a cross between brainstorming and a cause-and-effect diagram. It is based on a team's work in which every participant writes down his or her ideas and then groups these ideas by subject matter.

Tree Diagram

This is an extension of the value engineering concept of functional analysis. It is applied to show relations between goals and measures.

Matrix Diagram

This format is used in deploying quality requirements into counterpart engineering characteristics and then into production requirements.

Matrix Data Analysis Diagram

This diagram is used when the matrix chart does not provide sufficiently detailed information.

Process Decision Program Chart (PDPC)

This is an application of the process decision program chart used in operations research. This diagram was developed to optimize solutions and to avoid surprises.

Arrow Diagram

This is often used in PERT and the critical path method (CPM). It uses a network representation to show the steps necessary to implement a plan.

Information Discovery

This is an automated computerized search of a database to discover unexpected information and uncover hidden causes of quality problems (Parsaye and Chingnell 1993).

Data Visualization

Three dimensional (3-D) visualization of data adds the critical third dimension to graphic views of data, giving depth to charts and graphs and more fully exploiting human perceptual capability. The additional visual enhancements provide users with added help in interpreting information (Parsaye and Chingnell 1993).

Hypermedia

Quality assurance tools work best when they are linked together and/or compared with other tools for an analysis of detail that has been defined as appropriate. Hypermedia provides this type of capability and is the natural interface within which to embed the other quality tools (Parsaye and Chingnell 1993).

STATISTICAL PROCESS CONTROL

Statistical process control, otherwise known as SPC, is one of the most frequently heard buzzwords among government, industry, and service managers. What is it? How is it being employed, taught, tracked, and managed? Is it proving useful? Is anybody using it and getting the most out of it? Is it applicable to service?

Most people think of SPC as the use of statistical techniques such as control charts to analyze a process or its output so as to take appropriate actions to achieve and maintain a state of statistical control and to improve the capability of a process. Does this definition really describe it?

Statistics by itself is the collection, organization, analysis, interpretation, and presentation of data. The application of statistics to quality and other fields has resulted in the recognition of statistics as a field of its own.

Some people have become so involved in statistics that they have indeed become "technique oriented" instead of "problem oriented." The axiom "if it isn't part of the solution, it's part of the problem" may be applied to SPC just as easily as it can be applied to other managerial and production tools. Statistics is just one of may tools necessary to solve quality problems. It is not the only tool, however.

In this section, we will discuss SPC, its goals, its current utilization, and its untapped potential. Let's start with a definition. SPC is the application of qualitative and quantitative techniques to management of an operation or process. However, it involves the identification of events that are beyond the natural variation of the process and the systematic elimination of the causes of such events. When appropriate statistical techniques are built into the process or operation, management gains the ability to understand the nature of process variation and to bring that variation within desired limits.

The focus of SPC is the *process*. With the process control loop in place, emphasis is on closing the loop appropriately through the various techniques available, including charting. The product is not emphasized because there is a distinction between the two. The distinction between *process control* and *product control* was shown in Figures 2.1 through 2.4.

Product control is characterized as the traditional quality control method of improvement and is oriented toward a control cycle in a feedforward loop (in time mode). As a feedforward control system, the result is filtered output.

Product control fosters detection approaches and primarily focuses on containing problematic process outputs. Process control, on the other hand, is characterized as the new quality method for improvement and is oriented toward a control cycle based on a feedback system. Process control nurtures a prevention philosophy and primarily focuses on process improvement over time. The contrast between *process* and *product* can be seen in the following:

Measuring or Observing Data

Process Control	*Product Control*
View over time	Collapse into instant
Control chart	Picture in time
	Frequency curve
Now with a picture of process viability the source may be:	
Common sources (controlling limits)	Special sources
Maintain, reduce, or eliminate stability	Eliminate
Improvement	

SPC is the most effective method of process management. It eliminates subjectivity and provides a means of comparing performance with clearly defined objectives. Immediate feedback is the key to the success of any SPC system. **SPC is not solely a quality function; rather, it is a function of everyone in the organization.**

The responsibility for control is in the hands of the user. This provides the dual advantage of giving the operator a better understanding of what is expected as well as providing a means of detecting undesirable conditions before it is too late.

Advantages

1. SPC eliminates subjectivity and provides a means of comparing performance with clearly defined objectives.

2. Through application of statistical techniques, the need for "fire fighting" is eliminated. Problems are identified, quantified, and solved at the source in an optimum time.

3. SPC methodologies provide immediate feedback if utilized correctly.

4. SPC logically identifies responsibilities and accountabilities and helps eliminate "finger pointing."

Disadvantages

1. If not introduced carefully into an organization, SPC may be costly, in both dollars and time.

2. Production employees may feel frightened or threatened by SPC if not properly taught or introduced to it.

3. Going "overboard" in utilizing SPC methods may swamp both management and employees. Instead of being part of the solution, SPC charts/graphs become part of the problem.

4. Management may be too eager to start without proper understanding of the concept and the benefits of SPC.

Goals of SPC

The goals of SPC are surprisingly no different than most major corporate goals. The following six goals are believed to be very critical:

1. Improve overall quality and reliability of products and service without increasing costs. The reduction of variability in a process will reduce cost while increasing the quality of the product being produced.

2. Increase productivity and reduce costs. SPC can reduce rework, scrap, and inspection costs and increase efficiency.

3. Provide a practical working tool for directing and controlling a process.

4. Establish an ongoing measurement and verification system. By establishing a meaningful measurement of process parameters, a comparison of performance to target objectives may be assessed.

5. Prioritize problem-solving activities and help management with decisions on allocation of resources for the best return on investment.

6. Improve customer satisfaction through better quality, reliability, and performance to schedule.

Approach to SPC

So far, we have implied that for a SPC program to work, it is imperative that two attributes stand well above the rest:

1. Communication

2. Honesty

With proper communication, the process will be able to be adjusted via a "control" to solve it before it starts. With honesty, the entire model of SPC will be perpetuated as a dynamic tool to solve quality control problems at the operating floor level. For this to be implemented, it must be recognized that it would require a totally new top management climate and could succeed only if the company fully accepts at least five beliefs.

1. Acceptance of change. It must be recognized that quality is here to stay and, accordingly, the proper changes must take place.

2. All employees must be treated as equals. All employees have something to offer, and as such, they have to be encouraged, trusted, and motivated to do a good job the first time by their respective management.

3. Total employee involvement in productivity. Unless all levels of management show concern about quality, employees will dismiss the entire program as "well, here we go again with another lip service program." After all, true commitment is shown by action and not by words. Involvement alone will not do it.

4. Use of motivating work structures that accommodate both human and company needs. One of the most mishandled areas of quality control today is the emphasis on company needs over the needs of employees. (The term "human resources" is deliberately used here because the author believes that humans are not resources. They are much more than that and provide much more than a specific use. They have feelings, attitudes, opinions, knowledge, experience, and many other attributes that resources of any kind do not provide other than use.) In identifying motivating work structures within the quality control parameter, employees must be informed why they are doing a particular task and how they are performing. The significance becomes an intrinsic motivator and in fact contributes to quality performance.

5. Use of creative and quality approaches to managing workloads. Some form of SPC has been used by managers for a long time, in areas where graphics were required to depict a particular trend or visualize relationships between attributes. Today, however, for many managers, SPC is a set of techniques based upon mathematical statistics and applied to quality situations by a very small group of specialists. To others, it is simply a new name for inspection and testing. To still others, it is something very powerful which customers insist upon and which has a major effect on customer relations. Yet others believe that SPC is a passing fad and that it is solely responsible for the quality of products as well as workmanship.

What does this acceptance mean to an organization? Simply stated, it means that a given organization, under the auspices of SPC, emphasizes and uses the motto "quality means conformance" as a beacon for its overall quality program. The emphasis on conformance converts the concept of SPC from a mystical complexity into a quantitatively measurable tool. The approach that this conformance takes is of particular interest in at least two areas:

a. It allows a company to supply products to customers that conform to their requirements. This is not to suggest that one should go through the motions of fulfilling the letter of the law, but rather should fulfill the intent as well. For example, one major company's customer requested that the producer of its product be well acquainted with SPC and have a formal organization with SPC personnel. The producer, to satisfy the customer, processed over 1000 employees through a two-day training program in SPC over a 12-month period. It even created a department for SPC with two full-time staff, a secretary, and five rotating trainees. In the meantime, no one in the entire organization used systematic SPC principles and/or procedures. The producer fulfilled the obligation in terms of conformity, but that conformity was superficial and erroneous from a true quality perspective.

A second example is when a customer asks for a particular chart, and the producer, in all eagerness to satisfy, loses track of the intent of the information. As such, even though it is recognized that the chart and information are irrelevant and outright incorrect, the producer proceeds with the construction and delivery of the information requested. Both examples illustrate that when SPC is misused, it can in fact lose its credibility.

b. To minimize quality costs. As a general rule, SPC begins with problem-solving techniques and a control chart to study the variability of a process. This may not be necessarily the best or optimum way to approach costs. Another way may be to collect the appropriate data, perform a correlation analysis or plot the data on a scatter plot diagram to determine the relationships that exist between the chosen variables, and then perform an analysis of variance or a regression to identify the weights of the variables and to be able to predict and plan costs accordingly.

When using advanced statistical techniques however, remember the following adage: *figures don't lie, liars figure.* As anyone familiar with statistics knows, the variables and samples chosen and sometimes the techniques used cause different results to be reported, given the same probability of occurrence (confidence).

The outcome, of course, is loss of credibility. To avoid this, the SPC principles must be guarded with the following basic foundations in establishing the program:

1. **Simple:** Unless the implementation process is simple, the program will run into problems and most likely will not work.

2. **Flexible:** Unless the implementation process is flexible, the program will run into bottlenecks and most likely will not be implemented.

3. **Reliable:** Unless the implementation process has been proven reliable, the program will fail.

4. **Economical:** Even though the economic situation can be at either end of the scale (very economical or very expensive), attention should be given to this issue because it affects the bottom line of an organization directly.

5. **Acceptance:** Unless top management is behind the program 100%, it will not survive. Acceptance must be present even before implementation begins.

It may seem that these objectives are incompatible and that SPC would be concerned with achieving the best balance between (a) and (b). In practice, however, this is not so. The concepts of defect prevention and doing any task correctly the first time enable both objectives to be achieved simultaneously. What makes modern SPC important or at least a real tool for quality is the ability to solve quality problems while at the same time satisfying customers and minimizing costs. This is illustrated in Figure 9.4.

Although the figure shows the simplicity of the conceptual principles of SPC, it must be understood that for the majority of process problems, simple control charts and some advanced statistical techniques are required, none of which require the fancy mathematical modeling details of liner or nonlinear programming and/or simulation techniques.

The approach to SPC must be addressed from a corporate policy perspective. In order to be a workable policy, all employees (management and nonmanagement) must believe in it. It should not be seen as a morality issue, although it undoubtedly is. It should be accepted because analysis and experience confirm that a company should decide on its mission, goals, and values and take the required steps to fulfill them. A quality policy, especially SPC, that is halfheartedly attempted frequently leads to serious customer dissatisfaction and then to expensive and ineffective remedial action. The final costs are then higher than they would have been if a decision had been made at the start to achieve a quality product. The resulting disruption of production prevents schedules from being

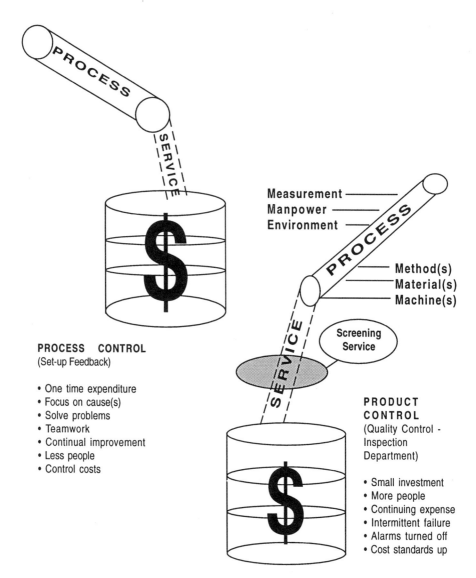

FIGURE 9.4   Important attributes of SPC

achieved and delivery dates from being met. At worst, market share is irretrievably lost.

By no means does this imply that SPC is the answer to all problems. In fact, the customer, product, and cost are related to SPC. However, in order to apply SPC principles effectively, they must go beyond these parameters. Error is possible in all human activities, and in the absence of planned error, prevention is almost inevitable. The consequence of error is either that the result of the activity is inferior to the aim or that more effort must be spent detecting the effects of the error and correcting it. A control chart is generated to identify and control the error, and the SPC program is well on its way.

All this does not mean that a quality policy for SPC should aim for the ultimate in technical performance or aesthetic elegance. It does mean, however, that a quality policy for SPC should exactly meet the defined requirements of the organization. As a minimum requirement, it should recognize the following:

1. Production employees need only a working knowledge of SPC. Overkill in statistical training is in many instances not warranted in the early stages of the program.

2. Generate only the quantity of data that your organization can digest. Generate only what you need and use it.

3. Concentrate on the areas with the greatest cost effect first. Use SPC on the "significant few" problems identified.

4. Realize that statistics is just a tool. SPC is a tool used to measure the process. The process is then evaluated based upon what was learned.

5. Statistics is not corrective action. Statistical analysis is just that—analysis. Control charts and capability studies should isolate (indicate) the problem (cause), so that a solution (action plan) to the problem (cause) can be achieved.

6. Work for continuous improvement. Push for quality and all the various forms it takes.

Historical Perspective of SPC

The control of product and process through statistical means is certainly not new. Rather than trace the complete historical development of SPC, some key moments in history which show the development of SPC are as follows:

- Eli Whitney accidentally made the first crude efforts late in the 18th century as he tried to mass produce muskets for the U.S. government. Gauges and formal inspection practices were not introduced until 1820–40. This was the first instance of formal "go–no go" limits.

- In the early 1900s, E.C. Molina introduced probability theory in switching engineering. The first real giant step was made by Shewhart, who developed the first control charts in 1924 while at Bell Laboratories.

- W. Edwards Deming, among many others, conducted classes across the country during World War II. The classes conducted for employees involved in the frantic race to produce arms were given significant credit for improved reliability and productivity.

- J.M. Juran published his classic *Quality Control Handbook* in 1951, which really put forth the notion of the *prevention of problems* instead of the *sorting of defects.*

- Ishikawa, president of JUSE, directed the unified Japanese quest for excellence through statistical quality process control. The rest is history.

The concept of SPC has been around for some time. However, American industry has only recently (early 1980s) begun to emerge from its lethargic state and become an active participant, once again, in the race to regain its "world-class" status in the marketplace. The use of SPC has been part of American industry's attempt to better serve the customer and, as of late, is making inroads in the service industry as well. It has tapped into service organizations with some noteworthy changes. These changes have helped in identifying and/or defining at least the following:

- Process team concept

- High-technology manufacturing and assembly methods

- Process versus product control

- Highly educated work force

- Elimination of all end-line inspection

- Establishment of fewer bargaining job classifications

- Early purchasing/supplier involvement

- Establishment of measurement systems capability

- Dimensional control plans for every service/product/process

CONTROL CHARTS

In the early 1920s, Shewhart found that the normal distribution curve appeared when the average of subgroups from a constant cause system were plotted in the form of a histogram. What is important here is not so much the shape of that constant cause system, but the sample size. It must be reasonably large. As long as the sample is large, then the averages of different sized subgroups selected from these distributions (populations, universes) will follow the normal curve. This is the concept of the Central Theorem, which is the foundation of control charting.

A control chart is a statistical device (tool) primarily used for the study and control of a repetitive or continuous process. The control chart tests the arbitrary or nonrandom arrangement of points to determine whether they behave as if they were random.

A process is any combination of:

- Machines

- Material

- Manpower   Structure

- Method   or   Process

- Measurement   Outcome

- Environment

employed to attain the qualities desired for products and/or services. Control, on the other hand, is the managerial process of establishing and meeting specific standards. The basic control device is the feedback loop (see Figure 2.1). Its main objective is to detect adverse changes, identify those changes, and take steps to eliminate their causes. Whereas the histogram is a tool to investigate the process as a "picture in time," the control chart is an investigative tool "over time." This time element allows the control chart to detect "variations" in the process.

Variation is the difference between parts and/or any of the components of a process. Some variation, of course, is expected. It is natural, is part of the system, and occurs in a random fashion. Other variation is due to "assignable causes" or specific causes of the process that can be identified. Examples of both kinds are:

Assignable	*Random*
Mixed	Homogeneous
Erratic	Single distribution
Shifting	Stable
Different	Consistent

Natural variation is called a "stable system of chance causes," or common variation, and represents the minimum possible amount of variation. In other words, this variation is always present, and a large effort is needed to eliminate it. When a process is working with only common variation, it is said to be stable and in control, as in Figure 9.5a.

Processes that are in control are also:

- Repeatable

- Stable

- Consistent

- Predictable

A process that is in control is not necessarily good or bad. It simply means that only random causes are present and repeat themselves. In no way does it imply that the process and/or products meet specifications. This is illustrated by the skeleton control charts in Figure 9.6.

Another type of variation in a process is called "special" variation. This variation is not part of the system and is not planned. It may happen in one or more parts of the process, and its source could be any one or combination of machine, method, material, manpower, measurement, or environment. Special causes are usually traced to a single factor, since they are not part of the operation. In order for such variation to exist, the operation must have changed. If we were to draw a curve depicting an out-of-control operation, we would notice the following characteristics about the process:

- The process would be changing

- The process would be unstable

- The process would be unpredictable

A graphic presentation of such conditions would look like Figure 9.7. Notice that these distributions have different shapes, and this condition may be due to different spreads (range or standard deviation) and/or location (mean).

Another way to view the control chart is to think of it as a continual test of a hypothesis. As such, even though no points fall outside the control limits and there is no evidence of nonrandom variation within the limits, this does not mean that assignable causes are not present. It means that the hypothesis that chance causes alone are at work is a tenable hypotheses and that it is likely to be unproductive to look for special assignable causes (Duncan 1986).

To facilitate the understanding of control charts, think of them as graphs that sort variation in a process. In other words, they distinguish special from common variation. These graphs also have summary statistics for analysis and evaluation of the process. Past observations are used to help us look at the future. To do so,

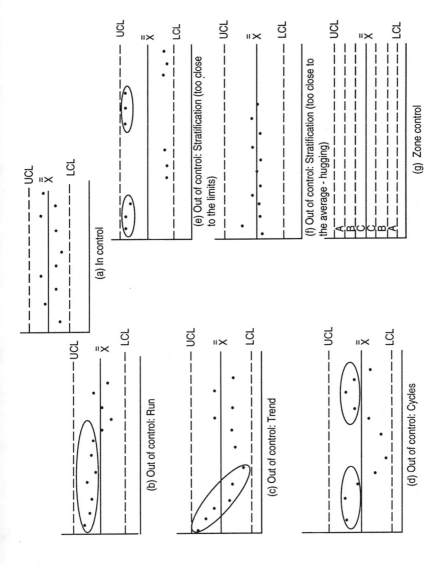

FIGURE 9.5 Sample situations for a process in control and out of control

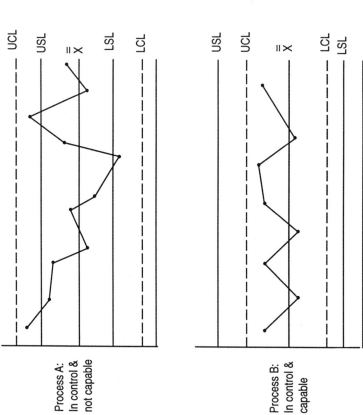

FIGURE 9.6 Relationship between control limits and specifications

ESTABLISH &
REFINE THE
PROCESS

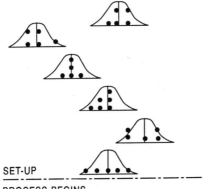

SET-UP

PROCESS BEGINS

DEFINE &
EVALUATE
THE PROCESS
POTENTIAL

Lo Spec   Hi Spec

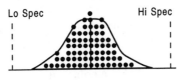

MINI-CAPABILITY STUDY
• 25 consecutive cycles
  1 part/cavity
• Measure each critical
  dimension
• Stability:
  Cavity to cavity
    differences
  Capability, short term
    ±4 99.994%

MAINTAIN
THE PROCESS

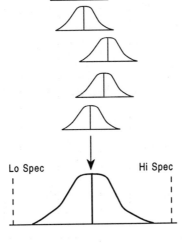

ONGOING PROCESS
CONTROL
• Randomly select
  5 parts hourly
• Xbar and R chart

CERTIFY
THE PROCESS

Lo Spec   Hi Spec

PROCESS CAPABILITY ANALYSIS
• Select probability
  distribution; normal,
  Pearsonian, etc.
• Estimate % out of spec.
  Compare estimate with
  mini-capability; note &
  explain discrepancies
• Accept/reject lot or
  portions; ship parts
  with data to customer
• Customer confirms
  capability & accepts
  product

FIGURE 9.7 Overview of process control and capability

we use probability theory since specifications do not help. The reason for using probability instead of specifications is that:

- Control charts are process dependent

- Specifications are customer dependent

In addition to this dichotomy, specifications do not rate stability or control of a process.

Control Limits

In designing control charts, one of the critical decisions is to specify the control limits. Moving the limits further from the center line decreases the risk of a type I error. In this context, there is a risk that a point will fall beyond the control limits (out-of-control condition) when no assignable cause is present. In addition to a type I error, the risk of a type II error also increases as the limits are widened. In this context, there is a risk that a point will fall between the control limits when the process is really out of control (Montgomery 1985). If the limits are moved closer to the center line, the opposite effect results (i.e., the risk of a type I error increases, while the risk of a type II error decreases).

The convention in the United States is that control limits are based upon a multiple of the standard deviation. This standard deviation is plus (+) or minus (−) 3σ and is called the 3-sigma limit (Duncan 1986).

Even though 99% of the distribution is accounted for, there are situations where 99% assurance is not good enough. Examples are abundant in the banking, hospitality, pharmaceutical, medical, food, electronic, and other industries. To put this in context, consider the following. At 99% assurance, there is:

- 200,000 wrong prescriptions per year

- No telephone or television 15 minutes per day

- Nine misspelled words on every page of a magazine

- No electricity, water, or heat 15 minutes per day

- Unsafe water 4 days per year

Control Chart Goals

All control charts—both variable (measurable) and attribute—are utilized to detect change(s) in a process. Specifically, a control chart will:

1. **Find unusual process change.** It will find the cause of special variation. You must always react to this kind of variation. Remember, how-

ever, that just because there is change does not mean that the change is bad. In fact, the change could be an improvement. If so, record it and try to repeat it.

2. **Define the process norm.** Once consistency has been achieved, the process (system) is working as it was designed to. At this point, systematic changes can be introduced as needed to improve the system.

3. **Identify characteristics that will provide answers to specific problems.** The source of identification may be the customer (via specifications), regulatory agencies (via safety items), and/or internal concerns (via the team process) for continual improvement.

4. **Identify the earliest production point at which testing may be done to confirm assignable causes.** This may be done with the help of a process flowchart.

5. **Choose the type of control chart.** This may be done once the characteristics of the process have been identified. Figure 9.8 illustrates the selection process.

6. **Choose appropriate sampling techniques.** This will allow you to make sound decisions about the process. The idea here is to recognize the variation but to spread it throughout in such a way that the sampling is indeed random and a true representation of the process under study. Special consideration should be given to the following:

- Equal time intervals

- Equal quantities of product produced

- Representation of subgroups (composition, size, and frequency)

- System for collecting data

Control Chart Development

A general process for developing and reading a control chart is as follows.

Normalize the process. This is one of the most important stages in control charting. Here, all concerned try to solve the clear-cut problems first, recognize the customer's specifications, record *all* key process events, and keep a log of the process. This log becomes part of the production task and will facilitate studying the process in a stable and unchanging operation.

State the purpose of the control chart. Unless the purpose is known ahead of time, the choice of control chart may be the wrong one. There are two basic groupings for control charts:

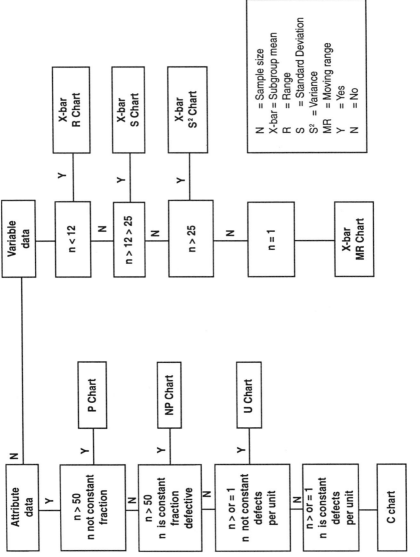

FIGURE 9.8 Guide for choosing control charts

- Variable
- Attribute

Some examples of each type are:

Data Type	Chart Type	Plotted Values
Attributes	p chart	Proportion defective
	c chart	Number of defects
	np chart	Number of defective units
	u chart	Average number of defects
Variables	Xbar and R chart	Sample mean and range
	Xbar and S chart	Sample mean, standard deviation
	Median and R chart	Median and range
	X and moving R chart	Individual observation and moving range

The variable-type chart needs the following:

- Measured data
- Detailed information
- Skillful reading of data

In addition, it is characteristic specific, uses small samples (three to ten measurements per subgroup, five being the most common), and warns the user of any changes in the process. Such a chart would be used to:

1. Learn about special variation
2. Judge whether or not the process is fit to meet specifications (again, this is a capability concern)
3. Know when to accept input
4. Determine the need to change measurement methods
5. Learn how to improve the process over time

The attribute-type chart, on the other hand, needs:

- Large sample size
- Count-type data

In addition, it sums up the overall quality level, is easy to make and read, and is less responsive to changes in the process. Such a chart would be used to:

1. Define the reject rate

2. Spot a specific quality level in the process

3. Find the average quality changes on rates in the process

4. Find possible uses for variable-type charts

Collect data from the process.   Before actually starting to collect data, the characteristic of the study must be chosen. The exact feature must be determined and made the focus of the control chart. Once this has been done, then you are ready to collect the data. Consideration should be given to the following:

1. **Customer concerns:**   This is the top priority. If neglected, the organization may in fact go out of business if the customer is not satisfied. The customer here means the next operation in line or the end user. The customer's concerns may be identified via past experiences and/or definition of critical characteristics. By definition, the critical characteristics should be charted.

2. **Process waste:**   Find the biggest and costliest problems by utilizing Pareto charts. Examples of waste are scrap, rework, inventory, etc.

3. **Causal links:**   Use scatter diagrams. Studying causal links in a process sometimes gives feedback faster than measuring the process results.

4. **Points of data collection:**   They should be early in the process, so that they are the leading signs of quality outcomes. A process flowchart may be helpful to identify such points.

5. **Sampling plan:**   The sample size and frequency should be thought out at some length before the actual collection begins. The sample size should be weighted against the risk. A large sample will be sensitive to changes. This is called confidence. However, it is costly to carry out. A smaller sample size may cost less but it risks weak control. The type of data is a second consideration. Variable data are more efficient and contain more information per measurement; therefore, they can use smaller samples. A constant sample size is recommended for variable control charts. Attribute data are not as efficient as variable data and need a larger size to get the same confidence.

   There must be three to five defective parts in each subgroup. Not all attribute-type control charts need equal subgroups. Examples are p and u charts. Those most quickly produced do need equal sample sizes. Examples are np and c charts.

When frequency is considered, do not lose sight of the goal of the control chart, which is to find important changes in the process over time. Therefore, the time between samples is important. The time interval should be small enough that differences between subgroups are identified, while at the same time differences between selected and unselected subgroups are very minor. The frequency for sampling usually takes the form of 100% sampling at the beginning of the study; as information and confidence are gained, the amount of time between samples is increased. If time is not a good indicator for sampling, then consider production volume in its place. This will give a good and steady sampling frequency.

Measurement error.   When a control chart is developed, care must be taken to ensure that a standard task is plotted and the data always have the same meaning for everyone. When there are differences in measurement, then there is an error somewhere in the system (the operator, the process itself, or the measurement instrument). Too much error will cause problems in identifying the source as well as the solution to the problem(s). In addition, this error will make the control chart miss meaningful changes in the process.

Because of the importance of measurement error in the control charting process, it is imperative to adhere to the following:

- Collect the data steadily

- Collect the data honestly

- Take enough time

- Have the right training

- Have the right measurement instruments

Calculate control limits from the process data.   Control limits are process dependent and therefore come from process data. Control limits show how much variation to expect if only common variation exists in the process. Control limits are not specifications. The actual calculations may be found in Gitlow et al. (1989) and Grant and Leavenworth (1980).

Study process variation for stability and control.   The process must have all the points within the control limits and must follow a random pattern (see Figure 9.5a). When these two conditions are not met, something is happening in the process. The system is out of control. Study the *why* and understand it. A process that is out of control is not stable because it is not following the expected pattern. Be careful, however, because not all out-of-control conditions are bad. If the out-of-control conditions are good, make them part of the process; if they are bad, identify them and then systematically eliminate them.

Study the process data for capability.   Process capability compares the estimated distribution of a product to specifications. Currently, a capable process is said to be when 99.73% of the population is within specifications. In the near future, this percentage is expected to increase to 99.94%. It is important to recognize that unless the process is stable and in control, you cannot talk about capability. As the process becomes out of control, different characteristics are encountered. It is useless to estimate their capability levels because each individual set of data will have its own capability. No generalization is possible, since the study has zero (0) confidence.

Plan to continue the process improvement.   Control charts are only a tool to help in both planning and continuing the improvement process. This improvement, however, must be developed as a habit and worked into the process on a regular basis. You must plan, schedule, and evaluate the improvement so that the customer is satisfied. Improvement work goes on even when every part of the process is within specifications. The goal here is to reduce common variation until the process achieves (nears) the best possible distribution.

Control Chart Interpretation

Common variation.   A process with only common variation is predictable, consistent, and stable. A process under these conditions is said to be in control. An example of such a process is displayed in the control chart in Figure 9.5a.

Looking at this control chart, it is easy to see that all points are within the control limits and follow a random pattern. This is the ideal and very desirable condition in every control chart.

Special variation.   Unlike common (inherent) variation, a process may also have variation due to some special cause. This means that some part of the operation has changed in some degree and/or fashion. In other words, the present process is not part of the old one. This change shows up on a control chart by the following signals:

1. **Points beyond control limits:**   When this shows up on the chart, it means that the sample was collected from at least two different distributions of the process. Again, note that a change in the process may in fact be an improvement. The point is that this condition should be investigated and appropriately recorded in the process log.

2. **Run of seven points:**   Even though all the points in the distribution are within the limits, this condition on a control chart shows that there has been a shift in the process average. That shift may be above or below the average and it must contain at least seven points in a row. When this happens, it is called a run. This is a special case and it should be highlighted on the control chart itself. If it continues for at least 25 subgroups, the process has changed enough to recalculate the limits and the process average. An example of a run is shown in Figure 9.5b.

3. **Trend of seven points:**   A trend is a special run of seven points that increase or decrease steadily. Think of it as drift in the process setting. Depending on the drift, an increasing trend is called a "run-up," whereas a decreasing trend is called a "run-down." An example of a trend is shown in Figure 9.5c.

    Note that in this special case, there are two signals of concern: (1) the downward trend and (2) the run below the process average. It is not uncommon to have more than one signal in a control chart.

4. **Cycle of points:**   A cycle is a repetition of a pattern. It may have more than one cause and is very easy to spot as well as correct. One of the easiest ways to solve a cycling problem is to study the process through a process flowchart or a team effort approach. An example of a cycle is shown in Figure 9.5d

5. **Unusual variation or stratification of hugging:**   This is one of the most difficult signals to spot because it is easy to misinterpret as a good chart. The cause of this signal is not in the variation of the process, but rather it may be in the sampling itself or the scale of the plotting. It is very important to note that in looking at the chart, the first impression is that it is "too good to be true" or "something is just not right." From a statistical point of view, this is referred to as a zone control problem. There are two main reasons for this unusual variation:

    • Basic changes have occurred in the process

    • Process streams have had an effect on the overall process

    An example of unusual variation is shown in Figure 9.5e. An example of stratification is shown in Figure 9.5f.

Zone control refers to a control chart divided into three equal zones (each zone is one standard deviation). Zone control is shown in Figure 9.5g. In zone control analysis, take note of and examine what has changed and possibly make a process adjustment if there are:

1. Two points out of three successive points on the same side of the center line in zone A or beyond

2. Four points out of five successive points on the same side of the center line in zone B or beyond

3. Seven successive points on one side of the center line

4. Seven successive points increasing or decreasing

5. Fourteen points in a row alternating up and down

6. Fifteen points in a row within zone C (above and below the center line)

REFERENCES

Berwick, D. M., Godfrey, A. B., and Roessner, J. (1990). *Curing Health Care*. Jossey-Bass, San Francisco.

Brassard, M. (1989). *The Memory Jogger Plus*. GOAL/QPC, Methuen, Mass.

Burr, J. T. (1989). *SPC: Tools for Operators*. Quality Press, Milwaukee.

Duncan, A. J. (1986). *Quality Control and Industrial Statistics*. Irwin, Homewood, Ill.

Feldman, D. and Arnold, H. J. (1983). *Managing Individual and Group Behavior in Organizations*. McGraw-Hill, New York.

Ford (1987). *Team Oriented Problem Solving* (2nd Ed.). Power Train Operations, Ford Motor Company, Detroit.

Fulmer, R. M. (1974). *The New Management*. MacMillan, New York.

Gitlow, H., Gitlow, S., Oppenheim, A., and Oppenheim, R. (1989). *Tools and Methods for the Improvement of Quality*. Irwin, Boston.

Grant, E. T. and Leavenworth, R. S. (1980). *Statistical Quality Control*. McGraw-Hill, New York.

Hays, W. (1981). *Statistics* (3rd Ed.). Holt, Rinehart and Winston, New York.

Ishikawa, K. (1987) *Guide to Quality Control*. Kraus International, White Plains, N.Y.

Juran, J. M. (Ed.) (1979). *Quality Control Handbook* (3rd Ed.). McGraw-Hill, New York.

Kepner, C. H. and Tregoe, B. B. (1981). *The New Rational Manager*. Kepner-Tregoe, Princeton, N.J.

Likert, R. (1961). *New Patterns of Management*. McGraw-Hill, New York.

Mizuno, S. (1988). *Management for Quality Control: The Seven New QC Tools*. Productivity Press, Cambridge, Mass.

Montgomery, D. C. (1985). *Statistical Quality Control*. John Wiley & Sons, New York.

Osborn, A. F. (1963). *Applied Imagination*. Charles Scribner's Sons, New York.

Palm, W. J. (1983). *Modeling, Analysis and Control of Dynamic Systems*. John Wiley & Sons, New York.

Parsaye, K. and Chingnell, M. H. (September 1993). "The Eighth, Ninth and 10th Tools of Quality." *Quality Progress*.

Rowe, H. A. H. (1985). *Problem Solving and Intelligence*. Lawrence Erlbaum Associates, Hillsdale, N.J.

Ryan, B. F., Joiner, B. L., and Ryan T. A. (1985). *Minitab: Handbook* (2nd Ed. rev.). PWS-Kent, Boston.

Summers, I. and Major, D. E. (1976). "Creativity Techniques: Toward Improvement of the Decision Process." *Academy of Management Review*. Vol. 1, p. 193.

Tribus, M. (1989). *Deployment Flow Charting*. Quality and Productivity, Los Angeles.

Whiting, C. S. (1958). *Creative Thinking*. Holt-Reinhold, New York.

10

ISO AND SERVICES

This chapter addresses the quality system in terms of the ISO quality standards for the service industry. Our focus in addressing ISO 9004-2 is to show that indeed all services can and should follow the building blocks of quality as identified by the ISO structure.

OVERVIEW OF THE GUIDELINES

The ISO 9000 series is a bundle of standards that define quality in minimum terms and allow an organization to deal in international markets. Within the structure of ISO, there are certifiable and noncertifiable standards. The certifiable standards are ISO 9001, ISO 9002, and ISO 9003. All others provide the rationale, support, interpretation, and general guidelines for the certifiable standards.

Therefore, it is important to recognize that ISO 9004-2 is not a certifiable standard. Nor it is a prescriptive standard. Rather, it is a guideline for all services to follow in their quality quest for continual improvement. The guideline provides the basic blocks of quality for all services and encourages them to focus on customer satisfaction. Some of the criteria identified in the guidelines may not apply to your own organization.

The guidelines provide a very systematic path for defining service, delivery, and how an organization can go about improving its quality system in the short and long term. All services can be included, if they are indeed interested in quality. All services can be improved, if they focus on the customer and the customer's needs. The ISO structure provides the path for that improvement. Examples of service industries which can be active participants in ISO are:

Hospitality services	Financial
Health services	Communications
Professional	Administration
Maintenance	Technical
Purchasing	Scientific
Trading	Utilities

QUALITY MANAGEMENT AND QUALITY SYSTEM ELEMENTS

The focus of this section is to review and summarize each of the clauses in the guidelines and to provide the reader with the structure and a general overview of what service quality is all about from the ISO perspective.

Section 1: Scope.   This guideline establishes the need for implementing a quality system in the service industry.

Section 2: Normative references.   This guideline provides for the references which are used to define service quality.

Section 3: Definitions.   In this section the specific vocabulary for the service is defined based on ISO 8402. ISO 8402 is the accepted *dictionary* of the ISO language. It is highly recommended that upon embarking on implementation of either TQS or ISO, an organization should have a copy of that document.

Section 4: Characteristics of services.   In this section, the guideline provides an overview of what service and service delivery characteristics are all about. Furthermore, this section defines the control of services and service delivery characteristics.

Section 5: Quality system principles.   This section delineates the key aspects of the quality system and identifies each of the components as:

- Management responsibility
- Quality system structure
- Personnel and material resources
- Interface with customers

Section 6: Quality system operational elements

Section 6.1: Marketing process

Section 6.1.1: Quality in market research and analysis. This section defines the responsibility of marketing and promotes the need and demand for service. The clause also expects management to establish procedures for planning and implementing market activities. In addition, it identifies the following as associated elements:

- Establishment of customer needs
- Complementary services
- Competitor analysis
- Review of appropriate legislation and standards
- Analysis and review of customer requirements
- Consultation with all affected functions to confirm the commitment and ability to meet service quality
- Ongoing research to examine changing market needs
- Appropriate application of quality assurance/control

Section 6.1.2: Supplier obligations. This clause requires supplier obligations to customers to be noted and communicated to the service organization and the customer. The obligations should be consistent with:

- Related quality documentation
- Supplier capability
- Relevant regulatory requirements

Section 6.1.3: Service brief. This clause reiterates the need for a definition of the customer's needs and the capability of the organization to provide the identified needs.

Section 6.1.4: Service management. This clause defines the responsibility of management in terms of:

- Development and withdrawal of the service

- Ensuring appropriate resource allocation

- Planning

Section 6.1.5: Quality in advertising. This clause reflects the requirement of *customer's perception* as a service specification and recognizes the liability of offering exaggerated or unsubstantiated claims for the service.

Section 6.2: Design process

Section 6.2.1: General. This clause delineates the concept of service brief. Specifically, it defines the service to be provided, delivered, and controlled.

Section 6.2: Design responsibilities. The clause defines specific responsibilities to management such as:

- Planning, preparation, validation, maintenance, and control

- Specifying products and services to be produced

- Implementing design reviews for each phase of the service design

- Validating that the service delivery process meets the requirements

- Updating the service specification

In addition to design responsibilities, it is important to recognize the service, quality, and delivery specifications during the design. Specific considerations may be in the area of:

- Plan for variations

- Create a "what if" scenario with both systematic and random failures

- Develop contingency plans

Section 6.2.3: Service specification. This clause identifies the need for clarity in the description of the service and allows for standardized acceptability for each of the service characteristics.

Section 6.2.4: Service delivery specification

Section 6.2.4.1: General. This clause defines the requirements of delivery. Specifically, it identifies guidelines for optimum results, such as:

- A clear description

- A standard of acceptability

- Resource requirements

- Skills of personnel required

- Reliance on sub-subcontractors

Needless to say, these guidelines should follow both delivery specifications as well as legal requirements for health, safety, and the environment.

Section 6.2.4.2: Service delivery procedures. This clause provides for flexibility in the service to subdivide the process into separate work phases.

Section 6.2.4.3: Quality procurement. This section provides some strong guidelines for the requirements of procured products and services. Some of these guidelines are:

- Purchase orders should provide for descriptions and/or specifications

- Selection of qualified subcontractors

- Agreement on quality requirements

- Provision for disputes

- Incoming product and service controls

- Incoming product and service quality records

In addition to the general guidelines, this clause provides some parameters for selecting a subcontractor:

- On-site assessment and evaluation of the subcontractor

- Evaluation of subcontractor samples

- Past history of subcontractor

- Test results of similar subcontractors

- Experience of other users

Section 6.2.4.4: Supplier-provided equipment to customers for service and service delivery. This clause states that when supplier equipment is provided, it must be suitable for its purpose and written instructions must be given, as required, for its use.

Section 6.2.4.5: Service identification and traceability. This clause reminds us about the awesome responsibility of identification and traceability.

Section 6.2.4.6: Handling, storage, packaging, delivery, and protection of customer's possessions. This clause reiterates the need for effective controls for the handling, storage, packaging, delivery, and protection of the customer's possessions for which the service organization is responsible.

Section 6.2.5: Quality control specification. This clause defines the scope of quality in service and provides specific guidelines for the appropriate design of quality control specification.

Section 6.2.6: Design review. This clause reminds us of the need for design review against the service brief. The design review should be consistent with and capable of satisfying the requirements of:

- Items in the service specification

- Items in the service delivery

- Items in the quality control

Participants at each design review should include representatives of all the functions that affect service quality. The design review should anticipate problem areas and inadequacies and initiate actions to ensure that:

- All specifications meet the customer's requirements

- The quality control specification is adequate to provide accurate information about the quality of service delivered

Section 6.2.7: Validation of the service, service delivery, and quality control specifications. This clause defines when and how validation should be carried out and under what conditions. In addition, it recommends that validation should confirm that:

- The service is consistent with customer requirements

- The service delivery process is complete

- Resources are available to meet the service obligations

- All applicable codes, practices, and standards are satisfied

- Information to customers in the use of the service is available

Section 6.2.8: Design change control. This clause not only defines the objective of design change control but also recommends several points to ensure it. The points are:

- Know the need for change
- Plan changes
- Appropriate personnel always participate in the functions affected by the change
- Notification of customers when changes will affect them
- The impact of change should be evaluated

Section 6.3: Service delivery process

Section 6.3.1: General. This clause reiterates the need for management to assign specific responsibilities to all personnel implementing the service delivery process.

Section 6.3.2: Supplier's assessment of service quality. This clause emphasizes the need for quality to be part of the operation of the service delivery process. This includes:

- Measurement and verification
- Self-inspection
- A final supplier assessment

Section 6.3.3: Customer's assessment of service quality. This clause reiterates the importance of the customer's assessment and indicates that unless measures are taken to identify and measure the quality of a service, there may be some customer reaction.

Section 6.3.4: Service status. All work done should be recorded to identify the achievement of the service specification and customer satisfaction.

Section 6.3.5: Corrective action for nonconforming services

Section 6.3.5.1: Responsibilities. This clause puts the responsibility on each individual to identify and report all nonconforming services. Corrective action should be defined appropriately.

Section 6.3.5.2: Identification of nonconformity and corrective action. This clause recommends that nonconformities, when detected, should be recorded and action should be taken to analyze and correct them.

Section 6.3.6: Measurement system control. This clause emphasizes the need for establishing, monitoring, and maintaining procedures for service measurement.

Section 6.4: Service performance analysis and improvement

Section 6.4.1: General. This clause discusses the need for continual evaluation of the operation of the service processes which should be practiced to identify and actively pursue opportunities for service quality improvement.

Section 6.4.2: Data collection and analysis. This clause emphasizes that the decisions of the service organization should be based on data from the service operation.

Section 6.4.3: Statistical methods. The use of statistical methods is encouraged in this clause, as well as processes that are in control and capable.

Section 6.4.4: Service quality improvement. This clause recommends the existence of programs that support the continual improvement process in service quality, including an effort to identify:

- The most important characteristics to the customer

- Any changing market needs

- Any deviations in a specific service

- Opportunities for reducing cost

The activities recommended in this clause address the need for both short-term and long-term improvements and include:

- Identifying relevant data

- Data analysis

- Reporting periodically to senior management

IMPLEMENTATION OF THE ISO STANDARDS IN THE SERVICE INDUSTRY

The implementation process for the ISO standards in any service industry is exactly the same as in any other organization. The basic steps for implementation are the same as those identified in Chapter 5. For more detail on implementation strategies, see Stamatis (1995), Peach (1994), and Lamprecht (1993, 1994).

REFERENCES

ISO 9001:1994, Quality systems—Model for quality assurance in design/development, production, installation and servicing.

ISO 9002:1994, Quality systems—Model for quality assurance in production and installation.

ISO 9003:1994, Quality systems—Model for quality assurance in final inspection and test.

ISO 10011-1:1990, Guidelines for auditing quality systems—Part 1: Auditing.

ISO 10011-2:1991, Guidelines for auditing quality systems—Part 2: Qualification criteria for quality systems auditors.

ISO 10011-3:1991, Guidelines for auditing quality systems—Part 3: Management of audit programs.

ISO 10012-1:1991, Quality assurance requirements for measuring equipment—Part 1: Management of measuring equipment.

Lamprecht, J. L. (1993). *Implementing the ISO 9000 Series.* Quality Press, Milwaukee.

Lamprecht, J. L. (1994). *ISO 9000 and the Service Sector: A Critical Interpretation of the 1994 Revisions.* Quality Press, Milwaukee.

Peach, R. (Ed.) (1994). *The ISO 9000 Handbook* (2nd Ed.). CEEM, Fairfax, Va.

Stamatis, D. H. (1995). *ISO 9000 Implementation and the Basic Blocks to Quality.* Marcel Dekker, New York.

APPENDIX A

HOW TO DESIGN, IMPLEMENT, AND MANAGE A SUPERIOR CUSTOMER SERVICE PROGRAM

This appendix provides a practical generic program for developing a superior customer service program.

I.   Elements of a superior customer service program
A.   The service imperative
1.   Define your business as service
2.   Manage the flow of external and internal information flows
3.   Treat complaints as opportunities
B.   Is the customer always right?
1.   Develop a written service mission statement
2.   Set realistic service standards
3.   Understand and control dissatisfaction
II. Develop the right service strategy
A.   Internalize what you are all about
1.   You cannot be all things to all people
2.   Keep abreast of competitive service programs

        3. Develop a professional orientation toward service

    B. Plan for service quality

III. Establish the service program

    A. Define the program

        1. Provide appropriate incentives for customer service

        2. Audit customers on a regular basis

        3. Use the audit information in a positive way

    B. Define the tools

        1. Benchmarking

        2. Surveys

        3. Focus groups

IV. How to use customer service as a weapon

    A. Stress consistency throughout the service cycle

        1. For your own people

        2. For your marketing and salespeople

        3. For third parties

    B. Use audit information to generate opportunities

        1. Gain and hold versus buy and lose

        2. Impact of customer service on sales volume

            a. High volumes

            b. Improved customer relations

            c. Possibility of repeat business

            d. Greater customer referral

        3. Use service information for market opportunities

            a. Build market share

            b. Crack new accounts

            c. Find new market niches

    C. Customer service as a profit center

        1. Profit center versus cost center

        2. Customer service as a profit center

V. Setting service standards for service performance

    A. Factors for service success

        1. Problem solving

        2. Quick recovery systems

        3. Spontaneous people

        4. People who CARE:

           C credible

           A attractive

           R responsive

           E empathetic

    B. Strategies for keeping abreast of the competition

        1. Hire away competitive personnel

        2. Use of sales force

        3. Talk to your customers

        4. Internal monitoring of competitive service programs

    C. Seek best organizational position for customer service

VI. Customer service quality and improvement

    A. Continually differentiate your service from the competition

        1. Primary

        2. Secondary

    B. Do Task Breakdown Structure (TBS) analysis of your service cycle

        1. Task breakdown structure analysis

        2. Performance standards

        3. Job descriptions

        4. Customer service manual

    C. Set service standards

        1. Know your customer service operation

        2. Know what has to be monitored

        3. Know what can be monitored

        4. Know what levels of performance are realistic from the customer's perspective

        5. Know what level your people will accept

VII. Can you teach change?

    A. Manage stress

        1. Employee recognition programs

        2. Day off

        3. No-phone hour

        4. Quite room

        5. Dress-down day

        6. Visit a customer site

        7. Dinner out

        8. Mirrors at desks

        9. Gymnasiums

    B. Develop a customer service plan

        1. Strategic plan: six months to a year

        2. Tactical plan: three to six months

        3. Operational plan: one to three months

        4. Establish mission statement and identify support elements

        5. Perform a company service scan

           a. Internal service cycle

           b. External service cycle

        6. Develop a tactical plan

        7. Develop the operational plan

        8. Establish customer service standards

    9. Review and establish controls

  10. Formalize and update plan

C. Handle customer queries in a professional way

    1. Identify and classify complaints

    2. Do not overlook negative word of mouth

    3. Do not be intimidated when handling a complaint
   - Have no fear of customer's organizational position
   - Placing the blame is not important—finding the solution is the key

    4. Do not panic because of problem severity
   - Avoid excess sympathy with the problem
   - Treat all complaints objectively
   - Do not become emotionally involved

    5. **Do not always assume customer information is correct**
   - Many problems are caused by customers because they do not understand the product or service or how to use it or apply it
   - Have your own people investigate the problem before developing a solution
   - Contrary to public wisdom, the customer is not always right

    6. Explain complaint procedures

    7. Stay away from familiar problem-solution syndrome

    8. Reassure customer and follow up
   - Always act concerned about a customer's problem
   - Customer goodwill can be lost if a customer service representative (CSR) does not sound concerned about a problem, no matter how minor it may be
   - Always report back to the customer as to what action is being taken to solve a problem; even if you only have a few things to report, a callback measures a firm's service orientation
   - All customers expect to hear back from a firm

    9. Preserve the customer's right of appeal
   - Set up an appeal mechanism for customer complaints
   - Do not insulate top management from customer problems
   - Executive action should only be used if the problem cannot be resolved at a lower level
   - Provide customers with the information they need to handle complaints for the types of products they buy from your firm

  10. Tell the customer how to complain, including consumers
   - Can save the organization money
   - Create goodwill
   - Make the customer complaint procedure convenient
   - Let the customer know who to talk to or call

- Avoid personal on-site visits by customers to complain
11. Set criteria for automatic adjustment of small items
    - Avoid investigating problems involving small sums of money or replacement of small quantities of the product
    - Avoid small problems reaching the supervisory level—they create unnecessary paperwork and are a poor use of management time
    - Delegate minor problem resolution to CSRs (a dollar value or quantity can be used to determine the level of delegation)
12. When handling a complaint, be sure you are talking to the right person
    - When seeking a solution, talk to the person who made the complaint
    - Complaints are frequently routed through several layers in a firm's organization
    - Before getting to the manager who can work out a solution, a lot of time and resources can be wasted
13. Capitalize on the hidden value of complaints
    - Supporting a proposal—a high incidence of customer complaints about a specific problem can often be turned into an advantage by justifying expenditures for training, improved information systems, changes in ordering procedure, lead times, and so on
    - Educating customers—a complaint can be used to educate customers about new procedures; a customer who complains is highly motivated to listen
    - Winning friends—a complaint properly handled cements relations and makes lasting relationships
D. Motivate your people to be service oriented
    1. View customer service in a positive way
    2. Get top management involvement
    3. Recognize good service performance
    4. Hold in-house service seminars put on by customers
    5. Develop a mission statement and communicate it throughout the organization
    6. Promote good service performance by employees
    7. Emphasize that excellent service performance impacts the bottom line
    8. Give all employees ownership in the customer service effort—empower them
    9. Spell out the role of each department in the customer service effort

APPENDIX B

KEY COMPONENTS OF CUSTOMER SERVICE

This appendix provides a partial list of factors that define customer service.

Frequency of delivery

Time from order to delivery

Reliability of delivery

Emergency deliveries when required

Stock availability and continuity of supply

Orders filled completely

Advice on nonavailability

Convenience of placing order

Acknowledgment of order

Accuracy of invoices

Quality of sales representation

Regular calls by sales representatives

Manufacturer monitoring of retail stock levels

Credit terms offered

Handling customer queries

Well-stacked pallets

Easy-to-read use-by dates on outer packaging

Quality of inner package for in-store handling and display

Consults on new product/package development

Review product range regularly

Coordination between production, distribution, and marketing

APPENDIX C

HOW TO ESTABLISH
A CUSTOMER SERVICE PLAN
FOR YOUR COMPANY

This appendix provides the sequence for a generic plan for customer service.

Step 1. Establish mission statement and support elements (system)

Establish a mission statement and a support system that will differentiate your company from other organizations.

Step 2. Company scan

A. **External cycle of service:** Diagram the cycle of service and include all points of contact between the external customers and company personnel.

B. **Internal cycle of service:** Diagram the internal service and include all of the critical points of contact between internal customers. This means the departments that are involved with customer service. The scanning (evaluation) may be performed with either process mapping and/or process flowcharts.

Step 3. Perform a comparison analysis

A. **Using a comparison analysis:** Scan the company to determine the strengths, weaknesses, opportunities, and threats facing your competition and the individual operating companies. The comparison process is divided into separate sections:

 1. **Strengths:** Identify any service area that the company of comparison excels in.

 2. **Weaknesses:** Identify those internal areas where service weaknesses may exist.

 3. **Opportunities:** Identify market opportunities where your organization may be able to apply.

 4. **Threats:** Identify any market challenges or threats from competitors, government, and so on that may exist and must be considered in developing the service plan.

B. **The comparison:** It is not necessary to compare your organization with your competition. What is necessary is to perform the comparison with the best at the time. The idea is to learn as much as possible from the best and then transfer that knowledge to your organization. The process can be represented as follows:

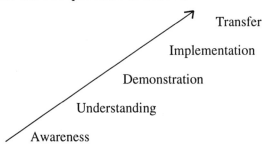

Some companies that your organization may want to compare its customer service with are:

Federal Express	American Express
Nordstrom	Dayton
Boeing	McDonald's
Rubbermaid	Caterpillar
Hewlett-Packard	American Standard

As part of this step, conduct a service audit to determine what customers currently think of your service and that of your competitors. This information can then be used as a basis for developing the tactical plan.

Step 4. Tactical plan

A. Establish specific goals and objectives for the organization.

B. Lay out the organizational structure of the program.

Step 5. Operational plan

A. Spell out the resources necessary to achieve the objectives in Step 4. For example: manpower, budget, and systems.

B. Lay out the specific strategies and programs that will be used. For example: 800 'numbers, customer advisory panels, and so on.

C. Establish an incentive scheme for rewarding good service performance and meeting service goals.

Step 6. Establish customer service standards

A. List areas as shown in the cycle of service (Step 2) that are to be monitored.

B. Establish a monitoring mechanism.

C. Set service standards based on customer audit results developed in Step 2.

Step 7. Review and control

Measure service performance based on standards established in Step 6.

Step 8. Formalize and update plan

Review preliminary results and compare actual performance to standards. Update the plan and change service standards if needed.

APPENDIX D

THE CUSTOMER SERVICE TEST

This test will provide you with a cursory overview of where your organization is "right now" in terms of customer service. This test is not meant to be an in-depth analysis of the organization; rather, it provides a "quick and dirty" evaluation. For a more in-depth analysis, contact a consultant and/or develop your own measurement instrument.

Directions: Read each question thoroughly. After reading each question, evaluate it based on a scale of 1 to 5 (1 = low, 5 = high). Write down your evaluation.

1. Are your front-line service employees caring? _____

2. Is your top management service oriented? _____

3. Is customer service seen as a positive force? _____

4. Are your front-line service employees empowered to solve problems? _____

5. Is customer service a dead-end position in your company? _____

6. Do the other departments in your organization understand the function of the customer service function? _____

7. Does the sales force in your company frequently overstate   _____
what customer service can do for customers?

8. Do you audit your customers on a regular basis (at   _____
least twice a year)?

9. Do you set customer service standards to ensure consis-   _____
tent service performance?

10. How successful have you been in managing the stress   _____
level in customer service?

11. Do your service personnel understand how customer ser-   _____
vice impacts the bottom line?

12. How cooperative is your top management in giving cus-   _____
tomer service the resources it needs to handle the service
responsibility?

13. Do you have a customer service mission statement?   _____

14. How well do your service personnel handle customer ser-   _____
vice queries and complaints?

The following question is worth 2 points if you respond yes
and 1 point if you respond no.

15. Do you have an incentive system for customer service?

                                 Yes (2 points)   _____

                                  No (1 point)   _____

Score: Add all the points together. Place the total here.   _____

The total points will determine your organization's orientation toward customer
service.

72–65	Superior customer service
64–50	Good customer service
49–40	Fair customer service
39–15	Poor customer service

APPENDIX E

HOW TO IDENTIFY
THE CURRENT CONDITION

This appendix provides a structure and a set of questions to determine the current status of a process and provide information to evaluate it appropriately.

1. Using a flowchart or map process, study the:
    *   Process steps
    *   Process inputs
    *   Process outputs
    *   Process interfaces
    *   Process feedback loops

2. Ask the following questions about all of the above:
    *   Are any components missing?
    *   Are any unnecessary or misdirected? Do they add value?
    *   Can anything be improved? Where? How?
    *   Can anything be simplified or standardized?

3. Identify root cause(s) of all areas of concern.

4. Label all areas of concern and try to develop a matrix of relationships.

5. Group all areas of concern and plan for appropriate action.

APPENDIX F

A GENERIC CONTINUAL IMPROVEMENT TOOL MATRIX

In Chapter 9, the six steps in the problem-solving process were identified as:

1. Identify and define the problem

2. Generate alternative solutions

3. Evaluate the alternative solutions

4. Decision making

5. Implement the decision

6. Follow up and evaluate the decision

In this appendix, these steps are referenced and some of the most common tools for continuous improvement in service organizations are indicated. The list is not exhaustive, but it provides the impetus for a starting point to both investigate and resolve specific problems. Note that some of the tools may be used in multiple steps without losing their effectiveness.

Step	*Process*	*Tools*
Preliminary steps	Form a team Cross-functional Multidiscipline Goal oriented Motivated Appropriate training	Team building Facilitator skills Continuous improvement process
1	Identify all services over which you have a direct effect and control	Focus group
	Analyze each service for its impact on the total organization	Role playing Cost–benefit analysis Matrix diagram
	Select one service to be your first project for applying the concepts of quality	Pareto analysis
2	List your customer(s)	
	List all customer requirements	Brainstorming
	Conduct a formal audit, survey, etc. (in person, phone, or written)	Role playing Customer survey Focus group Interview Histogram
	Reconcile/evaluate data	Interview
	Translate each customer requirement into real action plans	QFD
3	Identify the current requirements	Brainstorming Histogram Pareto chart
	Identify standards for each input	Matrix diagram
4	Determine the first starting point	Check sheet
	Identify all entities that are involved in the process from start to end	Process mapping Interview Focus group

Step	Process	Tools
	Create a column of your findings and label it "current"	Process mapping
	Verify this column with the entities that are involved in the process	Focus group
	Identify procedures and instruments to measure the "current" level	Pareto chart Control chart Histograms Cause-and-effect diagram Check sheet
5	Analyze the "current" processes	Sampling Run chart Benchmarking Process evaluation Force field analysis Cause-and-effect diagram Check sheet Control chart Brainstorming Role playing
	Project the "should be" state	Process mapping Benchmarking QFD Focus group Cost–benefit analysis
	Identify or revise measurement instruments to evaluate the "should be" state	Pareto chart Cost–benefit analysis Control charts Run charts Cause-and-effect diagram Sampling
	Review and revise	Focus group
	Implement and evaluate	Interview
6	Monitor process	Use any or all of the tools mentioned in previous steps

APPENDIX **G**

EXAMPLES OF
COST OF QUALITY ITEMS
IN SERVICE

This appendix provides a sample of the items that a service organization may want to monitor. The list is representative rather than exhaustive.

Accounting
Percent of late reports
Incorrect computer input
Errors in specific reports as audited
Percent of significant error in reports; total number of reports

Administrative
Success in maximizing discount opportunities through consolidated ordering
Success in eliminating security violations
Success in effecting pricing actions
Time spent in locating filed material
Percentage of correct purchases

Clerical
Accurate typing, spelling, etc.

Decimal points correctly placed
Correct calculations in bills

Data processing
Rerun time
Computer downtime
Data entry errors
Promptness in output delivery
Effectiveness of scheduling
Program debugging time

Finance
Billing errors
Accounts payable deductions missed
Timeliness of financial reports
Accuracy of predicted budgets
Payroll errors
Discount missed

Forecasting
Are budgets realistic?
Is cash flow appropriate for the needs of the organization?
Methods for finance and cost control
Assets control
Clear operating policies
Completeness of financial reports
Effectiveness of cost negotiations
Assistance to line organizations

Legal
Amount of paper used versus finished pages produced
Misdelivered mail
Misfiled documents
Delays in execution of documents
Patent claims omitted
Response time for request for legal opinion

Marketing
Success in reducing complaints through customer surveys
Success in capturing new business versus quotations
Responsiveness to customer inquiries
Accuracy of marketing forecasts
Responses from news releases and advertisements

Success in response to customer inquiries
Effectiveness of market intelligence
Achieving new order targets
Operation within budgets

Management
Success in minimizing use of overtime operations
Evaluation of capital investment
Errors in applying appropriate standards to processes
Effectiveness of work measurement programs
Effectiveness of reward programs

Material
Savings
Late deliveries
Purchase order errors
Material received against no purchase order
Delays in processing material received
Damaged or lost items
Complaints about improper packing of shipments
Errors in travel arrangements
Accuracy of route and rate information on shipments
Premium freight and/or mail cost
Success in estimating inventory requirements
Items in surplus
Effectiveness of material order follow up
Courteous treatment of customers

Personnel
Hiring effectiveness
Employee turnover
Employee participation in company functions
Effectiveness of administering company programs
Accident prevention record
Processing insurance claims
Accuracy of records

Project management
Quality of proposals
Backlog
Coordination of support activities
Soundness of project plans

Publications
Compliance with requirements
Errors corrected
Thoroughness of material
Quality of production

Quality assurance
Inspection errors
Sampling program errors
Timeliness of reports
Accuracy of supplier quality ratings
Customer complaints

Security
Security error clearance
Accurate processing of visitor identification
Effectiveness of security program

General
Promptness in replying to requests
Quality of service rendered

SELECTED BIBLIOGRAPHY

_____ (March 5, 1990). "Japanese Marketing Strategy Makes 'The Customer King.'" *Insight.*

_____ (March 1992). "Outrageous! Master the Art of Everyday Showmanship." *Success.*

_____ (March 1992). "What's the Bottom Line Payback for TQM." *Journal for Quality and Participation.*

_____ (July 1992). "Executive Skills." *Successful Meetings.*

_____ (October 1993). "Get It Straight from the Customer." *Success.*

_____ (June 1994). "Best-in-the-World Practices." *Training and Development.*

_____ (June 6, 1994). "Dayton's Is Top Retailer in Customer Satisfaction Survey." *Marketing News.*

_____ (August 1994). "Survey Reveals Quality Bonuses." *Quality.*

Aaron, H. B. (1986). "Measure for Measure—An Alternative to Goodness, Motherhood & Morality." Speech given at the conference of Automack Australia, Society of Manufacturing Engineers.

Albrecht, Karl (1990). *Service Advantage: How to Identify and Fulfill Customer Needs.* Dow Jones-Irwin, Homewood, Ill.

Albrecht, K. and Bradford, L. J. (1988). *At America's Service: How Corporations Can Revolutionize the Way They Treat Their Customer.* Dow Jones-Irwin, Homewood, Ill.

Bahl, Don Lee (Ed.) (1987). *Close to the Customer: An American Management Association Research Report on Consumer Affairs.* American Management Association, New York.

Baldwin, L. (January 1990). "Implementing a Software QA System." *Quality Progress.*

Balm, G. (August/September 1993). "Taking Aim at World-Class, Mature Quality." *Continuous Journey.*

Barner, R. (June 1994). "Enablement: The Key to Empowerment." *Training and Development.*

Batson, R. G. (October 1988). "Discovered: Quality's Missing Link." *Quality Progress.*

Bemowski, K. (January 1991). "The Benchmarking Bandwagon." *Quality Progress.*

Berry, Leonard L. et al. (1989). *Service Quality: A Profit Strategy for Financial Institutions.* Dow Jones-Irwin, Homewood, Ill.

Blankenmeier, B. (April 1994). "Quality Management: What's in It for Sales?" *Quality.*

Bleuel, William H. and Bender, H. E. (1980). *Product Service Planning: Service Marketing Engineering Interactions.* American Management Association, New York.

Bolongaro, G. (January 3, 1994). "Delphi Technique Can Work for New Product Development." *Marketing News.*

Booher, D. (June 1988). "Quality or Quantity Communication?" *Quality Progress.*

Booher, D. (August 1994). "Holding Your Own in Meetings, But Working as a Team." *Training and Development.*

Brache, A. P. and Rummler, G. A. (October 1988). "The Three Levels of Quality." *Quality Progress.*

Bridges, K., Hawkins, G., and Elledge, K. (August 1993). "From New Recruit to Team Member." *Training and Development.*

Buffington, P. W. (March 1990). "Hints of Suspicion." *Sky.*

Burke, R. J. (July/August 1969). "Methods of Resolving Interpersonal Conflict." *Personnel Administration.*

Burney, R. (January 1994). "TQM in a Surgery Center." *Quality Progress.*

Camp, R. C. (1995). *Business Process Benchmarking.* Quality Press, Milwaukee.

Carnegie, D. (1981). *How to Win Friends & Influence People.* Simon & Schuster, New York.

Carr, C. (March 1994). "Empowered Organizations, Empowering Leaders." *Training and Development.*

Carroll, S. (January 3, 1994). "Questionnaire Design Affects Response Rate." *Marketing News.*

Carry, M., Kay, B., Orleman, P., Robertshaw, W., Ross, G., Saunders, D., Wallace, W., and Wittenbraker, J. (June 1987). "The Customer Window." *Quality Progress.*

Caruso, T. E. (June 8, 1992). "Kotler: Future Marketers Will Focus on Customer Data Base to Compete Globally." *Marketing News.*

Christopher, Martin (1979). *Customer Service and Distribution Strategy.* John Wiley & Sons, New York.

Clinard, H. H. (1985). *Winning Ways to Succeed with People.* Gulf Publishing, Houston.

Cocheu, T. (1993). *Making Quality Happen: How Training Can Turn Strategy into Lasting Improvement.* Jossey-Bass, San Francisco.

Conlin, J. (February 1993). "Age Old Problem." *Successful Meetings.*

Conti, T. (December 1989). "Process Management and Quality Function Deployment." *Quality Progress.*

Conway, W. E. (January 1988). "The Right Way to Manage." *Quality Progress.*

Cunningham, N. (April 1994). "Deming and the Vindication of Knowledge in the Philosophy of C.S. Lewis." *Quality Management Journal.*

Czepiel, John A. et al. (Eds.) (1985). *The Service Encounter: Managing Employee/ Customer Interaction in Service Business.* Lexington Books, Lexington, Mass.

Davidow, William H. and Uttal, B. (1989). *Total Customer Service: The Ultimate Weapon.* Harper & Row, New York.

DePaulo, P. J. and Weitzer, R. (January 3, 1994). "Interactive Phone Technology Delivers Survey Data Quickly." *Marketing News.*

Desatnick, R. L. (March 1987). Building the Customer-Oriented Work Force." *Training and Development Journal.*

Desatnick, R. L. (1987). *Managing to Keep the Customer.* Jossey-Bass, San Francisco.

Dew, J. R. (November 1993). "A Quality Quest: Cross-Functional Teams." *Quality Digest.*

Dillman, D. A. (1978). *Mail and Telephone Surveys: The Total Design Method.* John Wiley & Sons, New York.

Duff, J. L. (January 1989). "The Structure of the Quality Revolution." *Quality.*

Dunkel, Jaqueline and Taylor, B. (1988). *A Business Guide to Profitable Customer Relations: Today's Techniques for Success*, International Self-Counsel Press, Vancouver, Canada.

Easley, M. and Schlick, J. D. (December 1988). "2.9 Million Reasons for Quality" *Quality Progress.*

Edwards, D., Gorrelli, J., Johnson, S., and Shedroff, S. (January 3, 1994). "Typical Definition of 'Satisfaction' Is too Limited." *Marketing News.*

Einstein, Arthur W. Sr. and Einstein, A. W. Jr. (1966). *What You Should Know about Customer Relations.* Oceana Publications, Dobbs Ferry, N.Y.

Eisenburger, Kenneth (1977). *The Expert Consumer: A Complete Handbook.* Prentice-Hall, Englewood Cliffs, N.J.

Elgin, S. H. (1989). *Success with the Gentle Art of Verbal Self-Defense.* Prentice-Hall, Englewood Cliffs, N.J.

Emmanuel, M. (March 31, 1994). "The Right to Basic Amenities." *The Star.*

Fightmaster, B. (1993). *Transforming Busines.* Council for Continuous Improvement, San Jose, Calif.

Flohr, J. R. (October 1987). "The S-Curve—How a Company Can Evaluate Its Technological Health and Determine What Types of Training It Needs." *Quality Progress.*

Ford, D. J. (June 1993). "Benchmarking HRD." *Training and Development.*

Francis, A. E. and Gerwels, J. M. (October 1989). "Building a Better Budget." *Quality Progress.*

Fuchs, E. (October 1993). "Total Quality Management from the Future: Practices and Paradigms." *Quality Management Journal.*

Fuller, S. J. (October 1993). "Selection of a Stratified Random Sample." *Quirk's Marketing Research Review.*

Furnham, A. (March 28, 1994). "Seven Strategies to Deal with Change." *Business Times* (Singapore).

Garfein, R. T. (Fall 1987). "A Company Study: Evaluating the Impact of Customer Delivery Systems." *Journal of Services Marketing.*

Geddes, M., Hastings, C., and Briner, W. (1993). *Project Leadership.* Gower Publishing, Hampshire, England.

Giaimo, D. (1993). *Total Quality Implementation.* Council for Continuous Improvement, San Jose, Calif.

Glasersfeld, E. V. (1983). "Learning as a Constructive Activity." *Proceedings of the Fifth Annual Meeting of the North American Chapter of the International Group for the Psychology of Mathematics Education* (Vol. 1). J. C. Gergeson and N. Herscovics, Editors.

Gold, C. S. and Speilberg, F. (1983). *Solid Gold Resource Guide.* Prentice Hall, Englewood Cliffs, N.J.

Goldman, S. L., Nagel, R. N., and Preiss, K. (1994). *Agile Competitors and Virtual Organizations.* Van Nostrand Reinhold, New York.

Goldstein, R. (October 1988). "The Roots of Unquality." *Quality Progress.*

Graham, J. R. (January 3, 1994). "Customer Service Redefined: It's What You Know, Not What You Sell." *Marketing News.*

Green, S. (September 1978). "Conjoint Analysis in Consumer Research: Issues and Outlook." *Journal of Consumer Research.*

Haddock, P. and Manning, M. (March 1990). "Ethically Speaking." *Sky.*

Haiter, J. (1993). *Integrating Quality.* Council for Continuous Improvement, San Jose, Calif.

Harbour, J. (November 1990). "Quality—Real or Perceived." *Automotive Industries.*

Harrington, H. J. (1987). *Poor Quality Cost.* Quality Press, ASQC, Milwaukee.

Hays, R. H. and Wheelwright, S. C. (1984). *Restoring Our Competitive Edge.* John Wiley & Sons, New York.

Heil, G., Parker, T., and Tate, R. (1994). *Leadership and the Customer Revolution.* Van Nostrand Reinhold, New York.

Herman, R. and Segal, S. (December 1990). "Rainbow Effects on Office Planning." *Office Systems 90.*

Hillkirk, J. (October 15, 1990). "W. Edwards Deming: On Mission to Revamp Workplace." *USA Today.*

Hoexter, R. and Julien, M. (January 1994). "Legal Eagles Become Quality Hawks." *Quality Progress.*

Holpp, L. (October 1989). "Achievement, Motivation and Kaizen." *Training and Development Journal.*

Honan, M. and Karp, P. (1989). *Customer Satisfaction: How to Maximize, Measure, and Market Your Company's "Ultimate Product."* American Management Association, New York.

Hunter, S. J. (Spring 1989). "Statistics and Quality: It's Only a Beginning." *Statistics Division Newsletter.* ASQC, Milwaukee.

Kalinosky, I. S. (June 1990). "The Total Quality System—Going Beyond ISO 9000." *Quality Progress.*

Kaplan, G. (February 1994). "Researchers Talk About Customer & Employee Satisfaction Surveys at the American Quality Congress." *Quirk's Marketing Research Review.*

Karabatsos, N. A. (January 1986). "World-Class Quality." *Quality Progress.*

Keller, M. (November 1990). "Lessons from Lexus." *Automotive Industries.*

Kennedy, D. A. and Young, B. J. (October 1989). "Managing Quality in Staff Areas." *Quality Progress.*

Kenny, A. A. (June 1988). "A New Paradigm for Quality Assurance." *Quality Progress.*

Klock, J. J. (June 1990). "How to Manage 3,500 (or fewer) Suppliers." *Quality Progress.*

Klooster, N. (Winter 1989). "God, Give Me Patience, and I Want It Now!" *Statistics Division Newsletter.* ASQC, Milwaukee.

Kotter, J. P. (June 1988). "Managers Must Be Leaders Too." *Modern Materials Handling.*

Kotter, J. P. (1988). *The Leadership Factor.* Free Press, Boston.

Kramlinger, T. and Huberty, T. (December 1990). "Behaviorism versus Humanism." *Training and Development Journal.*

Lawton, W. H. (Winter 1992). "Design, Marketing and Quality Management: Parts of a Whole." *Statistics Division Newsletter.* ASQC, Milwaukee

Lefevre, H. L. (December 1990). "Variation in the Service Sector." *Quality Progress.*

Longmire, L. (1993). *Who to Benchmark.* Council for Continuous Improvement, San Jose, Calif.

Lowe, T. A. and Mazzeo, J. M. (September 1986). "Crosby, Deming, Juran: Three Preachers, One Religion." *Quality.*

Luecke, R. (April 1994). "The Emperor as CEO." *Sky.*

Maass, R. A. (September 1988). "Supplier Certification—A Positive Response to Just-in-Time." *Quality Progress.*

MacStravic, S. (February 1994). "Scale Scoring in Health Care Customer Surveys." *Quirk's Marketing Research Review.*

Marash, S. A. (September 1993). "The Key to TQM and World Class Competitiveness." *Quality.*

Marken, G. A. (February 1989). "Presentations to Get Your Message Across." *Office Systems 89.*

Marquardt, D. W. (Winter 1989). "Quality Audits in Relation to International Business Strategy—What Is Our National Posture?" *Statistics Division Newsletter.* ASQC, Milwaukee.

Marquardt, I. A. (August 1992). "Inside the Baldrige Award Guidelines." *Quality Progress.*

McCord, S. and Bjork, R. (1993). *Friendly Competition.* Council for Continuous Improvement, San Jose, Calif.

McCormick, E. J. (1979). *Job Analysis: Methods and Applications.* AMACOM (a division of American Management Association), New York.

McDermott, L. (1993). *Caught in the Middle: How to Survive and Thrive in Today's Management Squeeze.* Prentice-Hall/Simon & Schuster, Englewood Cliffs, N.J.

Merron, K. A. (January 1994). "Creating TQM Organizations." *Quality Progress.*

Miller, C. (January 1994). "Health Care Marketers Plot Strategy in Face of Reform." *Marketing News.*

Moen, R. D. and Nolan, T. W. (September 1987). "Process Improvement." *Quality Progress.*

Monroe, A. (March 1994). "Benchmarking: How to Spy on Your Rivals." *CFO.*

Nadler, P. S. (August 10, 1987). "Banks Must Charge Off Authorization Woes." *American Banker.*

Nehrenz, T. (1993). *Benchmarking Logistics.* Council for Continuous Improvement, San Jose, Calif.

O'Connor, J. (January 1994). "Defining Quality Service." *Market Share* (Newsletter of the American Marketing Association, Detroit Chapter).

O'Reilly, M. (1993). *University of Texas Quality Center.* Council for Continuous Improvement, San Jose, Calif.

Osborn, P. (1993). *Information Strategic Planning.* Council for Continuous Improvement, San Jose, Calif.

Parasuraman, A., Zeithamel, V. A., and Berry, L. L. (Fall 1985). "A Conceptual Model of Service Quality and Its Implications for Future Research." *Journal of Marketing.*

Patterson, M. L. (1993). *Accelerating Innovation.* Van Nostrand Reinhold, New York.

Peritz, J. (May 24, 1993). "Retailers Who Keep Score Know What Their Shoppers Value." *Marketing News.*

Perry, P. M. (July 1994). "How to Avoid the Seven Most Costly Errors When Evaluating Your Employees." *Office Systems 94.*

Phillips, S. R. (April 1988). "The New Time Management." *Training and Development Journal.*

Pisek, P. (June 1987). "Defining Quality at the Marketing/Development Interface." *Quality Progress.*

Piselli, R. (December 1989). "Quality Leadership Through Education." *Quality Progress.*

Piskurich, G. M. (March 1994). "Developing Self-Directed Learning." *Training and Development.*

Poe, R. (December 1991). "The Nero Effect: How Leaders Destroy Themselves." *Success.*

Pope, J. (March 1990). "What Are Really the Best Questions for Measuring Customer Satisfaction." Speech at the 2nd Annual Customer Satisfaction and Quality Measurement Conference, Arlington, Va.

Powers, V. J. (August/September 1993). "Quality Hurdles: Barriers that Keep Organizations from World-Class, Mature Quality." *Continuous Journey.*

Powers, V. J. (August/September 1993). "Survey Says…What People Are Saying about World-Class Principles and the Organizations that Practice Them." *Continuous Journey.*

Press, G. (September 2, 1991). "Benchmarking: Is Your Research Department Best." *Marketing News.*

Pyzdek, T. (April 1994). "Total Service Systems Engineering." *Quality Management Journal.*

Rosenberg, D. (April/May 1994). "The Making of a Facilitator." *Continuous Journey.*

Rubinstein, S. P. (April 1988). "Quality and Democracy in the Work Place." *Quality Progress.*

Russell, J. P. (1991). *Quality Management Benchmark Assessment.* Quality Press, Milwaukee.

Ryan, J. (December 1989). "Is U.S. Quality Competitiveness Back?" *Quality Progress.*

Sarazen, S. (October 1988). "Quality Plan Development: A Key Step toward Customer Enthusiasm." *Quality Progress.*

Satir, V. (1988). *The New People Making.* Science and Behavior Books, Mountain View, Calif.

Scheef, D. (September 1993). "Deck for Success." *Training and Development.*

Scheffler, S. (August/September 1993). "What Is World-Class, Mature Quality? A Center Survey Explores the Meaning of World-Class." *Continuous Journey.*

Schlossberg, H. (January 3, 1994). "Road to Success Paved with Service that Exceeds Customer Expectations." *Marketing News.*

Schultz, D. E. (October 25, 1993). "Maybe We Should Start All Over with an IMC Organization." *Marketing News.*

Schwarz, R. M. (August 1994). "Ground Rules for Groups." *Training and Development.*

Schwinn, D. R. and Schwinn, C. J. (November 1989). "Converting Training into Action." *Quality Press.*

Shafer, D. W. (November 7, 1986). "Managing the 'Fifth P' Leads to Teamwork." *Marketing News.*

Shelton, S. and Alliger, G. (June 1993). "Who's Afraid of Level 4 Evaluation?" *Training and Development.*

Skrabec, Q. R. (November 1990). "Ancient Process Control and Its Modern Implications." *Quality Progress.*

Spechler, J. (May 1989). "Training for Service Quality." *Training and Development.*

Spechler, J. (1991). *When America Does It Right: Case Studies in Service Quality.* Industrial Engineering and Management Press, Norcross, Ga.

Spendolin, M. J. (1992). *The Benchmarking Book.* Quality Press, Milwaukee.

Squires, F. H. (February 1975). "Comments on a Motivation Survey." *Quality Management and Engineering.*

Squires, F. H. (March 1986). "What Motivates?" *Quality.*

Stamatis, D. H. (September 21–24, 1987). "A Model of Job Redesign" *TMI Innovations in Quality: Concepts and Applications. Proceedings* (Vol. 2). ESD, Detroit.

Stamatis, D. H. (September 21–24, 1987). "Qualitative Methodology: A Quality Tool for Standard Operating Procedures." *TMI Innovations in Quality: Concepts and Applications. Proceedings* (Vol. 2). ESD, Detroit.

Stamatis, D. H. (1995). *Failure Mode and Effect Analysis: FMEA from Theory to Execution.* Quality Press, Milwaukee.

Stevens, D. P. (December 1993). "Avoiding Failure with Total Quality." *Quality.*

Still, T. (February/March 1992). "Applying Project Management to Training." *Technical and Skills Training.*

Stowell, D. M. (October 1989). "Quality in the Marketing Process." *Quality Progress.*

Stratton, B. (June 1988). "The Low Cost of Quality Lodging." *Quality Progress.*

Sullivan, L. P. (Spring 1989). "Company-Wide Quality Control as the Operative for Taguchi Methods and Quality Function Deployment." *Automotive Division Newsletter.* ASQC, Milwaukee.

Tague, N. R. (1995). *The Quality Toolbox.* Quality Press, Milwaukee.

Turino, J. (1992). *Managing Concurrent Engineering.* Van Nostrand Reinhold, New York.

Vasilash, G. S. (March 1988). "Buried Treasure and Other Benefits of Quality." *Production.*

Walonick, D. S. (November 1989). "Questionnaire Design—Some General Considerations." *Quirk's Marketing Research Review.*

Walton, R. E. (March–April 1985). "From Control to Commitment in the Workplace." *Harvard Business Review.*

Wargo, R. (August/September 1993). "How May I Help You? Customer Call Centers Share Secrets of Success." *Continuous Journey.*

Waterbury, R. C. (December 1993). "The New Management Paradigm." *INTECH.*

Watson, G. H. (August/September 1993). *Strategic Benchmarking.* John Wiley & Sons, New York.

Wilemon, D. L. (1973). "Managing Conflict in Temporary Management Situations." *The Journal of Management Studies.*

Williams, G. and Reid, L. (April 1994). "Enhancing Customer–Supplier Relationships." *Quality.*

Wormald, K. (July 1994). "At Your Service." *Office Systems 94.*

Young, B. J. (December 1989). "Managing Quality in Staff Areas." *Quality Progress.*

Zaclewski, R. D. (January 1993). "Instructional Process Control." *Quality Progress.*

Ziaja, J. (1993). *Community Competition for Quality.* Council for Continuous Improvement, San Jose, Calif.

INDEX